LEAP INTO LEGEND

*Donald Campbell
and the complete story of
The World Speed Records*

Steve Holter

SIGMA PRESS
Wilmslow

Published by
Sigma Press, 5 Alton Road, Wilmslow, Cheshire SK9 5DY, England.

British Library Cataloguing in Publication Data
A CIP record for this book is available from the British Library.

ISBN: 1-85058-804-X

Typesetting and Design by: Sigma Press, Wilmslow, Cheshire.

Cover Design: Sigma Press, based on the painting "Leap into Legend" by Arthur Benjamins

Printed in the United Kingdom by Cambrian Printers

Foreword
– by Jean Wales (née Campbell)

As the daughter of Sir Malcolm Campbell and the sister of Donald Campbell, I feel that the real story behind these two great men should be told. There has been much written about my brother, and with the raising of his *Bluebird* boat and the subsequent finding of his body, interest is as keen now as it ever was. He has rightly achieved legendary status and I am proud that he is still considered to be a national hero in the true meaning of the word.

I felt that it was a shame to disturb the crash site in Coniston and wished that the whole enterprise had never been started. However, I suppose that technology has moved on and that sooner or later somebody else would have raised the boat and his body – and then who knows what might have happened? Although at present we have the mammoth task of trying to save the boat, if only people had thought of the consequences of their original actions! At least the family were able to give Donald a true Christian burial and for that at least we must be thankful.

I first met Steve, with my husband Charles and son Donald, when he was the curator at a local museum and he came across as having a huge amount of knowledge about the family, more in fact than I have ever known! He explained that watching the tragic crash in 1967 was the last thing he did with his father, who died shortly afterwards and this had a lasting effect on him.

Steve came to visit me on a number of occasions and during one of those I suggested that he should write all his information down in a book to help others see the real story and help them to understand the struggles involved with all such endeavours of this nature. It seems that he took my advice and has produced this superb book.

I know that over the years Steve has taken great effort to track down and to talk to those of us that are left and has not left a stone unturned to get the proper feel of the man who constantly placed himself in great danger. Donald understood those dangers but overcame his fear and still carried on when lesser men would have given up – a truly very brave and courageous man.

Steve has helped to capture the spirit of my brother and has written, as far as I am concerned, an excellent factual account of his life.

Mrs Jean Wales

Ken Norris,
co-designer of Bluebird K7:

It gives me great pleasure to give a foreword to this book. I have known Steven for many years, and the content, accuracy, and detail and readability are amazing. Everyone interested in speed record breaking should have it on his or her bookshelf, for reference and not least for the story it tells. Well done Steven, a great sleuth, who seeks only 100% accuracy and appears to have succeeded in that goal.

A mine of information for the minds of fascinated fans of speed records.

Ken Norris

Preface

We never quite know from where our interests come – or what fires an inquiring mind, and what sustains it. On the morning of January 10th, 1967, I was awoken by my brother, Gary, who told me that our Auntie Joan had arrived and her Triumph Vitesse was parked across the road. Auntie Joan's visits always culminated in sixpence so, without a second thought that we should be getting ready for school, my brother and I rushed downstairs. A lot of people were there, but the atmosphere was heavy, and no-one was smiling. "During the night," my mother told us, "your father was taken ill, and died". As a seven-year-old it was difficult to comprehend. In the following months and years, I began to realize that my dad wasn't there, and that it was permanent. I began to remember things I had done with him, and the things he had said. How he taught me to draw "Stingray", how I sat with him and watched the television as Henry Cooper floored Cassius Clay. And how he had dragged me from playing with a model of a BRM to watch what he told me was "The end of an era, and of a very brave man". The date was January 4th 1967, and it was the last thing I can remember doing with my dad.

I went on to collect tiny model *Bluebirds* from boxes of cornflakes, and it was this that triggered my own interest in big blue cars, fast blue boats, and the very brave man to whom my father had introduced me. A school project convinced me to dig further, and a letter was sent to Norris Bros, whom, I found, had designed the *Bluebird* boat. Over the years, I met many of the people who were involved first-hand with both water and land speed record attempts, and my pile of notes grew beyond what I had ever needed for my project. I would proffer books for them to sign as keepsakes, and always got the same response along the lines of "You don't want to take any notice of that book, that's the one that says it happened like this, and it didn't. I know, I was there". Through this, my inquiring mind was sustained. I wanted to know it all, but I wanted to know the 100%, accurate truth.

Having been asked by Donald Campbell's sister, Jean, to "put the record straight" – a very apt way of putting it – I felt honour bound to do just that. But this is no rose-tinted glasses account, just the facts as told to me by those who knew that neither man was perfect, but neither were the ways that many books and newspapers had portrayed them. It is intended to be a comprehensive account of how the land, water and even the air speed records (for without the Rolls-Royce R-type, Sir Malcolm might have been less successful, and Donald might never have sought to follow his father) culminated in one disastrous run on Coniston Water on 4 January 1967. An account, therefore, of how Donald Campbell ran his *Bluebird* ever faster, for no other reason than to keep Britain and the family name where he felt they belonged.

I realize how fortunate I have been to meet and talk to – and in many cases become friends with – people who at one time were just names in books. All, without exception, told me that, without even knowing it, they had all known or been part of an exceptional family. To witness the interest that still exists in the exploits of Donald and Sir Malcolm never fails to amaze me. I felt, and still feel, extremely honoured to have learned first-hand from the family, friends and team members of both men. The compliment of being sought out by these same people to clarify points to which they felt I knew the answers, steered me to writing it all down, as honestly as I was able.

When, in the early 1990s, Ken Norris first asked me to help archive his paperwork it was one of those moments when one steps back, and has a reality check. Had I really been asked by the man who designed *Bluebird* to help him? After all the help I had received from him, it was a pleasure to repay his generosity. I came down to earth, however, when I found a letter filed in Ken's archives, asking for his help with a school project. It was the letter I had written some 25 years before, and was signed by a then thirteen-year-old Steven Holter, 217 Broderick Road – the address of the house where my father had died. It was my mother who, having read all that I had done, persuaded me to write it all again in a form that someone who had not been involved, or knew nothing of these events, would want to read it. And she kept persuading me until it was completed in 1992 – fortunately, before she died.

My father gave me a gift without knowing what he had done, or how it would help me throughout my life. My mother showed me how anything was possible: you just had to work at it and meet any set-back with the courage and the conviction of your ways. Remarkably the lives of Sir Malcolm and Donald Campbell have taught me the same lesson.

Steve Holter, Eastbourne

Dedications and Thanks

This book is dedicated to:

My father Ron – like the man to whom he introduced me, I only came to know through the recollections of others – but who inspired me just the same.

My mother Joan – whose never-ending encouragement and bravery is an example for which I will always be grateful.

My sons Charlie and Ross – for putting up with a father whose head always seems so firmly buried in the past!

My partner Debbie – who has put up with so much (including me), and met it all head-on.

My thanks are due to many people, some who are no longer with us, who took the time to speak to me from when I was an inquiring schoolboy, to today, and on whose first-hand accounts this book is based: Leo Villa, Lady Dorothy Campbell, Gina Campbell, Tonia Bern-Campbell, Jean Wales, Don Wales and his ever-tolerant wife Francesca, Ken Norris and his ever-helpful secretary Barbara, Tim Villa, Tony James, Ted Hammel, Bill Izatt, Peter Pateman, George Eyston, Peter du Cane, John Line and Ray Wheeler of Westland Aerospace (formerly Saunders Roe), L.G. Brown of Vosper Thornycroft, Mike Evans and Rolls-Royce, Lord Montagu and The National Motor Museum, Sir Stirling Moss, Dory Swann, Bert Denly, David Tremayne, Arthur Benjamins, Gino Felicetti, Phil Rorke, John Ackroyd, Frank Aldridge, Mark Harley, Ken Burville, Vera Cobb, David de Lara, Kevin Desmond, Joyce Villa, Howard Statham, Neville Duke, Clive Glynn, Anthony "Robbie" Robinson, Lord Mishcon, Mrs. U.E. Goldie Gardner, Pam Cripps, Bill Smith, John Gould, Daphne Harvey, Goodyear, Mobil Oil, Chris Openshaw and Sue Pesch of BP, Dunlop, Geoff Hallawell, Fred Harris, Paul Foulkes-Halbard, John Shinton, Robin Richardson and the Speed Record Club, the K7 Club, Richard Noble and the 633 Club, John Stollery, Bill Maloney MRINA, Lord Bolton, Dorothy McKegg, John Cooper, The Rt. Hon Lord Shawcross, Graham Adam Ltd, Lepp Transport, Col. Bowser, Castrol Oils, David Benson, Lionel Rapson, Amherst Villiers, Mark Tidy, Ray Govier, Michael Ware, and to the many others whose input, although smaller, was no less important.

Also to Graham Beech, Andy Griffin and The Speed Record Group.

Publisher's Note:

The name of Steve Holter is well-known to all those with an interest in fast cars or boats, so we are delighted to publish this book – a very worthy companion to "The Bluebird Years" which we published in 2001, just a few weeks after the wreckage of *Bluebird K7* had been recovered so expertly from Coniston Water by a diving team led by Bill Smith. The remains of *Bluebird*'s driver, Donald Campbell, were found by the same team and his funeral was held in Coniston's parish church – near to where he died in his attempt to take the water speed record past 300 mph in 1967.

There are many different aspects of the Campbells and their boats. Therefore, each chapter in this book is presented as a separate story. The first three chapters provide historical background to the world of record-breaking, with Sir Malcolm Campbell and Donald Campbell making relatively brief appearances. These chapters also include considerable technical information on the engineering innovations that went alongside speed record attempts.

Chapter 4 is an insight into the life of Leo Villa, chief engineer to both Malcolm and Donald. Uniquely, Steve Holter has had access to Leo's diaries, recollections and photographs. Here, for the first time, readers can discover how Leo regarded the people for whom he worked.

Chapter 5 – "Of Mice and Men" – looks in more detail at the personalities of Malcolm and Donald. This is an opportunity to find out what drove these complex personalities to risk their lives in the pursuit of speed – for this was not a simple quest for fame and fortune .

If *Bluebird K7* is your main interest, the final three chapters will be essential reading. Steve takes you from the earliest scale models, through the design and testing of *Bluebird K7*, to the fatal crash in 1967 and an analysis of its likely reasons.

In addition to this feast of information, there are comprehensive photographic sections containing pictures that are informative, fascinating, and poignant recollections of a golden age. Many of these have never been seen in any other book.

So – enjoy the chapters in the order that appeals to you, or simply start at the beginning and continue to the end of a book that is concerned with two of the most famous record breakers of all time.

Graham Beech

Contents

1.

Pioneers of Speed

It is an interesting coincidence that the collective name for the population of the Earth is 'The Human Race' – for it has always been in man's nature to compete against fellow humans, animals, or the elements of nature. Competition of this sort was based on the challenge of simply staying alive but, as man became more sophisticated and the machines that he invented were improved upon, death while competing became more of a rarity.

There is, however, one very special aspect of competing: from the earliest times, if man has had a moving object at his disposal, it has been raced. This has led to many benefits that have improved the lot of the everyday man and the consequence of the desire to race is to *win* – for one man has to be faster than all others. Some, however, have been above the simple competition of their fellows, and have challenged the very laws of physics to face only the steady ticking of the clock in a solitary quest for speed. In the field of the motor car, the fastest person on earth had captured the 'Land Speed Record', and similar awards were made for those who chose motor boats or aeroplanes to push against the natural boundaries. The histories of these pioneers of speed, be they on land, water, or in the air, are the seeds of a story: a story that reached a dramatic climax on 4 January 1967. For this was the day that Donald Campbell died in his *Bluebird* jet boat while trying to take the World Water Speed Record past 300 mph. Just as Buddy Holly's untimely death was regarded by some as 'The day the music died', this was the day, for many, that ended a remarkable period of British heroism and engineering.

Speed on Land

The first recognised race between automobiles is usually accepted as the Paris, Bordeaux, Paris contest, which was won by Emile Levassor over three days in June 1895. At the planning meeting for this event held by Count de Dion, was one Count Gaston de Chasseloup-Laubat, the man generally acknowledged as being the first holder of the Land Speed Record. On 18 December 1898, on a 2km (1.2 mile) track that had been carefully laid out in Agricole Park, Achères (near St Germain, just north of Paris) he trundled his 36 hp Jeantaud electric car to record a speed of 39.24 mph. This was the beginning of a saga that is nearly as long as the history of the motor car itself.

The first years of the Land Speed Record were peculiar, in that there were others to compete against on a regular basis. The technology of the car was new, and development rapid. There was room for the ingenious, the brave, or the foolhardy to increase the record quite rapidly, and so the days between new attempts were few.

Camille Jenatzy, the man who was to become revered as the 'Red Devil' of early motor racing, had been unable to take part in the first speed competition. He threw down a challenge to Chasseloup-Laubat that brought them together on the same Achères course on 17 January, 1899. Jenatzy drove his electric-powered car, carrying his own name, to record a new mark of 41.42 mph, only to see it fall instantly to Chasseloup-Laubat's 43.69 mph. This was to stand for ten days, when Jenatzy returned alone to Achères and set a new record of 49.92 mph. Chasseloup-Laubat's efforts to regain the honours set a good example of what was to beset challengers in the future: unpredictable weather, and mechanical gremlins. Eventually on 4 March, with his Jeantaud displaying what could loosely be described as the first attempts at streamlining, Chasseloup-Laubat wrested the record from Jenatzy at 57.60 mph.

Jenatzy's reply was to set a precedent for future contenders, as his next car was purpose-built for nothing other than raising the record – it was the first Land Speed Special. If ever a car's name could give an insight into the thinking of a land speed contestant, this was surely the one: 'Le Jamais Contente', The Never Satisfied. The thinking behind building a purpose-built vehicle for record-breaking was settled on 29 April when Jenatzy smashed the record with a fair degree of ease, at a speed of 65.79 mph.

The electric car was an ideal vehicle for these early attempts in everything other than the enormous weight of the batteries. The power was delivered reasonably instantly and smoothly and, to an extent, the huge weight played its part as the inertia helped to maintain onward progress, once top speed had been reached.

The next challenger, however, saw a different means to the end with the development of a steam-powered car, which was to bear the name, 'Ouef de Paques', or the 'Easter Egg'. Again a crude attempt at streamlining had been made, but much like Jenatzy's 'Jamais Contente' it appeared that the designer considered the driver to be suitably aerodynamic, for there he sat, from the waist up, out in the elements! On 13 April 1902, at the annual 'Speed Week' held on the Promenade des Anglais, in Nice, the car's creator, Leon Serpollet drove his white 'egg', to a record of 75.06

mph. It was to be a short-lived reign, as on 5 August the first non-European name appeared on the slate, that of William K. Vanderbilt. Vanderbilt had, for some time, been recognised as the fastest driver using a petrol-driven car and, on a course marked out in Ablis, he set a new record of 76.08 mph. This it seemed was the signal for a sudden rash of records, as Fournier, Augières and then Duray raised the record from Serpollet's 75 mph to 84.73 mph. The Land Speed Record had come of age, sufficiently to tempt the Americans into entering the fray.

This new age of record-breaking also led to years of confusion. The Automobile Club de France (ACF) had, until Duray's record, timed and verified all record attempts, which was not surprising when one considers that all but one of the successful attempts had been made in France. So when, in January 1904, Henry Ford reached a speed of 91.37 mph on the frozen Lake St Clair and Vanderbilt pushed his Mercedes to 92.30 mph at Daytona Beach, USA, the new 'American' records were not recognised – at least not in Europe, as 'unauthorised' timing equipment had been used. Although it might have been a little autocratic of the French, it at least meant that eventually, everyone would be bound by the same rules.

As for the 'official' Land Speed Record, it remained intact only until 31 March 1904 when Louis Rigolly moved the target up to 94.78 mph only to see it surpassed in May by Baron Pierre de Caters with 97.25. It was tantalisingly short of the first great barrier of 100 mph, but within two months both record and barrier had been broken, again by Rigolly, at 103.55 mph.

Already, advances in automobile technology were such that increments in raising the record were becoming very small, and to hold on to the Land Speed Record for any length of time became quite an achievement. Indeed, it was only a matter of two months before Paul Baras moved the goal posts yet again with a speed of 104.52 mph.

Meanwhile, on the beach of Daytona, the Americans were going their own way, claiming speeds from 104.65 mph right up to 121.57 mph, but still timed with equipment that the ACF refused to recognise. Of the American cars claiming to have exceeded the speeds of their European counterparts, two were 'specials', built solely for the purpose of gaining the record. 'The Flying Dutchman', a Mercedes with two 60 hp engines, and the extraordinarily advanced Stanley Steamer, 'Rocket'. These, with Jenatzy's torpedo-like 'Jamais Contente' had proved beyond doubt that the way ahead in the quest for speed in a straight line, was to engineer a car, either from an existing racing machine, or from scratch, for the sole purpose of breaking the Land Speed Record. Speed was all.

Regardless of the fact that the Stanley's record was not official, it took three years before it could be beaten, officially or otherwise. The new record-breaker was a petrol-engined car, driven at 125.95 mph by Victor Hemery (a distant relative of British Olympic gold medalist David

Hemery who, in turn, is related to Richard Noble's wife, Sally). His Benz was again a special: a 200 hp machine developed for record-breaking and hill climbing. In the United States, Barney Oldfield and Bob Burman, driving similar cars, were claiming much higher speeds but still using unapproved timing methods. The worth of the Benz special was confirmed on 24 June 1914, when L.G. 'Cupid' Hornstead achieved 124.10 mph, his record having been set by calculating an average speed from two runs in opposite directions, thus eliminating any wind assistance, or advantage gained from slopes. Although the likes of Tommy Milton and Ralph de Palma kept the unofficial American contingent in touch with European advances, this two-way calculation method was to set the 'official' precedent for record attempts in the future.

Enter the British

The days of French domination of the Land Speed Record were at an end, and it was to be the British that took over the mantle of increasing the speed at which man could travel in an automobile.

In May 1920, The Sunbeam Company announced they were to build a new 350 hp car, which although not solely for the intention of breaking the Land Speed Record, was to play an important role, not only in the history of record-breaking but also in the early career of Captain Malcolm Campbell.

The Sunbeam Company had learnt a great deal about aero engines during the course of the First World War, but was at pains to point out that their new car was not going to be constructed just by the simple expedient of installing a redundant pre-war aero engine into an elderly frame. This was to be an all-new venture, with not only a purpose-designed frame, but also a specially designed engine as well. The engine was based on the Manitou aviation unit, and drew on Sunbeam's wealth of aero engine experience, but to all intents and purposes was built from scratch for the car. Its aluminium cylinder blocks were cast in sets of three and then mounted into banks of six on a 60-degree angle. Steel liners were used with aluminium pistons, each with one scraper and three compression rings. The crankshaft, camshafts and connecting rods were all machined from solid billets of nickel-chrome steel. The timing train was by spur gears, mounted at the front of the crankcase, and the final departure from the Manitou was that these gears drove camshafts that operated one inlet and two exhaust valves per cylinder, via rockers. When finished, the unit had a bore of 120mm, and a stroke of 138.5mm, which gave it a capacity of 18,322cc, and produced 357 bhp at 2500 rpm. With its narrow single-seater bodywork, and advanced suspension married to this new hybrid engine, much was expected of the car, and much, eventually delivered. The first driver to take the controls of this fabulous new automobile, was Kennelm Lee Guinness (of the famous brewing family and inventor of the KLG spark plug) who, at the banked Brooklands track, recorded a speed of 133.75 mph on 17 May 1922.

Two years later, in 1924, the Englishman Ernest Eldridge with his ageing aero-engined Fiat, 'Mephistopheles', and Frenchman, Rene Thomas in his track-racer Delage, were locked in combat on a course in Arpajon, France. It was a conflict that saw the record increase to over 146 mph. Even this duel was not without acrimony, as Thomas refused to accept Eldridge's first effort because the giant Fiat was without a reverse gear. Necessity being the mother of invention, a simple friction wheel and electric motor were installed. Not for the last time were the rules circumvented. For all this, Eldridge only held the record for six days. His record fell to one Captain Malcolm Campbell, who had at first persuaded the Sunbeam works to lend him their 'wonder car', and then had pressured them into selling it to him. His first task was to give the car a coat of blue paint, and to name her, '*The Blue Bird*'. It was the first time that the names Campbell and *Blue Bird* had appeared on the land-speed roll of honour; it certainly would not be the last. Less than a year later, on Pendine Sands in South Wales, Captain Campbell increased the record to 150.76 mph. His fellow Britons, Parry Thomas, a brilliant engineer who lived in a bungalow at the Brooklands track, and Henry Segrave, a circuit racer turned record-breaker, regularly swapped the title of the world's fastest man on wheels until 1927. This was when the first purpose-built *Blue Bird* appeared, and raised the record to 174.88 mph.

The honour of being the first man to exceed 200 mph, however, fell to Segrave – but only after the death of Thomas on Pendine sands in his beloved aero-engined monster, 'Babs', caused when a rear wheel collapsed. This allowed one of the drive chains to flail wildly, decapitating poor Thomas who had a habit of driving with his head tipped to one side, out of the cockpit. Thomas must have died instantly, for the autopsy revealed that, 'the top of the skull was removed from above the eyebrow down to the nape of the neck'. When his mechanics arrived, 'Babs' was on fire, and one of them had to break Thomas's legs to get him out of the car. It was a tragic end to very fine gentleman.

The stage had also changed, and the venue for future land-speed attempts would be America, this time with properly sanctioned timing equipment. Sir Henry Segrave had arrived at Daytona Beach, Florida, with the twin-engined 1000 hp Sunbeam three weeks after the death of his friend Thomas. The four-ton, 50-litre monster had cost over £10,000 to build, and much was expected of it, but Thomas's death caused Segrave to hesitate. On his way to Florida, Segrave had the drive chains checked many times, fearing a repeat of Thomas's horrific accident. As the 'Slug', as the Sunbeam had been christened, was being prepared,

Segrave was surprised to receive a letter from a Mrs Mary McCann in England. In it, she claimed to have received a message from Segrave's dead friend, Parry Thomas, warning of a serious design fault with the Sunbeam. Mrs McCann was convinced that the message had come from beyond the grave. Segrave, a pragmatic man, felt uneasy about postponing his attempt on the instruction of a clairvoyant, but remembered that Thomas had voiced concern over the transmission when he had seen the original blueprints. Segrave had nothing to gain, and everything to lose, and asked his team to check the car carefully, but found nothing awry, although extra protection was given to the driver's cockpit. Segrave told friends on his return, 'I had no justification for postponing the attempt for another day, yet I had to admit that I was disturbed by the 'message' from England, particularly as it contained technical details which only Parry could have known'. Hours before the first run a telegram arrived from Mary McCann, it read, 'Further message from the other side. Check all steering bolts'. Segrave later wrote of the attempt, 'after the second message, two lads completely stripped the steering and found a fatal flaw, a bolt in the steering column was faulty, and would have snapped under the strain during the record. It was held by less than two turns of thread. The consequences don't bear thinking about'. On 27 March the record fell at 203 mph.

1927 to 1947: Britain is Best

Daytona Beach, Florida became *the* place for an attempt on the Land Speed Record, but it had very little in the way of home-grown contenders to cheer. Campbell arrived on the sands in March 1928 to be confronted by the two faces of engineering, finesse and brutality. On one side, Frank Lockhart's ingenious *Stutz Blackhawk* of only 3000cc, but 385 brake hp. Against this David of a car stood the Goliath of the *Triplex Special*. Built by Jim White, a millionaire wire manufacturer, the Triplex had no less than *three* 27,000cc Liberty aero engines, and a total power output of over 1200bhp. While Campbell raised the record, the Americans suffered mishap. *Blue Bird* had achieved 206.95 mph and was being unloaded in England a month later when the *Triplex*, driven by Ray Keech, managed to eclipse that figure by just short of one mile per hour. Sadly, Lockhart paid the price for impatience, and died while driving the *Blackhawk* at over 200 mph.

Segrave had not been idle and arrived in Daytona during 1929, with the car many consider to be the most beautiful land speed car of all time, the *Golden Arrow*. It is said that, so easily did the record fall, that this car has only ever travelled 20 or so miles in its entire life. Also on the sands was the Triplex, this time in the hands of Lee Bible, an inexperienced garage mechanic and part-time barber from Daytona. It was Bible's lack of experience that was to cost him his life. While travelling at over 150 mph, he lifted his foot from the throttle pedal too quickly, and put the Triplex in a slide that also claimed the life of Charles Traub, a cameraman who ran from his camera into the path of the wayward car. The camera continued to roll, capturing the car on film as it sped by, hitting Traub – who was sliced in two.

By 1931, Campbell's *Blue Bird* had been modified yet again, but this time by engineering genius Reid Railton, who had learnt much at the side of Parry Thomas. Railton had altered the drive train so that the driver sat along side the gearbox, which permitted a more satisfactory inclusion of a tail fin for stability. With a new, more powerful Napier Lion engine, Campbell was on a roll. The record was raised to 246.95 mph, then to 253.97 the following year. By 1933, Captain Malcolm Campbell, had become Sir Malcolm Campbell, and with this extra 'clout' managed to persuade Rolls-Royce to lend him one of their R-type racing engines. The record was pushed up to 272.46 mph, after which Campbell announced that he would break the 300 mark, and then retire. Railton again refined the *Blue Bird*, giving her an all-enveloping body and twin rear wheels to try to combat wheelspin. As the car neared completion, Sir Malcolm managed to purchase two Rolls R-type engines, and he finally realised his goal in September 1935, attaining 301.129 mph, on the salt flats at Bonneville, Utah. Sir Malcolm was good to his word and retired from the Land Speed Record, but not from record-breaking, as the names of Campbell, *Blue Bird*, Railton and Rolls-Royce moved from land to water.

From Land to Sea

As with the Land Speed Record, the early days of the Water Speed Record are shrouded in confusion. Again this may be due to the passing of time, or perhaps the whim of a biased reporter, but the result is the same, the Water Speed Record and its early history are confused and often contradictory.

Even before the turn of the century there had been many claimants to the title, 'the fastest man on water'. F.T. Haig claimed a speed of 24.36 mph as early as 1874, and the steam-turbine-powered *Turbinia*, is reputed to have attained 39.1 mph, in 1897.

When attempting to gain the Land Speed Record it was normal either to obtain the latest, or at least the largest engine available. In those early days, chassis and hull technology was almost non-existent, there was no substitute for horsepower. It was basically down to big engines, and brave men. Many of the early motorboat engines chosen for high-speed work were tuned and altered so much as to become almost new types. Often they were given new names, although this was not the case with 'Mercedes', a boat powered by a Daimler engine to a speed of 22.36 mph in

March 1907. It was not until 1910 that the unofficial mark left by *Turbinia* was bettered.

Ursula was owned by the then Duke of Westminster, and powered by two Wolseley engines. Built by Sam Saunders, she was as advanced as she could be, given that the only material available was 'God's plastic', but in the case of *Ursula*, the wood used was literally stitched together with annealed 16 SWG copper wire, a technique patented as *Consuta*, Latin for 'sewn together'. The Americans had claimed to have the fastest boat afloat in 1905, although it was clear that any competition would be between the two sides of the Atlantic. This was not to be until the late twenties, about the same time as the duel for the Land Speed Record was to become trans-Atlantic. The deciding factor in the Anglo-American joust for the water speed honours, was the Harmsworth Trophy, an event founded in 1903 by the owner of the *Daily Mail*, Alfred Harmsworth, for circuit-racing motorboats. The spoils were shared from 1903 to 1959 between the *Stars and Stripes* and the *Union Flag* and, as the winning boat had to be the fastest, it was no coincidence that the Water Speed Record was usually held by the Trophy-winning craft.

1911 saw an American boat, *Dixie IV*, piloted by Fred Burnham set the target at 45.21 mph, but it took nearly a year to raise the record by one mile per hour, by British aviator Tommy Sopwith in another Saunders hull, *Maple Leaf IV*. Yet another year was to pass before Sopwith raised the speed again, by eleven miles per hour.

Although it seemed normal practice in the following years that record-breakers on land switched to water to continue their career, in the early days of the Water Speed Record it seemed that aviators were leaving their planes to become marine pilots. After Sopwith, there came the French aviator, Santos Dumont, the first man to 'loop the loop' over British soil. He and his fellow Frenchman, Victor Despujols, had built their own hydroplane, with which they recorded 59.96 mph in 1914. Yet again it was to take nearly a year for the American, C.C. Smith in *Miss Minneapolis*, to add a little over six miles per hour to the record.

As is often the case, the onset of war caused a surge in the development of arms, the pay-off being that along with the advances in aircraft design came a huge improvement in their engines. This not only benefited the builders of the purpose-built land speed cars, but also the builders of high-speed boats.

It fell to Casey Baldwin, in a hydrofoil designed by Alexander Graham Bell, to be the first to use aero engines in a successful record attempt. On 9 September 1919, he slated a speed of 70.86 mph using two brand-new Liberty V12s in *Hydrodome IV*, on Bienn Bhreagh, in Nova Scotia.

Wood and *Miss America*

Of all the Americans that aspired to the Water Speed Record, one stands above all others. Garfield Arthur Wood, or as he was more commonly known, Gar Wood, was born in Mapleton, Iowa, in 1880, the second oldest of twelve children. His first taste of handling boats came when the family moved to Minnesota, where Wood's father was a harbour pilot. His initial encounter with a racing boat came as a spectator, when watching a craft called *Leading Lady*. She had been built by a house carpenter from plans found in the *Motor Boat* magazine, drawn up by George Crouch. Power came from a six-cylinder, two-stroke, Emerson of 589 cubic inches. Instantly Wood knew she was not running well and volunteered his electrical know-how, repairing the ignition system, and then riding as *Leading Lady's* mechanic. By 1916, he had amassed a fortune from his patent for a hydraulically operated dump truck, and in that year's Gold Cup races, a then-unknown G.A. Wood entered a boat called *Wood Hydraulic*. The race was for cruisers, but Wood's craft was a thinly disguised Hacker monoplane with an improvised 'cabin'. The result, when Wood finished well ahead of the field, was vigorously protested, and although Wood withdrew his boat, it was a good indication of Wood's 'win at all cost' philosophy.

Wood bought his way into the C.C. Smith Boat and Engine Company. While Chris Smith, at the suggestion of Wood, was building the hull of a new boat to be called *Miss America*, Wood set about obtaining a batch of Liberty aero-engines. Wood was an expert in milking the stunt-crazy American media, and winning the Harmsworth Trophy (nine times) the Gold Cup (five times) and even racing express trains down the Hudson River, earned him the following of his country and the title 'The Speed King'. It was no surprise that the name of Gar Wood should find its way onto the Water Speed Record roll of honour.

On the 18 September 1920 *Miss America's* twin Liberties powered her to a speed of 77.85 mph. The following year, *Miss America II*, fitted with four Liberties, reached 80.57 mph.

The next increase fell to the French in the shape of Jules Fischer, another aviator, driving Maurice Farman's *Hydroglider*. One can only describe a hydroglider as an extremely low-flying seaplane, so the regulations governing such craft, became very complicated. Was a hydroglider a boat or a seaplane? There was no official governing body to decide, and in complete reverse to the discord between the French and the Americans over what constituted a Land Speed Record, Gar Wood and his homeland refused to accept it as a Water Speed Record. Eventually, the International Yacht Racing Union laid down the rules that have become the standards by which all records have had to be set. Everybody then knew where he or she stood, and battle could commence in earnest. It was indeed a Wood who set the next record, but this time it was Gar's brother, George who, at the controls of *Miss America VII*, attained 92.84 mph. Gar Wood and Chris Smith had designed this new boat around two Packard engines, the hull being built by Napoleon Lisee and, although he never said it publicly, Gar Wood believed his brother had not got the best from her. Six months later, on 25 March, Gar gunned *Miss America VII* down Indian Creek, but managed to add just 0.28 of a mile per hour to the record.

As with speed on land, it was clear that any increases in the Water Speed Record would be hard won. It became apparent to the British challengers that it was no longer enough to build big boats to house big engines. Finesse, clever design and thinking were to become the British answer; the duel was between American brute force and British ingenuity.

'England Expects'

Sir Henry Segrave was not the first racing motorist to decide to try his luck with high speed boats, and had already been handling small motorboats at the time of his land-borne success in the 1000 hp Sunbeam. After driving his *Golden Arrow* to a record of 231 mph in 1929, he more or less retired from driving racing cars and record-breakers. At about the same time as Segrave was setting his last Land Speed Record, The British Power Boat Company, owned by Hubert Scott-Paine, was having a good deal of success with a single-engined hydroplane, designed by Fred Cooper. Like most of Cooper's designs, she was revolutionary. She was only 26 feet in length and her Napier Lion aero engine spun her single prop at an unheard of 6500 rpm. With help from Scott-Paine it was with this craft that Segrave started his motorboat racing in 1929 – the boat was called *Miss England*.

Fred Cooper was born in 1898, and it was always his childhood ambition to design, although during his formative years his passion was for aircraft. During the First World War he was a sub-lieutenant in the RNVR and at the end of the hostilities, served an apprenticeship with Thornycrofts at Basingstoke. It was here that Cooper developed his perfectionism in the design of boats, under the tutelage of Sidney Porter – previously the chief draughtsman at Saunders Ltd, where Cooper went to work after finishing his apprenticeship. He assisted in the design of Miss Betty Carstairs' 1-litre hydroplane *NEWG* and, during 1928-29, while working for the British Power Boats Company with Scott-Paine, designed *Miss England*. He became increasingly annoyed at Scott-Paine's claims that he alone had been responsible for the lines of this craft, and resigned to set up as a freelance.

The performance of the first *Miss England* convinced Segrave that if he was to be successful in taking the Harmsworth Trophy, and the Water Speed Record, his next boat must be another Cooper design.

The project was generously sponsored by Lord Wakefield of Hythe, chairman of the Castrol oil concern. Cooper starting design work in November 1929 and Saunders Roe were entrusted with the construction, which commenced in December 1929 – even though it was planned to be on Windermere in June of the following year, a little over six months later.

The vessel was to be powered by two Rolls-Royce R-type engines, of the kind that had just won the Schneider Trophy for Britain in the Supermarine S6 seaplane. Accordingly, a contract was signed early in 1930 between Lord Wakefield and Rolls-Royce. The two engines were specially built for marine use, the major difference being the inclusion of water-cooled exhaust manifolds. The power output of these engines was dependent on air being forced down into the rear-mounted supercharger, requiring a blast of over 180 mph to have any effect on the power output. In its 1929 specification, with an air induction of around 100 mph, the aero version was good for about 1115 bhp at 2200 rpm. The specially built engines for the new *Miss England* were improved by using a supercharger gear ratio of 7.47, increasing the power output to 1842 bhp.

One of Cooper's main concerns stemmed from the problem of having two engines spinning at high revolutions, and the torque reaction that would arise, not only within the hull, but also if they were driving two separate props. Added to this was the fact that if the engines were to spin at even slightly different speeds, the boat would want to travel in a great arc, instead of the straight line required. These problems were solved in typically clever Cooper fashion. The first step was to fit a single propeller, although Segrave took some convincing that a prop could be made to spin at 12,000 rpm. But from past experience and common-sense reasoning, Cooper was convinced that it was possible. He decided that the drive from the engines could be taken forward to a gearbox in the bow, and then returned by a single prop-shaft to the propeller. A second advantage of this would be the reduced drag, having only one shaft and its necessary brackets trailing in the water. The second problem was easily solved. The ENV Engineering Company were entrusted with the manufacture of the gears for the forward gearbox, built by Rolls-Royce, and requested that for ease and weight saving it would help if the two engines turned in opposite directions. Originally, a method of counter-gearing was considered, but the excessive weight penalty led to the idea being dropped. Instead, of the two engines built at Rolls' Derby plant, one of them, R17, became the only counter-clockwise unit, requiring a completely different crankshaft, cam-shafts and ancillaries. Along with its sister engine R19, R17 was installed in April 1930. Two four-inch tubular shafts were connected between the engines and the gearbox, while the single prop-shaft was of $1^5/_8$-inch diameter, 120 tons per square inch solid steel. Brackets housing 'Cutless' rubber bearings supported the shaft and, in spite of spinning at 12,000 rpm, this shaft, and especially its balance, never gave trouble.

Miss England II was also equipped with two rudders, one forward, on the trailing edge of the planing step, and one aft, inter-connected by an Arens control (a system of solid links and levers). Two seventy-five gallon fuel tanks were hidden in the bilge, either side of the engines.

At rest, *Miss England II* displayed the most elegant of lines. From her purposeful bow, back to the beautiful sculptured 'duck tail' stern, she was a masterpiece. She was built upside down on six trestles, holding her mahogany frames firmly fixed during construction, and nothing was spared in making her as rigid as possible. Her forward step had been designed as a fully adjustable surface, and was bolted on with eighty specially made stainless steel nuts and bolts. This step was to play a major role in the events at Windermere in the June of 1930.

She arrived at Windermere bang on time and trials preceded almost immediately. In the first few days, a few minor cooling troubles were encountered, but these were easily solved. After a run on the evening of Thursday, June 12th, it was decided that the attack on the World Water Speed Record would take place the next day, Friday the 13th. In his hotel room on the night before the record attempt, Segrave sat at his writing desk and typed a letter to his sponsor, Lord Wakefield. In it, he was critical of the standard of the propeller being supplied for the attempt, but insisted that the attempt would go ahead. The last paragraph read: 'We will go for the record tomorrow as planned, and I will telex you to let you know how we get on.'

Miss England II had been conceived as having only two crew, Segrave, the pilot and a riding mechanic to look after the engines. The mechanic was Michael Willcocks, who had originally been suggested by Fred Cooper as supervisor during *Miss England's* construction. He was trained at Coventry Technical College, and while working in his family engineering business, raced small class boats. He had already told Segrave of his interest in the project, and an interview was arranged. He told his future employer that he didn't even wish to be paid; all he wanted to do was 'beat the damn yanks'. Segrave offered him four pounds, ten shillings a week, plus expenses, and after a week of soul searching, Willcocks accepted the offer.

Victor Halliwell, a Rolls-Royce engineer, whose most recent job had been leading the bench tests on the Rolls R-type engine, and who was fully used to the complex warming procedures of the engine, had been responsible for the conversion to marine use of both of *Miss England's* power plants. When the decision was made that two riding mechanics should be on board, one for each engine, Halliwell was chosen as the ideal candidate to partner Willcocks.

As the sun rose on the morning of Friday, June 13th, it appeared to be a perfect day to break the record. It is said by some that the crew were so confident, that as Segrave, Willcocks, and Halliwell stepped aboard, none was wearing a life jacket, although some contemporary photographs show the team donning them before a run. It is more likely that these were standard 'jackets' as only one of the special reinforced jackets ordered for the record attempt had arrived. Segrave, not wishing to single anyone out for preference, decided that it would be better that none of the crew should wear the one jacket they had. It is also strange to note that Segrave had suddenly decided to abandon his 'hard' crash helmet, of which he was a pioneer in motor racing, in favour of a linen helmet.

At first the attempt went well, but the plan was changed. As Michael Willcocks recalled after the attempt: "On the way out, Sir Henry made an alteration in the programme. Instead of returning to the boathouse after a run in each direction to fit the other propeller, he decided to do two runs at only just over record speed. 'You and I, Halliwell, will take the times of the first run, and if not good enough for the average I will increase slightly on the return. Then if everything is OK, I'll run her up again all out, and see how much over 120 she'll do. I hope to God she behaves herself'."

She made two high-speed runs, and turned to make one more at full throttle, hitting an estimated 120 mph. Just short of the marker for the end of the measured mile, *Miss England* struck a water-laden log, which pierced a hole in the forward step. The water pressure at such a speed was such that, in the words of one witness, 'she seemed to be gripped by an unseen hand'. The sudden deceleration to one side of the hull forced *Miss England* to swerve violently, and cartwheel over. For a few seconds her engines screamed underwater, then the deathly silence that descends over such scenes fell as the horror hit those watching. Seconds later a white-overalled form weakly rose to the surface, and a wet balding head glistened in the brilliant sunshine. It was Segrave. A Mr King dived in, fully clothed, from a launch, and swam to the limp figure. He was suffering from a punctured lung, and in great pain, but his first reaction was to ask about his companions. Just as he did so, Willcocks came to the surface, suffering only from very bad bruising. Segrave was taken to a private house, still fully conscious and suffering badly. He asked if they had succeeded in their quest and managed to smile a little on hearing of 'their' new record. He died after three hours; he was 34 years old. Two days later, Halliwell was found. It was said that he was still wearing his goggles and clutching his pencil and clipboard. He had drowned.

Segrave's plans after capturing the Water Speed Record were to win the Harmsworth Trophy and then win the Schneider Trophy in a plane he had helped to design and which had already been entered. From there, the air speed record was to be his crowning achievement. These dreams died with him that day, but were to be echoed later by a man called Malcolm Campbell.

The Anglo-American Joust

While *Miss England II* was being refurbished at the Rolls-Royce works at Derby, the Water Speed Record was being wrested back to the United States by Gar Wood, and yet another *Miss America*. Powered by two Packard engines and built by Napoleon Lisee, Wood steered her to 102.25 mph on Indian Creek, but it was to be a short tenancy of the record.

The helm of the reconditioned *Miss England II* was handed to Kaye Don, the son of Polish parents (his name being shortened from Donsky). He was another racing driver making the switch to water, although in Don's case it was after an embarrassing failure on the land-speed record in the Sunbeam *Silver Bullet*. Some of the mechanics and engineers who had been with Segrave, and who had spent the last months bringing *Miss England II* back up to first-class condition, were shocked that anyone else would be allowed to take the helm after the late Sir Henry. Some openly voiced their alarm, but she belonged to Lord Wakefield, and ultimately it would be his decision. One mechanic, whose name has not been recorded, is said to have crawled up to the inside of the bow, where he fixed a photograph of Segrave – the intention being that, when *Miss England II* broke her next record, it would be Sir Henry who crossed the line first.

After trials on Ireland's Loch Neagh, *Miss England II* and her crew were taken to Brazil where, on the River Parana, just over one mile per hour was added to the record.

Three months later, on Lake Garda, Northern Italy, Don added a further seven miles per hour, but felt it was the limit of the boat's performance. 1932 saw the record return to the United States, and Gar Wood, again in *Miss America IX*. Wood raised the record to 111.71 mph, spurring further activity on the other side of the Atlantic. Lord Wakefield had already commissioned Fred Cooper to improve on *Miss England II*, the third craft to carry the name and which was being built by Thornycroft. She retained many of the features of her predecessor, including the Rolls-Royce R-types, tuned to 1931 specification, but *Miss England III* had twin props making the counter-rotating R17 an absolute necessity. Five months later, Kaye Don recovered the laurels on Loch Lomond at a speed of 117.43 mph. Not satisfied, Don had another couple of runs later in the day and left the mark at 119.81 mph. Wood knew that America did not have a comparable engine to the Rolls R-type, and the only solution he could think of was to simply multiply the engines he was using. *Miss*

America VIII and *IX* were stripped of their supercharged Packards and a new craft was built to house all four units. For all this, *Miss America X* could only add 5 mph to the record, leaving it at 124.91 mph.

Make Way for the Campbells

Wood had held the record for three years when Sir Malcolm Campbell retired from the Land Speed Record, but his plans to regain the laurels from the Americans had been put in motion three months before his last land-borne success in September 1935. By 1937 Malcolm Donald Campbell was 54 years old (seven years younger than Gar Wood) but had every intention of beating the record using sound British engineering. Between them, Railton and Fred Cooper had designed a craft worthy of the name *Blue Bird*, the first craft built for the record that would seat a lone pilot. This first *Blue Bird* speedboat was conceived around the Rolls-Royce R-type engine, and much thought had gone into keeping her size and weight down to the absolute minimum. She was ready for trials by September 1937. Sir Malcolm had advertised on several occasions for a length of water suitable for a record attempt, and finally decided on Loch Lomond, where Kaye Don had taken *Miss England III* for her successful attempts of 1932, and where the measured mile surveyed for that attempt was still laid out. Sadly, the Loch proved totally unsuitable, and a speed of only 85 mph was recorded, although it did give Campbell a chance to remedy a few teething problems. Lago Maggiore on the Swiss, Italian border was finally selected for the record attempt, and *Blue Bird*, then registered as *K3*, successfully raised the record over two days to 129.5 mph. The following year *K3* raised the record again to 130 mph, but had proved beyond doubt that she was stretched far beyond her capabilities. The year before Campbell had complained of *K3*'s instability, and Railton and Cooper had already started setting out the lines for her successor, which was to be designed on the three-point principle.

Meanwhile, T.E. Lawrence (better known as Lawrence of Arabia), and Edward Spurr, a 26-year-old research engineer, were planning their own attempt on the Water Speed Record. But Lawrence's mysterious death in a motorcycle accident robbed the project of much of its initial impetus. Finally, after troubled runs in 1938 'their' boat, called *Empire Day*, returned to Windermere in September 1939 for further trials. *Empire Day* was still unable to reach anywhere near the Water Speed Record and Spurr had problems with fumes entering the cockpit, with the dagger-like rudder, and with the propeller flattening out as the speeds rose.

At more or less the same time as *Empire Day* was at Windermere, the new *Blue Bird* arrived at Coniston Water for her first attempt at the record. The lines of *Blue Bird K4* were originally laid down by Fred Cooper, but he had become more and more dissatisfied with the conditions imposed upon him, so the design was completed by Peter du Cane of Vosper (later to be Vosper Thornycroft), and Reid Railton. She arrived in the Lake District on 13 August, but was not ready to run until the 17th. After a few cooling problems had been sorted out, she made two further runs on the 18th and by noon of the 19th the record had fallen to Campbell again at 141.74 mph. It was that easy. But within a month, Britain was at war with Germany.

The Thrust to 200

By June 1948 *Blue Bird K4* had changed considerably. Gone were the smooth lines, as had the piston engine that once lived inside them. Sir Malcolm had decided to have another go at his own record more or less at the same time as the war had ended. Having sought out Peter du Cane, it was decided that the old R engines must be at their limit, and that the new Merlin and Griffon engines that Rolls-Royce were building would only increase the record marginally. So it was that *Blue Bird* arrived at Coniston fitted with a De Havilland Goblin jet, and a completely new look. She was at once nicknamed *'The Slipper'*, but that was all she did – having been coaxed into planing, she then showed a frightening tendency to yaw uncontrollably off-course. The suggested modifications took over three months to complete, and, after a few secret runs in Poole harbour, she returned to Coniston. But Sir Malcolm was beginning to show his 63 years. He suffered from bouts of kidney trouble, and his eyesight was failing due to glaucoma. It seemed that even the task of piloting *Blue Bird* was becoming a chore, especially as her handling was so poor. At speeds of 100 mph she began to porpoise violently, and Sir Malcolm actually began to think it was a lost cause. Eventually *Blue Bird* was returned to Vosper for yet more modifications, but these were incomplete when Sir Malcolm died on New Year's Eve, 1948.

It was not long, however, before Sir Malcolm's son, Donald, decided to follow in his father's footsteps. Wherever his motivation came from, by August 1949, *K4* had been returned to her pre-war form, and another Campbell was attempting to set a World Water Speed Record. After many trials and tribulations, however, Donald Campbell's camp was shattered to hear that Sir Malcolm's record had been beaten by a completely unknown boat called *Slo-Mo-Shun IV*, driven by Stanley Sayres – and by a considerable margin. Far from being outdone, Donald set about finding as much information as he could about this new threat, and followed it up by further modifying *Blue Bird* to attempt the record yet again. But these efforts finally culminated in an accident (see page 87) that put *K4* beyond further use.

A Step Back

The *Blue Bird* car had been silenced in 1935 when Sir Malcolm Campbell retired from Land Speed Record-breaking. As the names of Campbell and *Blue Bird* switched to water, the names of Eyston and Cobb came to the fore on land. George Eyston, a first-class engineer, had been active in record-breaking for some years, and saw Campbell's 'retirement' as his opportunity to add the outright Land Speed Record to the numerous class records that he already held. To this end, he set about designing and building *Thunderbolt*, an enormous, twin-engined, eight-wheeled brute, that weighed in at a colossal seven tons. It was Eyston's thinking that this huge weight would counteract the wheel spin that had dogged Sir Malcolm Campbell's attempts in the past.

John Cobb, on the other hand, had a liking of handling large powerful cars, and had already visited the salt flats of Bonneville with his 24 litre, Napier Railton. It was a simple step up to have Reid Railton design a larger version of the Napier for Cobb to have a crack at Campbell's record. Railton probably relished the opportunity of starting a design from scratch, rather than the constant, cost cutting modifications of Campbell's *Blue Bird*. Eyston had already worked out that with the weight penalty of his huge car, he would require the most powerful engine available and, as Campbell had already used one of these to set the current record, his idea was simply to use *two* Rolls-Royce R-types. Cobb, however, had access to two Napier Lions that were over twenty years old, and had seen active service in Betty Carstairs' Harmsworth Trophy motorboat *Estelle*. Eyston had nearly 4000 bhp at his disposal, while Cobb was restricted to about 2400 bhp – but in Railton's active and inventive mind, this was no handicap.

Only a month after Campbell had reached his 300 mph goal, Railton was hard at work on the calculations for project Q.5000, Thomson and Taylor's in-house code name for Cobb's Land Speed car. He had already formulated the idea that four-wheel drive was a better solution to wheel spin than the simple expedient of weight, and had designed an ingenious 'S' shaped beam chassis with the engines slung from each side at 10 degrees to the centre line. The rear engine powered the front pair of wheels, and the front engine the rear pair.

Five scale models were made to test various body forms, these being put to the test in the Vickers wind tunnel at Brooklands. The purpose was to find the best body shape to enclose the mechanics of the car, while still presenting the smallest frontal area. These shapes were listed as: '*Three Wheeler*'; '*Cigar*'; '*Blue Bird with troughs*'; '*Long tail*'; and '*The Bun*'. After further tests at the National Physical Laboratory, the 'Bun', was chosen, in spite of its slightly larger projected area. To counteract this, the car was planned as being 'crab tracked', that is to say the rear track was narrower than the front (the actual track measurements were: front 5ft 6ins, rear 3ft 6ins). Railton's skilled assistant, R.H. Beauchamp, another top-class engineer whose first job had been under Parry Thomas, was soon joined by a Mr Hobbs, and together they translated Railton's thinking into the necessary working drawings. John Thompson Motor Pressings Ltd made the chassis in four sections, which were hot rivetted together, while the body was made by master craftsman, Bill Masters, with the help of one assistant, who worked from simple plywood formers made from Hobbs' drawings. The whole one-piece all-enveloping body could be lifted on and off by six men, The body was devoid of holes as the cooling was taken care of with a seventy-five-gallon ice tank. Because of the unusual engine layout, the car required two three-speed gearboxes, manufactured by David Brown & Sons of Huddersfield. When complete, the *Railton Special* weighed in at a very light 7000lbs and, although Cobb had financed most of the project himself, twenty-eight companies had given invaluable help.

In contrast, Eyston's car had several major backers. Lord Wakefield was tempted into supporting the venture, and was instrumental in obtaining the loan of two of the most powerful Rolls-Royce R-types for the car. One had won the Schneider Trophy while the other had held the air speed record twice. The Bean works at Tipton undertook construction of the design that had been hatched between Eyston and the French coachbuilder and aerodynamicist, Jean Andreau, the whole machine being constructed in just six weeks. Regardless of its size, and the speed with which it materialised, *Thunderbolt* was no Heath Robinson device, and it bristled with innovation. Of her eight wheels, the front four were inter-linked to form a twin-steer system, with a slightly different ratio for each pair of wheels so that the rear pair followed the front pair perfectly. The four driven wheels were on a common axle driven by a single three-speed gearbox. The two V12 engines were linked by a gearset in an effort to turn them into one twenty-four-cylinder unit, these being mounted behind the driver, much like today's modern Grand Prix car. Braking was also very similar to today's racing cars, with disc brakes all round, the similarity continuing to the point where the front discs were mounted inboard, to save on unsprung weight. These were supplemented by 'air brakes', mounted in the body, and which were hydraulically operated. Apart from the gaping maw required for the forward mounted radiator, *Thunderbolt* differed from the *Railton Special* in one further aspect. Mounted on the tail was a large aerodynamic tailfin for stability, something that Railton considered unnecessary.

Thunderbolt arrived on the salt of Bonneville in October 1937 and broke Campbell's mark with 312.00 mph on 19 November. It was not a large increase, but the problem of linking two V12s into one 24 cylinder had not been the hoped-for success. A temporary solution involved allowing the clutches to slip, thus allowing the crankshafts to take alternate positions. It worked, but the slipping clutches lost a good deal of speed. By the time Eyston returned in 1938, the body had grown in length, the cockpit was fully enclosed, and the radiator intake had become more refined. The car had also become nearly a ton lighter, thanks to the replacement of the original leaf springs, with smaller and lighter coil springs. It was enough to see the car to a new record of 345.50 mph, but only after the side of the car had been painted black to ensure being picked up by the electric eye timing device after the complete failure of the system on a previous run.

Cobb, who had arrived just after Eyston, took no chances and had the sides of his car painted black before his first run, which brought to light a few teething problems, which were restricted to alterations to carburation and ignition, due to the altitude, and the use of cork floats in the carburettors. After the first high-speed trial, airflow pressure dents were found in both the top and bottom of the tail section, and wooden reinforcements were screwed to the inside of the body. The extraordinary body shape of the Railton was unlike anything yet seen on the salt, and one team member heard a woman spectator comment to her friend, "Let's go around the back, and take a look at the front".

Eyston's presence on the salt was of great concern to Railton, as he considered the potential of his car as just 350 mph, an increase of only five miles per hour over Eyston's new record. On 15 September, Railton was proved right, and Cobb set the mark at 350.20. Most of Cobb's team were set for the return journey to England on a German liner by the name of *Bremen*, but Ken Taylor, of Thomson and Taylor, decided it might be best, in view of the growing hostilities in Europe, to travel on a British ship. The journey home was made on the *Olympic*, sister ship to the *Titanic*.

Eyston responded to Cobb's record by improvising a ice-cooling system of his own, allowing him to fully enclose the front of *Thunderbolt* for better streamlining, in addition to the removal of the tailfin and the lengthening of the body tail section. The black paint on the sides had only been a temporary measure, and was replaced by black arrows with yellow discs at their centre. The day after Cobb had set his record, Eyston replied with a new record of 357.50. Cobb returned in August, with sponsorship from the American Oil Company, Gilmor, and, having had the gearing for the superchargers increased, hit 369.70 mph. The return to England was made just before the onset of the Second World War.

Out from the Ruins

In the summer of 1946 the body and chassis of the *Railton Special* were recovered from the country barn where they had been stored during the war years. They had been thoroughly lacquered to prevent salt corrosion, but still looked tired, being covered in years of dust. The engines had been kept in storage by the car's builders, Thomson and Taylors for seven years, along with Sir Malcolm Campbell's Rolls-Royce R-types. They had all benefited from careful attention, and were in tiptop condition. In its pre-war guise, the *Railton* had suffered from stalling between gear changes, due to the lack of flywheels on the elderly aero engines, and Railton devised a clever ancillary drive to keep the engines running. He was pleased to find that Cobb, with backing from the American oil giant Mobil, was keen to have another crack at the record. Napier agreed to overhaul the engines completely at their works in Acton, London, although both units were found to be in excellent condition, requiring no major work. The axles and gearboxes were also stripped; it was found that the front axle casing had suffered hairline cracks, and this entire casing was re-made in a lighter RR53 alloy with different ratios installed front and rear.

The car arrived back on the salt flats of Bonneville in August 1947, but the course was in a terrible condition. To make things worse, a failure of the new anti-stalling device on the test bed had meant that new camshafts (the gears for the anti-stall device were contained inside the camshaft housing) had to be made and dispatched from England, and then fitted on site along with a replacement head. The old carburettor trouble resurfaced, but Railton was on hand to sort them out. He also advised an alteration to the ignition timing as well as calculating how much ice should be put in the cooling tanks (previously the 75-gallon tank had only been half-filled). The body of the car was given a half-degree nose-up attitude and much attention was paid to the Greecen tachograph recorder. Thanks to these careful preparations, the record fell to Cobb at 394.20 mph, having broken the 400 mph barrier on one of his two runs.

Cobb goes to the Water

Cobb knew that the *Railton Mobil Special* as the car had become known, was very near her limit. He sat back for a year, during which he and Railton sketched out three successors. Cobb was not unlike other record-breakers before him, and having watched Sir Malcolm Campbell wrestle with the jet-engined *Blue Bird* hydroplane, asked Railton to give the idea of a jet-powered boat some thought. In April 1949, Railton wrote to Peter du Cane, giving him the outline of the plan, remarking that, "It would be foolish for us to embark today (1949) on any project aimed at less than 200 mph, which would mean designing for aerodynamic safety up to at least 250 mph. If you agree on this, it seems inevitable that our first line of approach must be to think up some 'body shape' which would combine the necessary aerodynamic properties with adequate accommodation for man and machinery, and then (and only then) to try to work in the necessary buoyancy and planing surfaces etc."

Railton envisaged a seaplane-type of hull to support the engine and pilot, and to give the necessary buoyancy. For stability, outriggers were to be included at the stern, producing what he described as a tricycle effect, with one 'wheel' at the front, and two at the rear. During model tests, Mr Gawn of the Admiralty-run Haslar Experimental Tank gave Peter du Cane invaluable help (as he did with Sir Malcolm, and Donald Campbell throughout their careers), but it still took until January 1952 before design work on the full-size craft began in earnest. In July 1952 the project was announced to the public and construction work begun. It was to cost Cobb in excess of £15,000 before the craft was launched. On the strength of the successful tank and free-running model tests, Major Halford of the De Havilland Engine Company, persuaded the Ministry of Supply to loan the project a 5000lb thrust Ghost jet engine, and with that the last piece of the jigsaw fell into place.

The construction made use of a mixture of high quality birch plywood and high tensile aircraft aluminium alloy. Peter Crewe, chief hydrodynamicist at Saunders Roe Ltd, assisted in the calculations of the forces likely to be encountered on the planing surfaces, while Railton kept a close eye on the whole project. Within days of the green light, Vosper took delivery of the birch ply that was to be used in the majority of the hull from William Mallison and Co. Two skins of this ply were cross-laid onto spruce longitudinal stringers, which were in turn notched to birch ply bulkheads and sawn to shape, much like a giant model boat. The more highly stressed sections, in particular the planing surfaces, and the hoops used to locate the engine and rear mounted sponsons were of the aluminium alloy. Dr Corlett of the British Aluminium Co, who later gave great assistance to Donald Campbell, suggested an alloy known as DTB610B, which gave a strength of 32 tons per square inch for the beams that, in full-throttle trim, would be supporting the entire craft.

Cobb decided to call his boat *Crusader*, because as he put it, "In the old days a Crusader was a man who liked to get away from his office and go out and have some fun". The first runs of *Crusader* (registered with the international racing number *K6*) were attempted by du Cane on the upper reaches of Portsmouth harbour, near the Vosper works at Portchester, but only to check basic controls, and to find at what speed she would start to plane. She was taken to Loch Ness where modifications were made to ensure that water would not enter the engine intakes. Cobb had yet to arrive, and project manager George Eyston suggested that du Cane give *Crusader* her first run on the Loch. Du Cane was surprised at how quickly *K6* accelerated, but was more concerned about her tendency to hold her speed as the throttle was closed. Vosper had indeed found out during model tests that the resistance/speed curve became a horizontal line as soon as *Crusader* got up onto the plane, a phenomenon that was to have great repercussions later in the attempt. It was found that, during Cobb's initial trial runs, the flat bottom of the main hull was delaying the 'break away' from the water. A simple solution to this problem was effected by looping a piece of rope around the hull to disturb the water travelling under the hull, although on some occasions it was also necessary to use small speed boats to create an artificial rough spot at the start of the course. The speeds reached during September 1952 showed that the thinking behind *Crusader* was sound, but Peter du Cane, and Eyston were concerned about the strength of the forward planing shoe. In fact, du Cane offered to take *Crusader* back to Portsmouth and carry out any work needed, free of charge. Cobb, however, was determined not to hang around any longer, and signed a letter to du Cane promising not to exceed 190 mph, which would have been more than enough to have taken the record. On the morning of the 29 September, the weather conditions looked favourable, and the team was on stand-by at 4am. Just after 9am, *Crusader* was in her start position awaiting the all clear, but it was not until 11 o'clock that the attempt was given the go-ahead. Joyce Cronk was standing next to Peter du Cane as the run started and, in a letter written to him in October 1952, she recalled what happened:

> In case it is of any help to you and before my memory dims, I write this account of what I saw of the tragic accident to '*Crusader*'.
>
> As you know, I was standing by you. I later measured the distance from the first milepost (to ourselves) and found that it was 0.6 of a mile. I did not see the waves beforehand, as, from the moment when I heard my husband over the P.T. say, 'he's away', I was watching to see the boat round the point by Urquhart Castle. It was considerably nearer the north shore than on previous occasions and I remember remarking on the beautifully smooth way in which the boat was making the run. It was not until the moment of 'bucketing' that I saw he had hit what I realised must have been a wave, and then another, the forward part of the boat smacking down on the water with what from sight, must have been considerable impact. As far as I can estimate, the time between the impacts was about half a second and the position of the first bucketing just beyond us about 10 degrees past the direct view across the mile. He seemed to have weathered these and showed no sign of distress at that moment. Immediately afterwards, the boat slowed considerably and I next remember the spray rising (about 45 degrees past the direct line) the sound as of an explosion and pieces of debris flying out. From our angle of vision, the growing volume of spray hid any further sight of the boat and when it subsided there was nothing to be seen. I am afraid this is a bald account.
>
> Yours Joyce Cronk

Du Cane withdrew from public gaze for a short time after the tragedy, then threw himself into compiling a report on what had happened. His own statement has, until now, never been published and was written within hours of the tragedy:

On September 6th I was asked by George Eyston to give the boat a preliminary test to ascertain whether the particular difficulty of getting over the 'hump' (on to her planing shoes) had been overcome. I was gratified to find that after a relatively short period in the transition stage, and provided full thrust was applied, the boat would start to plane relatively easily. Once planing, the boat seemed to be very pleasant, bearing in mind that I did not at any time pass the 100 mph mark. My report at this stage was to the effect that I did not consider the rudder large enough. However, Mr Cobb then got into the boat and drove her with considerable dash, considering it was the first time he had been in her and in fact succeeded in turning her after a fashion. A day or two later, Mr Cobb took *Crusader* out in rather rough water and gave her a real 'work out' which revealed some minor weakness in the hull. At this stage he did not exceed more than 140-150 mph. A week or ten days later there were very good conditions on the Loch, to the extent that it was almost 'glass calm', which allowed Mr Cobb to run the boat at a much higher speed. His report was that he was easily able to reach 200 mph and, in fact, a bit more. The acceleration was terrific and full thrust could by no means be applied once this speed was reached. There was, however, difficulty in glass-calm conditions in getting through the transition stage, in fact speed boats had to used to ruffle the surface of the water at the appropriate place. A thorough investigation of this trouble was proceeding at the time of the accident, and the remedy was in fact discovered, although time had not been available to put this into practice. In the meantime, speedboats were used on such occasions to assist in solving this problem.

We had now reached about the middle of September and I asked for an opportunity to go over the hull very carefully and remedy to the best of our ability such defects as had revealed themselves up to date.

It will be appreciated that for a development of this nature, matters had been moving pretty quickly. About a week later I reported to Mr Cobb that I thought there was a reasonable chance of him taking the record this year, provided he was not over-ambitious in the matter of speed. From that time forward runs were to be timed officially.

The first occasion on which we timed runs was on Friday, 19 September. On this occasion we were unlucky because, although the boat was obviously running very fast, Mr Cobb found himself unable to hold her straight, due, in my opinion, to a 5-6 knot cross-wind. He did, however, even on this occasion accomplish one leg at 185 mph. It was decided to fit a larger rudder, which we had already, against the eventuality that the existing rudder proved too small.

No further opportunity for running occurred until Saturday 27 September, when the weather was far from ideal. However, the *Crusader* was run to prove the efficiency or otherwise of the new rudder. We were gratified to see that the boat was able to turn very convincingly at the end of the run at speeds in he neighbourhood of 100 mph.

We now come to Monday, 29 September, the day of the final run. Weather in the early morning had proved reasonably promising, but insufficiently good to justify an attempt being made on the record. However, at 11 o'clock conditions improved greatly and all concerned went to their stations again. About 15 minutes were allowed for various washes to die down and the *Crusader* was off. As far as I myself was concerned, I was half-way along the measured mile on the side of the road about 80/100 feet above the Loch and overlooking it on the north side. This position was, of course, ideal for observation.

We saw *Crusader* approach, running beautifully at extremely high speed. Unfortunately, a system of waves was creeping out into the Loch from the steep shores, and the *Crusader* went into these at extremely high speed with a smack which could be heard from where we were. The bow oscillated violently a few times and the engine was momentarily cut, and then put in again for a short time. From that time forward, the boat built up a gradually increasing instability or 'porpoise' culminating in the craft diving in. The exact cause of the trouble I am unable to give, but I am certain that the difficulty occurred after hitting the aforementioned washes as the boat was running perfectly hitherto. From the fact that the average speed of 206.89 mph was recorded, and that for a substantial part of the second half mile, the engine was cut, or at a very much reduced power, I should say that the speed was between 240/250 mph, at the stage when the waves were met. In my opinion more speed than this was available if it could be used."

Many theories were put forward for the accident that befell Cobb, most of which made much of the discussion between du Cane, Cobb and Eyston regarding the front planing shoe, but modern studies of the film and written evidence would point to a simple failure in stability. Du Cane had already voiced his fears about *Crusader's* tendency to hold her speed, and sometimes even accelerate, on a closed or partial throttle setting. As has been mentioned, the expected resistance/speed curve had become a flat line in reality, and this was borne out in du Cane's statement in his reference to Cobb throttling off at the onset of the trouble, but that his speed did not abate. Anyone who has seen the BBC film of the accident would be excused from believing that the front planing shoe did not, as some have said, collapse, or if it did perhaps it was only a partial distortion, which could well have put the boat out of her fore/aft balance. This being the case, and again relying on the BBC film, the official Vosper report and a statement made in the 1950s by Peter du Cane, it is more likely that the course of events was as follows:

Crusader entered the measured mile at approximately 190/200 mph, accelerating up to about 230 mph at the half-mile mark. It was at this point that she encountered what was probably the reflected wake of one of the support craft which had travelled up the loch some fifteen minutes before hand, and appeared in the form of three short waves, which du Cane calculated had a mean distance between peaks of no less than 50 feet. Cobb, sensing that the water had become less than perfect (he always likened driving *Crusader* to driving a London bus on corrugated iron, with no tyres, and at speed) lifted his foot from the throttle, only to find the craft continuing at the same speed. Having passed the first 'lump' Cobb found the water again smooth and re-applied the throttle. The first 'smack' against the wave formation altered the planing form of the front shoe, so that on the second wave the front of the craft pitched down more than it had before, and again Cobb lifted his foot, although *Crusader* was still holding her speed. This would account for what du Cane described as 'the momentary re-application of the throttle'. The natural buoyancy of the craft then brought the bow back up, and above its normal height and Cobb, sensing that all was not well, kept his foot completely off the power. It is then quite evident from the BBC film that, on encountering the third and last wave, the bow was high enough not to make any great contact, but the rear shoes were well down, and this led to what Peter du Cane later described as 'a kangaroo leap in comparison to the previous hops'. *Crusader*, obviously unsettled by the alteration to her hydrodynamic surfaces, and the partial collapse of her forward planing shoe, simply nose dived in, ejecting poor Cobb, who was found some 250 yards from the scene, floating in a standing position, barely alive. He died just under an hour later, mainly from shock.

2.

Vitesse Bleu

The accident that befell John Cobb came as a great shock to Donald Campbell who had known him from his very young childhood. After his own crash in *Blue Bird K4*, he had expected Cobb to secure the Water Speed Record and had visions of building a new *Blue Bird* to compete for the Harmsworth Trophy, but there was no Briton in a position to recover the Water Speed Record from the Americans, and the fuse was lit. Using all the information from the *Crusader* tragedy, there was to be a new *Blue Bird*, stronger and faster than any boat ever built. The name Campbell was yet again striving for the record.

It is surprising to some just how many *Blue Birds* and *Bluebirds* there have been, as Sir Malcolm and Donald Campbell were liable to use these names for nearly every motorised device they owned. Up until 1921 the name had been given to a succession of cars, ranging from Darracq, Schneider and Lorraine-Dietrich to Grand Prix Sunbeams, all raced at Brooklands and various beaches and hill climbs around Britain and the continent. The Sunbeam Motor Works had built a one-off special, to the design of Louis Coatalen, to challenge for the outright Brooklands outer circuit lap record, but the car, known to the general public as the 350 hp Sunbeam, was also used, successfully, to challenge for the Land Speed Record. The car became one of Sir Malcolm's periodic obsessions, and on purchasing the car direct from the works the Campbell workshop was put to the task of tuning the car for more speed.

The car featured a special engine based around the Sunbeam Manitou aero engine, which displaced 18,322cc. At first, only slight mechanical changes were made but, over a period of time, the car developed an ever-lengthening tail that was built over the original, more streamlined radiator cowls. It also had an assortment of wheel discs to improve air flow, but the car was never equipped with much-needed front brakes. In 1927, the name *Blue Bird* was given to a purpose-built record-breaker. In order to compete with the likes of engineering genius Parry Thomas, Campbell decided that the only approach was a special chassis designed to hold the best engine available, housed in the most aerodynamic body shape possible. Vickers Ltd built a chassis, to a design by Amherst Villiers, which was basically an enlarged, conventional chassis featuring leaf springs and wire cross bracing. On completion, the chassis was transferred to the Robin Hood Works in Kingston, Surrey where, under the supervision of Joseph Maina, a 24,000cc Napier Lion engine of 450 hp was installed. The construction at the Robin Hood works was not up to Campbell's pace, however, and the construction was moved to Campbell's own workshop at his home at Povey Cross, near Horsham. The mechanical parts, including Maina's gearbox, were fitted by a team led by Leo Villa (see Chapter 4), and the bodywork, developed in the Vickers wind tunnel at Brooklands, was fitted by a team of panel beaters. The car resembled an over-sized Bugatti, with wire wheels and four wheel brakes.

For 1928, the 450 hp Napier was replaced with a 900 hp version. The forward radiator became two, which were moved to a surface position on the tail, allowing a bluff aerodynamic nose. The tail also employed a removable tail fin, although it is doubtful if this would have served any useful purpose, as Campbell sat astride the gearbox, elevating him so high above the engine that the bodywork had to be built up to protect him from the air blast. Again the aerodynamics were honed in the Vickers wind tunnel but Mulliners, the coachbuilders, can hardly have thought it was the most attractive car once the body had been finished.

The appearance was not greatly improved for the 1929 attempt, the car retaining its barrel-like midriff. The radiator returned to the front of the car, housed in a pointed nose section with a small round orifice for cold air. The rear treatment was a mixture of bulges and lumps. The construction of this body was handed to Arrol Astors, in Dumfries, Scotland based around the same 900 hp Napier Lion. It was obviously no better than the previous year's effort as the car failed to beat the Land Speed Record. At this time even Sir Malcolm's aeroplane was called *Blue Bird* (as was the Hon Mrs Victor Bruce's Blackburn aeroplane with which she set many flying records with the help of Sir Alan Cobham who was instrumental in the development of in flight refuelling, and who lent his expertise to Sir Malcolm's efforts) although the name brought no extra luck to the biplane as it crashed while in use in South Africa.

Design work for the next rebuild was from the drawing board of Reid Railton, who learnt his trade at the side of Parry Thomas. Although the car retained its original chassis, slightly modified, Railton had designed an offset transmission and back axle, allowing Campbell to sit alongside the gearbox, much lower than before. Again, Vickers produced a new body in which the driver's headrest continued to form a tail fin. The engine was exchanged for a 1450 hp supercharged Napier Lion, requiring the radiator to be mounted on the extreme front of the chassis. In an effort to smooth the flow of air, the wheels had full width covers and fairings to their trailing edges. The design did have one curiosity on the body built by Gurney Nutting. Mounted at the front of the body was a duplicate rev counter, allowing Campbell to check his engine speed without having to take his eye too far from the sands rushing beneath him. So successful was this incarnation, that for 1932 the only modification was the reshaping of the radiator housing, which grew slightly in length with a smaller entry hole. Such was Sir Malcolm's standing that, for 1933, Rolls-Royce lent him one of their still secret R-type racing engines. This engine displaced 36,765cc and could produce 2500 hp, but differed greatly from the Napier in both size and frontal aspect. The bodywork was kept much the same as before, but because of the size of the engine, the front of the car developed a pronounced hump. On the Supermarine S6 Schneider Trophy aircraft, which used the same engine, the rocker covers were exposed in order to keep the bodywork as closely fitting as possible, and to aid cooling. This procedure was borrowed for *Blue Bird*.

The car was successful in raising the record, but mainly due to the extra power of the Rolls-Royce engine, so Railton had the luxury of over a year to effect a redesign to see Campbell first past the 300 mph barrier. As with any competitor for the Land Speed Record, one of the biggest enemies to success was wheel spin. To counter this, Railton developed a new rear axle that allowed for twin rear wheels, although this caused the wheelbase to differ from one side of the car to the other. The extra weight of this assembly was complemented by lead ballast bolted to the chassis rails. The radiator was retained at the very front of the car, but replaced by a lower, wider unit allowing a full width nose incorporating a shutter to improve airflow once the car had entered the measured mile. Again, the driver's headrest continued into a larger, more integrated tail fin and the tail section of the bodywork also housed air-operated braking flaps. The most obvious change was that the bodywork was continued out between the wheels, completely enclosing the leading and trailing edges. After succeeding in raising the record on Daytona Beach early in 1935, this car, still incorporating much of the original 1927 design, finally took the record past 300 mph.

Blue Birds on Water

Sir Malcolm Campbell had taken to the water long before his decision to take on the Americans for the World Water Speed Record honours, becoming a keen yachtsman. Sir Malcolm purchased his first yacht, *Blue Bird 1*, during September 1929. She was a 34ft cabin cruiser built by Thornycroft, and was originally called '*Billduan*'. She was powered by two Handy Billy petrol engines and had twin props. *Blue Bird 1* unfortunately vanished, oddly at about the same time as she went to Dunkirk, as part of the fleet of little ships used in the evacuation. Perhaps she was lost in action? *Blue Bird 2* was launched on 20 July 1931 and was again built by Thornycroft to Sir Malcolm's orders. She served the Campbell family for two years and was sold, eventually to be renamed *'Bluefinch'*, after she too had seen action at Dunkirk. After many years, she has now been fully restored and is moored on the Thames, renamed *'Blue Bird of Chelsea'*. Sir Malcolm's third motor yacht was a 73ft vessel built by Frank Bevan and originally called *'Frebelle 3'*. Sir Malcolm paid the sum of £7000 for her and she too went across the Channel to Dunkirk. After the war she was renamed *'Chico'* and probably retains this name to this day. *Blue Bird 4* was yet another Dunkirk veteran, she is still fully operational and retains the *Blue Bird* name, and can even be chartered by the enthusiast.

The first high-speed boat to have the name *Blue Bird* was christened by Lady Dorothy Campbell in 1937 and was given the international racing number *K3*. Built by Saunders Roe, and designed by Fred Cooper, she was to be powered by the same Rolls-Royce 'R'engine that had driven the last of Sir Malcolm's cars to 301 mph in 1935, the R-type R37. Cooper, who had previously designed the *Miss England* craft for Sir Henry Segrave decided that to utilise the power of the Rolls R-type, Campbell's first speedboat would have to be as compact as possible, therefore *Blue Bird K3* was designed for the helmsman only. To give the craft the necessary strength, the centrally mounted engine was bolted to longitudinal frames of Canadian rock elm boxed with diagonally jointed three-ply. This central armature was completed by the forward-mounted gearbox bolted to the frames. Attached to these members were lateral frames, much like the bulkheads on a scale model. These were cut from single sheets of seven-ply, eliminating the need for joints and the compromise in strength they would create. These frames were attached to the central runners by triangular Duralumin brackets with support members for the deck. The deck was then fitted using six-ply and the bottom of five-ply, the side planking being of cross-laid mahogany. The decking was finally covered with canvas and ply and an aluminium cockpit/engine housing built onto it. The drive was taken from the engine, through a dog clutch, forward to the gearbox, where the rotation was geared up by a ratio of three, and taken back to the propeller at the stern. All up, she weighed only 2½ tons, and measured only 22ft 3ins at the waterline, with a beam of 9ft 6in. Because of her wide, gently curved undersurface, her draught was a mere 1ft 9ins at rest, with a displacement of 4,945 lbs. Throughout her career, she proved an unstable, and difficult to manage craft, due in part to her single-step layout, and also because of the enormous torsional twisting created by the huge engine.

Blue Bird K3 was duly replaced by the Thornycroft-built *Blue Bird K4* in 1939, a craft whose design was originally laid out by Fred Cooper, but after a dispute between Cooper and Vosper, the design was completed by

Peter du Cane, and Reid Railton. The construction method was along exactly the same lines as her predecessor, employing the same use of plywood, but there was one very important difference, the increased use of Duralumin. This was to increase the torsional rigidity of the hull so that full use could be made of her new planing principle. During trials of *Blue Bird K3* at Lake Lucerne in 1938, Railton had mentioned a new technique for reducing the water drag of a single-step hydroplane. Working from drawings supplied by Adolf E. Apel of the Ventnor Boat Works, of Atlantic City, USA, the design incorporated a three-point system, in which the forward step was concave, which meant that as the hull rose out of the water it was supported on just the outer edges of the step, reducing the drag effect and increasing stability. Retaining all of the mechanical parts of *K3*, the new *Blue Bird* easily raised the record in August 1939. After the Second World War Campbell had *Blue Bird* converted to jet propulsion, but died before he could perfect the combination. Meanwhile, just before the war, Sir Malcolm did a part-exchange deal with his friend, John Simpson. *K3* was exchanged for a Lincoln car, with the promise that the engines, gearbox and rudder assembly would follow.

When Donald Campbell took up the challenge, he brought *K3*'s hull from Simpson as part of the deal to secure the R-type engines. She had received light damage in an air raid, but was basically in her pre-war condition. Even though the hull formed part of the engine deal, Campbell junior left the hull at Simpson's yard, where it remained until his death. Simpson's son Sammy used the battered hull for advertising and in the fifties there were noises that perhaps John Cobb might use the hull to gain valuable experience at handling high speed boats before driving *Crusader*. *K3* then moved to Lord Bristol, who had visions of displaying her alongside both of Donald's later *Bluebirds* in a museum. She now lies at Paul Foulkes-Halbard's Filching Manor Motor Museum in Polegate, Sussex. Having once obtained the original engines, Donald set off on his own speed odyssey using his father's *Blue Bird K4*. The jet engine removed, her appearance returned to that of 1939 until a second cockpit was installed for Leo Villa, and finally she metamorphosed into a two-seat prop-rider. The remains of her hull were burned after she sank in 1952.

Motive Forces

Nearly all British land and water speed record attempts had one thing in common – their engines. From the early 1920s onwards there were really only two engines to choose from, and without these Britain would probably never have held either record.

The early efforts of Segrave, Campbell and Hubert Scott-Paine had revolved around the Napier Lion aero engine, as had Britain's efforts in the Schneider Trophy of the 1920s. The Napier line goes back to before the reign of George III. Robert Napier (1726-1805) was the father of six sons, and one of these, Robert junior, was blacksmith to the Duke of Argyll at Inverary. His son, David, born in 1795, decided to make the move south, and opened an engineering plant just outside London in 1808, specialising in the manufacture of printing presses. David died in 1873, and the works were taken over by his son, James Murdoch Napier and, under his direction, the works began the production of motor cars. Their reputation for producing well-made, relatively fast cars was enhanced by the racing motorist, S.F. Edge, whose many feats included winning the 1902 Gordon Bennett race from Paris to Innsbruck, and setting many endurance records at Brooklands in Surrey. In 1903, D. Napier & Son Ltd moved to Acton, and in 1915 started production of the V12 RAF 3a, and V8 Sunbeam aero engines for the British war effort.

During 1916, Montague Stanley Napier, and chief designer A.J. Rowledge started work on an all-new engine to be designed, and built at the company's expense. This engine, originally called the '*Triple Four*' was to become the Lion. The design was a masterpiece. Early aero engines tended to suffer from crankshaft problems, and for that reason Napier and Rowledge decided that they could still have a twelve-cylinder engine, and maintain a short, and therefore stronger crankshaft, by planning a W12, or 'broad arrow' configuration. Thus, the engine comprised of three banks of four cylinders spaced at 60 degrees to each other.

The closely spaced steel cylinders were fitted, by means of spigots and flanges, to an aluminium crankcase. Each block had an integral combustion chamber and steel water jackets. The cylinders measured 5.5 inches x 5.125 inches (1,461 cu in engine capacity), and were topped by a monobloc aluminium head, each with two inlet and two exhaust valves. The centre, vertical cylinders had master rods connected directly to the short and virtually unbreakable crankshaft, while the two outer banks were linked by auxiliary rods, pivoting on the master rods by tapered 'wrist pins'. Compression ratios ranged from 5 to 1 to an extraordinary 10 to 1, the aero propeller being geared down by 0.6585 to 1 by nose-mounted reduction gears. Pistons were of aluminium alloy with two gas rings at the top, a scraper immediately below, and a second at the base of the piston skirt. Each bank had two camshafts, one for inlet, and the other for exhaust valve operation.

One curiosity was that on the starboard and centre banks, the inlet valve was on the left of the exhaust valve, while on the port bank this layout was reversed, something one assumes was worth remembering during a rebuild! Dry sump lubrication was used, oil being drawn up from a separate tank and pumped through oil galleries in the crankshaft, and then directed by drillings to lubricate the big ends, slave con rods and pins. From there, the oil was taken up through further galleries in the master rods from the big ends to the gudgeon pins and cylinder bores, which also benefited from splash lubrication from the big ends.

The engine first ran in April, 1917 and instantly gave a reliable 450 hp at 2000 rpm and, by the time production engines were running, most were geared to produce 570 hp at 2,585 rpm, though it was usual to limit the speed to 2,350 rpm. Eventually, when the Lion became the engine for racing and record-breaking, they were coaxed to run at 1,400 hp at nearly 4000 rpm.

Each bank was considered as a separate four-cylinder engine, their individual firing orders being a normal 1, 3, 4, 2. The complete engine was numbered from the front of the port bank, back down the centre bank toward the front, and then from the front to the rear of the starboard bank, making the firing order for the complete engine: 1, 5, 9, 3, 7, 11, 4, 8, 12, 2, 6, 10. One suspects that most mechanics wrote this down rather than commit it to memory!

The Lion was widely used in service, and was installed in such aircraft as the Vickers Virginia bomber, *Fairey IIIF*, and the commercial version of the Vimy bomber. But as with Rolls-Royce, and the famous R-type, it is the short life-span racing engines and their application that are of the most interest. Again, as with the Rolls-Royce R-type, initial tuning for racing was at the behest of the Royal Air Force High Speed Flight for use in the Schneider trophy, which it duly won in 1927, the year the Capt Malcolm Campbell used the same specification Napier Lion to gain the Land Speed Record at 174.223 mph on the sands of Pendine, South Wales. The following year was again successful for Campbell and the Lion on the beach of Daytona, USA. 1929 saw the Lion (in its Mk VII A 900 hp form) power first Segrave's beautiful *Golden Arrow* to a Land Speed Record of 231.446 mph, and a Mk V IID engine of 1,320 hp powered a Gloster VI N249 – coincidentally named the *Golden Arrow* – to an air-speed record, as well as an absolute record, of 336.3 mph. It was at this time that Segrave's thoughts were turning to speed on water in *Miss England*, also powered by a Napier Lion.

Other boats powered by the Lion included Hubert Scott-Paine's *Miss Great Britain III*, which was for some time the fastest single-engined boat in the world, and Betty Carstairs' *Estelle*, whose two Napier Lions would go on to power John Cobb's Railton to Land Speed Records in 1938, 1939 and 1947. A Lion was installed in the Edward Spurr/T.E. Lawrence (Lawrence of Arabia) boat, *Empire Day*, in 1939 for its unsuccessful attempt on the World Water Speed Record on Windermere. Unlike the Rolls-Royce R-type however, the Lion never managed to capture the outright Water Speed Record, regardless of the fact that although they gave 'only' 900 hp they could be geared to rev to 3,300 rpm, which was ideal for marine application. The engine was continuously updated and converted for different applications and power outputs, but it was such a good engine that its makers grew complacent, and it was soon overtaken by the opposition. The Lion's second lease of life came in the Second World War when it was marinised. Redubbed the *Sea Lion* it powered many high-speed naval vessels. Perhaps the W12 format of the engine was finally its downfall, but the arrangement was recently resurrected for the *Life* Grand Prix car, driven amongst others by Bruno Giacomelli, but with little success. The Napier Lion put Britain, and those that either drove or piloted for her at the forefront of racing and record-breaking, but like all things technically advanced, the engine was replaced by another that has a unique place in record-breaking.

The R-Type and the Triple Crown

In today's world of motor racing, the Triple Crown comprises the World Formula One championship, the Le Mans 24 hours, and the Indianapolis 500. As yet, the only holder of this accolade has been Graham Hill. In the days of old, however, the Triple Crown meant the air, land, and water speed records. Some men had the courage to contemplate attacking the Triple Crown, but their dreams never came to fruition. The most notable aspirants to the Triple Crown have been Sir Henry Segrave, and Sir Malcolm Campbell. Had their ambitions been realised, theirs would have been two names on a very short list. As it was, Segrave's death put an end to the development of the *Segrave Meteor*, an experimental aircraft built to prove the theory of his ultimate record contender's design, and Campbell's final obsession with perfecting the use of the jet in the water speed arena robbed him of the time to attempt the air speed record. It is ironic, therefore, that the only name to bridge all three mediums of speed should be there through the simple reason that they had built the best thing for the job, with no other intention than that of winning one race, in one year.

The 'Coupe d' Aviation Maritime Jacques Schneider', was offered by a French industrial entrepreneur, Jacques Schneider, in an attempt to accelerate the development of maritime aviation, and was announced to the public on 5 December 1912. Schneider was convinced that the continents of the world would one day be linked by a flying boat service and, in order to foster the idea, the regulations were written around the idea of proving seaworthiness as well as out-and-out speed.

The rules required that all entrants should go through elimination tests that included a navigation test and a water tightness exercise, which involved very little actual flying, but did call for the aircraft to stay afloat for anything up to six hours, having made several taxi-ing runs. Having successfully proceeded to the next round, the aircraft were called on to fly a triangular course of some 150 nautical miles, followed by a smaller circuit of about 30 miles. Although not a race (the competitors were started at intervals, having drawn lots) it was the fastest craft that took the prize for its nation's governing aero-club. The winning nation could then hold the next contest on home 'ground', so to speak and, as an added incentive, any country winning the Trophy three times within a five-year span, was deemed to have won the Trophy for all time. The Schneider Trophy was unique in that aircraft and aero-engine development were actively encouraged by the participating Governments to such an extent that only the following two world wars accelerated development any faster.

The first contest was won by France, in Monaco. The following year, Howard Pixton, in a Sopwith took the Trophy for Britain with a speed of 86.78 mph. In 1919, the event was declared void as not one entrant qualified as a finisher. The right to stage the next contest fell to Italy, simply because Sgt Guido Jannello was the only pilot to complete any laps at all, although all eleven of his circuits were done incorrectly! It was not until 1927 that Britain won again, by which time the winning speed was in excess of 281 mph. A win in 1929 would put a firm grip on the Trophy. Sadly, it would not be an event that Jacques Schneider would witness, as his death on 1 May 1928, in almost total obscurity, robbed him of the opportunity.

Since 1919, the only engine thought up to the task of powering Britain's entries to success was the already elderly Napier Lion, and success in 1929 would be dependent on a new, and more powerful engine. First tentative approaches to Rolls-Royce met with firm rejection due to a long-standing company policy of not supporting competitive motoring, or aviation events. One can only assume this dated back to the death of C.H. Rolls, in a flying accident after a career in motor racing, during which he had held the Land Speed Record. Finally, a direct approach was decided upon, and Commander Bird, of Supermarine, and G.P. Bulman, who was in charge of aero engine development at the Air Ministry, paid a personal visit to Henry Royce at his home in West Wittering, on the Sussex coast.

It has often been said that it was during a long walk on the beach that discussions imploring Royce to change his mind took place, and during which the idea of improving Rolls-Royce's already high reputation was to be Bird and Bulman's main line of attack. It is also said that, having capitulated to the pressure, Royce drew his first ideas into the sand with a stick. Having taken the decision, Royce had to settle on what form this new engine would take. He first looked to the idea of producing a 45-degree V16, and indeed the design scheme for the engine was completed, not in Royce's personal series – the LeC drawings (LeC stood for Le Canadel, his winter home in the south of France from 1913 onwards) but back in Derby in the DES series (Derby Engines Schemes). Unfortunately, time was short and eventually the idea was abandoned in favour of developing an already existing engine. The engine chosen had a pedigree that could be traced back to the very first Rolls-Royce aero engines.

This first aero engine was the Eagle, a 60-degree V12 of around 20 litres (20.32). Design work started in September 1914 and the Eagle first flew in late 1915, installed in a Handley-Page 0/100 bomber. A smaller version, the 14.22 litre Falcon was also produced, being basically a scaled-down Eagle. Shortly after, a third engine was produced, the Hawk (7.4 litre) which was, in effect, half an Eagle without reduction gear. Only about 200 Hawks, but thousands of Eagles and Falcons were produced, all playing a vital role in the First World War. Further development produced the Condor, a 35-litre monster with four valves per cylinder, but the finished design arrived too late to help in the allied victory in Europe.

The first part of the R-type jig-saw fell into place when, in 1921, A.J. Rowledge left D. Napier & Son, and joined Henry Royce as Chief Design Assistant, and set up the Derby Design Office. He introduced many features to the Condor that were to become almost standard issue for Rolls-Royce aero engines. Spur replaced epicyclic propeller-reduction gears, fork and blade supplanted articulated connecting rods and there was the addition of crankcase lateral bolts to support the crankshaft main bearings.

In 1925, Royce introduced the 'F' engine, a V12 which was later christened the Kestrel. It was a monobloc of about 22 litres, of about Eagle size, and was the first Rolls-Royce engine to incorporate supercharging. Soon after its introduction, and on the instruction of Royce, the Kestrel design was scaled up, the result of R.W. Harvey-Bailey's detailed draughtsmanship becoming the 'H' engine of 37 litres. Royce suggested that broad 'saddle studs' should be fitted to the crankcase to combat the expected higher loads (a possible clue to future racing use) and, in due course, the 'H' became the Buzzard, its main application being for flying boats. Only about 100 were built, and it was this engine that was selected to become the basis for the new Schneider Trophy power plant. Although originally coded the 'Racing 'H'', it soon became the 'R' – R for racing.

The experimental department, along with Rowledge and Harvey-Bailey, worked together to increase the Buzzard's 950hp, and testing commenced on 4 July 1929 when engine R1 produced 1656 bhp at 3000rpm. The next day, R7 managed 1718bhp. A short while later, the first batch of production R's was complete, and numbered R1, 3, 5, 7, 9, 11 and 15, there being no number 13 for superstitious reasons (indeed the number 13 never appeared as part of a chassis number, and never on an aero engine!). Air trials of the new engine, fitted in the Supermarine S6, a development of the older Napier-engined S5, started almost as soon as the first aircraft arrived at Calshot and, during practice for the contest itself, some of the mechanics and engineers that had been involved in its development were allowed to travel down to Southampton to watch the event. It was to be a very fortunate situation. During the first trials of the contest proper, 'Batchy' Atcherley's S6 (airframe number N248), was seen listing quite badly, and a messenger was dispatched to inform the plane's designer R.J. Mitchell (who later used the experience of the S5 and S6 to design the Spitfire) of the situation. Mitchell was in bed, sleeping off the effects of working several extremely long days, but once roused he motored down to see what could be done. The regulations insisted that once moored, the craft could not be touched for six hours. Mitchell decided that in his opinion the aircraft would still be afloat at the end of that period. He was proved correct, but once having repaired the leaky float, metal particles were found on two of the twenty-four spark plugs indicating that a piston failure was in the offing. Again, the rules were quite specific in that the original engine could not be removed, but parts of the engine could be replaced. Once again, messengers were sent all around Southampton to round up the mechanics and engineers from hotels and public houses. After a night of work, one block had been removed, the offending piston replaced, and the block renewed, all without removing the engine from the airframe. It was left to Flag Officer H.R.D. Waghorn to win the competition. To put the icing on the cake, Squadron Leader Orlebar seized the air speed record at 357.7 mph, on 12 September. Royce was rewarded with a baronetcy the following year.

During this time, two more R-types were built under contract for Lord Wakefield, financed by his company, Castrol Oil, to be installed in the newly completed *Miss England II* motorboat for Sir Henry Segrave to attack the World Water Speed Record. These were numbered R17 and R19 and, of these two, R17 was probably the rarest of all R-types, for it was the only engine built as a left-hand tractor (i.e. it rotated in the opposite direction, thus eliminating the problem of matching engine speeds in a two-engined craft), a fact that was to give Sir Malcolm Campbell a few headaches in the years to come. The Water Speed Record duly fell to Segrave at 98.76 mph, but in attempting to raise the record still further Segrave was to lose his life. It was a bittersweet 1930, not only for the engine builders, but also for Britain. *Miss England II* was salvaged and rebuilt by Rolls-Royce at Derby and the helm handed to Kaye Don and the record fell again, first at 103.49, and then at 110.28 mph. The engines were then installed in Lord Wakefield's new speedboat, *Miss England III*, and the record improved to 117.43, and finally to 119.81 mph.

On the night of the 1929 Schneider Trophy success, a banquet was held aboard the motor yacht, *SS Orford* to celebrate the victory. It was with great pride that Ramsay MacDonald, the then Prime Minister announced, 'We're going to do our level best to win again'. He may well have meant it in 1929, but by 1930 he, or his government, had changed their minds. The economic climate was such that the government felt that the contest could not be supported officially, a position that led to vigorous attacks by press, parliament, and the public, and it was left to an individual to change the government's mind.

Fanny Lucy Radmall was the daughter of a Camberwell cabinetmaker, but had married Sir Robert Houston, a wealthy shipping magnate. On his death in 1926, she had become the richest woman in Britain. She had a dislike for the way Ramsey MacDonald had treated the whole affair, probably borne out of the interest her late husband had shown in running a flying boat service around the world, much as Jacques Schneider had envisaged. After an approach from Colonel the Lord Sempill, she agreed to put up the necessary £100,000 to embarrass the government into an about-turn. The only drawback was that it left Rolls-Royce with a scant six months before the next contest to further develop the R-type to produce the extra power felt necessary. The experimental department (created and headed by Ernest Hives) set about wringing even more power from the trusty 'R', rather than designing a new engine.

For the 1931 contest, six more engines were built: R21, R23, R25, R27 and R31, bringing the production run up to 14 units. Time was short and, because of this, development work carried on night and day. Rod Banks, an expert in fuel mixes was entrusted with producing special sprint fuels, to give high power outputs, but for very short periods of time, well short of the specified one hour continuous test run that Royce demanded. The 1931 engines were physically different, having a more streamlined crankcase lower half. Internally, the R-type had been given sodium-cooled exhaust valves (visible as black at full power instead of cherry red, and a notorious weak spot in the early engines) and finally, and unknown to Royce himself, American Wellworthy pistons. These proved far more able to withstand the 13 tons of force every time a chamber fired. There was also a revision to master and articulated con rods, but the one-hour test proved difficult to complete. On 24 April 1931, R3 failed after only 17 minutes when the main bearings collapsed. On 1 May 1931, R3 again ground to a halt after only 2½ minutes, again with main bearing failure, allied to a connecting rod failure. R3 managed to run for $17^1/_3$ minutes on the 14th until the supercharger slipper bushes seized. The next day, poor old R3 was coaxed to run twice, once for 29½ minutes, then again for 18½ minutes, but both times the exhaust valves had broken. On 29 May, R3, fitted with the new sodium-cooled exhausts valves ran for 25 minutes, before the heads failed, possibly caused by the new valves.

Testing Times for Derby

The testing of an R-type engine required that as well as the test engine, three Kestrels be run simultaneously. These were required to reproduce the head wind necessary for the ram effect on the supercharger intake, the through-draft required to provide ventilation and clean air and another to provide sufficient cooling to the R's crankcase. The people of Derby had endured the sound of unsilenced, highly tuned engines before, but the cacophony of a screaming R engine and its three ancillary Kestrels being run day and night, began to put a strain on local feeling. Only after the intervention of the Mayor, who requested that they endure the noise for the sake of British prestige was a compromise effected that allowed testing to continue. If the people of Derby thought they were suffering, perhaps they should have been inside the factory, as it required eight men to be *inside* the test house, in the most inhospitable of conditions. One man was at the engine controls, one at the water brake controls, one checking tachometer readings and one checking cooling readings. There was a man checking fuel flow, another in charge of the Kestrel producing the head wind, one in charge of the 'double boost' Kestrel, the foreman in charge, and finally the chief tester, who gave all the orders and took down and logged all the readings. During the tests of the initial batch of R engines, this was the job of Victor Halliwell, who lost his life with Henry Segrave in the *Miss England* tragedy. Even using cotton wool as earplugs, these men became deaf for at least twenty-four hours after each half-hour test, and their ears rang for up to two days – and these tests continued for seven months.

Another problem was the incredible oil consumption. During a 25-minute run, the engine could consume, burn, or spit out of its breathers nearly sixty gallons of castor oil. This put consumption during these first attempts at the one hour run somewhere in the region of 112 gallons per hour. The test house becoming smothered on a regular basis, requiring milk to be served to the test house operatives twice a day as an antidote to the effects of castor oil. For each test, 200 gallons of fuel had to be mixed, some 80 gallons being needed just to get the circulation going, and then to run the engine up to working temperature. The normal test procedure called for a period of 5 minutes running at 1000-2000 rpm to stabilise the running temperatures, although slow running was an extremely low 450 to 500 rpm and was ensured by running each engine with a propeller of the same type as that being fitted at Calshot. Although the 'R'-type was provided with an air starter system, the test engines were started with an electric motor and a belt drive. Fuel was gravity fed from a tank, and lubricating oil was pre-heated by steam. These tests also allowed a detailed life history of every part to be recorded, enabling Rolls-Royce to predict accurately when parts would need reconditioning or replacing.

The speed of development accelerated to a phenomenal rate. On one occasion, a rod had come through the crankcase at 5pm. The engine was off the test bed by 5.30pm, dismantled by 7pm and new drawings made. By 8.30pm, completely new rods were in hand. Before lunch the next day, the newly rebuilt engine was being started up for test. Finally, on August 12th, R9 ran for the magical one hour. Outside, the ground was warm to the touch, and a fifteen-foot-wide hollow had appeared under the exhausts. A totally new crankshaft and rods had been incorporated and much re-designing had been necessary so that the white-metal big ends could withstand the increased loads that were being inflicted. These were enormous by any standards: nearly nine tons on the centre main bearing alone. There was also side-lashing of the big-end bearings, which could cause bearing failure, and this also had to be combated. And all this from a modest increase in revs of only 300rpm. After ten minutes' running it was usual to find that at least two valve springs had broken, and a special test rig was made to overcome this. After much experimenting, revolutionary springs were evolved, and another problem solved.

After its run, R9 was stripped to its bare bones and found to be in near-perfect order. Further research on combinations of different scraper rings and breather systems eventually reduced oil consumption to around 14 gallons an hour, reducing oil temperature to approximately 80 degrees inlet and 140 degrees outlet. The magnetos were also a cause for concern, as vibration had a disastrous effect on them. Added to this, oil found its way along the magneto drive shafts, eventually soaking the rotors and points. New seals were developed and, in the end, every nut and bolt had to be split-pinned. The components that always seemed to run faultlessly were the Lodge X170 sparking plugs. Under the microscope they showed signs of minute metallic particles, but not once did a plug fail. Race sets were given a duration test and sent back to Lodge for examination, re-polishing and fitting with new outer bodies.

* * * *

If the Derby experimental department was working double time, it certainly was no different down on the south coast at Calshot. Running an engine on a test bed was far removed from the forces encountered in a racing aircraft, and much research into the fuel and cooling systems became necessary. Supermarine built a complete fuel installation test rig to replicate as much of the stresses and strains as possible. Further problems arose with the new installation to the actual aircraft. One illustration of this was the carburettor mounted on the underside of the supercharger, which cleared the inside of the fuselage by a mere 0.15 in. Yet again, the only solution was for a mock-up to be made of the front of the Supermarine S6 to ensure the correct installation. The task of changing engines was also a difficult one, needing the transfer of much piping and requiring some six operatives no less than half an hour just to lower the engine the final six inches onto the bearers. In damp weather the engines proved extremely difficult to start, due to moisture in the compressed air wetting the plugs but, once started, the same plugs could be used throughout an airborne run. Even special methods of filling the wing radiators had to be adopted to prevent air pockets developing. It seemed as if every single facet of winning the Schneider trophy was to be rife with problems.

Finally, however, everything looked as if it was beginning to fit together, as R21 was installed into Supermarine S6, airframe number S1596 in readiness for the competition.

In contrast to the complexities of production and running the engines, the starting procedure was relatively simple. The engine was turned over using compressed air, drawing fuel through to the combustion chambers, where it was ignited by a spark created by a hand-turned magneto. The engine was warmed by running for 5 minutes on a weak mixture at about 1000rpm, and the oil coolers were vented. The mixture was then enriched and the throttle opened to about 245rpm with 22lb/sq in boost. During the first test flights, it was found that the air intake velocity was reaching 407 mph allowing the boost to be increased on the Derby test bed and unleashing yet more horsepower.

On the 9 September 1931, R15 produced a staggering 2783 bhp at 3400rpm, the highest figure ever attained from any R engine, but the next problem was about to rear its head just as test engines were being run to Calshot. Rod Banks, working with Rolls-Royce and the Ethyl Export Corporation had been experimenting with several fuel mixes, and had thought their work was finished, but it was found that the original sprint cocktail (petrol, benzol and methanol) dissolved the jointing compounds, thereby blocking the fuel filters. This was not the only problem, it was also found that any water content over 0.3%, rendered the fuel useless and an elaborate test procedure had to be devised to check for this. Eventually, Banks came up with a mix of 30% alcohol, 60% methanol, 10% acetone and 4.2cc of tetra-ethyl lead per gallon, while Rolls-Royce developed a non-setting jointing compound, Hylomar, that is still used in today's modern motor trade.

* * * *

As test engines were dispatched to Calshot, along with Rolls-Royce staff and Mr J. Pettitt-Herriot, the Air Ministry liaison officer between Rolls-Royce and Supermarine, it became necessary to return engines to Derby for rebuilding. In full sprint form, the 'R' was only really any good for about 15 minutes before the exhaust valves started to fail and so a special Rolls-Royce Phantom I with an engine cradle was made for the purpose. As most of its runs were made at night, and at high speed, usually to a suitably blind (and deaf!) police force, it became nicknamed '*The Phantom of The Night*'.

Two new S6Bs (S1595 and S1596), were joined by two S6As (N247 and N248) which were S6s brought up to S6B standard, as well as a Gloster IVA, a Gloster VI and two S5s, which arrived at Calshot for the Royal Air Force High Speed Flight to practise with. Sadly, during these trials Flying Officer Brinton died, when his S6A, N247 failed to take off cleanly on his first flight. The aircraft plunged nose-first into the sea after bouncing down onto her floats. After a very difficult underwater search, the wreck of the aircraft was located, but there was no sign of Brinton. After several days of checking local beaches and waterways, the mystery of the location of Brinton's body was solved. The shattered remains of N247 were loaded onto a transport barge and taken over to Calshot, where they were left to drain for a couple of days. A Supermarine engineer was then sent over to make an on the spot report. Extracts from his report show that he was pleased with the fact the major components of the aircraft, the fuselage and floats, had survived intact – if separated – but he was curious that the seat was missing. A torch was shone into the aircraft and the engineer noted that many of the bulkheads were damaged, and bent backwards toward the tail. A hole was cut in the fuselage just ahead of the tailplane, at the narrowest part of the structure. There in the tail, forced in by water pressure, was the seat, and the body of Monty Brinton. He had broken his neck.

It became a matter of history that Flt Lt J.N. Boothman won the Schneider Trophy for his country for all time at an average speed of 340.8 mph over the 217.5-mile course, the engine used was R25. The Schneider Trophy was accordingly presented to the people of Britain and tradition has it that Boothman, as the winning pilot, was the only man, allowed to hang his cap on the trophy. Even this apparently easy victory followed yet another careful set of operations to ensure the final result. Just before the race, the practice engines were removed and the race engines installed. These were then given a short ground run to check the installation. A short test flight was then made and the plugs removed so that each bore could be inspected. New plugs were fitted and the oil, boost and fuel gauge pipe lines blanked off to obviate trouble should they break during the race. The mixture setting was fixed and a final ground run made to test the new plugs, then the fuel system was cleaned throughout and filled with 140 gallons of Rod Banks' special fuel mix. The coolant tank was topped up, leaving a 1½ gallon air space or expansion, and 16½ gallons of castor oil, pre-heated to 60°C in special tanks on the quayside, were put in last. After the race the winning aircraft was checked over, where it was found that although it had consumed no water, it had used 110 gallons of fuel and 11½ gallons of castor oil in the 38 minutes, $22^1/_5$ seconds it had taken to complete the seven laps. Yet more was to come. R27 had been given a few additional tuning tweaks and, along with the new sprint fuel, the carburettor passages were opened up, fuel header tank pressure was increased and the fuel pumps geared to operate faster. Fuel consumption rose to 0.85 pints per bhp hour, which meant that when flat out she would be burning fuel at over 3½ gallons per minute (210 gallons per hour). The engine was then installed in Supermarine 6B no. S1595 (now in the Science Museum and the same aircraft that secured the Schneider Trophy) and on Tuesday, 29 September 1931 Flt Lt Stainforth set up a new airspeed record of 407.5 mph.

Production of the R-type did not finish there, however. In 1933 Sir Malcolm Campbell borrowed an R engine (either R25 or R31 according to factory despatch records) and set up a new Land Speed Record of 272.46 mph on Ormond Beach (now Daytona Beach), Daytona, Florida USA. It was a unique event. Until then the air, land and water speed records had been totally separate. Nobody had managed to leave the ground (or indeed the water) to take the air speed record, nor had any previous air speed holders attempted either the land or water speed records. On the engine front, the Liberty aero engine had held the Land Speed Record (this was in 1926 with Parry Thomas and *'Babs'*, and in 1928 with Ray Keach and *'The White Triplex Special'*) and the Water Speed Record (in 1919 with Casey Baldwin in *'Hydrodome IV'*, and with Gar Wood and *'Miss America' I* and *II*), although until 1928 there were no officially certified absolute records for motorboats but the air speed record was out of reach of this heavy mass-produced engine. The Napier, on the other hand, had also held the air speed record and had been used by both Campbell and Segrave to secure the Land Speed Record. Although a very successful motorboat engine, it had never powered any vessel to the outright Water Speed Record.

The Rolls-Royce R-type had originally taken the air speed record in 1929 (A.H. Orlebar in the Supermarine S6), the Water Speed Record in 1930 (Sir Henry Segrave in *Miss England II*), and now the Land Speed Record. It is a feat that has never been equalled. In late 1933, Sir Malcolm Campbell paid £5,800 to Rolls-Royce for the R37 that he installed in the newly streamlined *Blue Bird* car, raising the record to 276.82 mph, nowhere near his intended 300 mph target but, in September 1935, R37 powered *Blue Bird* to 301.13 mph. Campbell, having achieved his ambition, promptly retired from speed on land. As Campbell stepped down, so George Eyston stepped in and set about the construction of his huge car *Thunderbolt* for his attempt on the Land Speed Record. Eyston knew that Campbell had used the most powerful engine then available and taking the record would be a formidable task, but George had made two inspired decisions. The first was to use not one but two R-types and his second was to use R25 and R27 the fastest R-types yet built and still holders of both the Schneider Trophy and air speed records. It would appear that George's attempt on the Land Speed Record was off to a good start.

At the same time as *Thunderbolt* was nearing completion at the Bean works in Tipton (where, until recently, the Reliant car was made) a small 23-foot hydroplane was taking the name of *Blue Bird* from land to water. This is where the history of the R engine becomes a little involved.

Sir Malcolm Campbell had ownership of R37, and also had R39 as a spare lent to him by Rolls-Royce at the time of his 1935 land speed attempt. He had also been allowed by Lord Wakefield to select spares from the retired *Miss England III* motorboat and therefore R19 and the counter-rotating R17 were also spares. According to Leo Villa, Campbell then lent R17 to George Eyston who already had R25 and R27 and an option to use the factory spare R39 (all of these engines had been con-verted for use in record-breaking by the removal of any reduction gear driving directly through a new housing to a drive shaft). It would also appear that, although Eyston had obtained probably the most powerful R-types built, they had in fact been detuned, as Rolls-Royce quoted 'only' 2000 bhp for each unit against the 2350 bhp one would have expected. No matter, for Eyston while embroiled in his titanic battle with John Cobb at Bonneville raised the record three times to 357.5 mph before finally being eclipsed by Cobb in his Napier Railton fitted with two 'antique' Napier Lions.

Blue Bird and R-types

While Campbell's Land Speed Record was being broken in America, he and his new *Blue Bird* were taking to the water. On 30 June 1937 the *Blue Bird*, registered *Z-K30*, was timed at 85 mph and, according to Alf Poyser, the Rolls-Royce mechanic assigned to the project, the engine used was R19. This was left *in situ* until the record attempt proper at Lago Maggiore in northern Italy. According to Poyser's official report, and unknown to Rolls-Royce, his first task on arriving at the Italian lakes was to remove R19 and substitute it with R37. This was for two reasons: Campbell knew that the later 1931-spec engine had more power than the up-rated 1929 one and, also, he had developed the ambition of breaking both land and water speed records with the very same engine. While this was being done, Leo Villa was kept occupied changing the steering ratio from 9:1 to 10:1, as Campbell had found the steering sluggish. The first Italian run was merely a test lasting eight minutes, after which the gearbox thrust race was found to be dangerously hot. A cooling arrangement was made, comprised of a small water tank with a wick wrapped around the bearing and an air scoop, rumoured to have been made from the horn taken from Sir Malcolm's Rolls-Royce car. The first timed trials did not last long, however. On the first run, the engine could be heard backfiring very loudly. Campbell suggested that this had been caused by his throttling back too quickly, but it soon became apparent that it was due to the engine overheating. Sir Malcolm was convinced that at no time was the engine temperature over 70°C. After a static run, the engine was prepared for a high-speed test. *Blue Bird* had only travelled two-thirds of the measured mile when the engine cut out. From the jetty, Leo Villa, Alf Poyser and the rest of the team set out to find *Blue Bird* drifting, and a very red-faced Campbell standing in the cockpit proclaiming that he had, 'boiled the ruddy engine'. It was apparent that the cooling scoop had risen clear of the water at speeds of over 100 mph and robbed the engine of its vital cooling for the sealed system header tank. Poyser's report was short and to the point:

> Too much oil was thrown out of the breathers. Several tappet clearances had taken up. Both cylinder blocks were removed and they were both cracked around the valve seats. Two pistons, 'A' bank no. 3 and 4 were very badly scored and several piston rings were broken. Two new pistons, and eight rockers were scrapped due to very bad wear on the pads. The cams require cleaning up and should be tested for hardness.

Not surprisingly, R37 was removed and R39 installed along with several other modifications. The engine header-tank cooling scoop was lowered 1½ inches, and the exhaust cooling was separated from that of the engine with its own five-gallon header tank equipped with a relief valve pressure of 2lbs, plus a warning light mounted in the cockpit. Finally, and especially after Sir Malcolm confessed that he only ever looked at the rev counter, the exhaust thermometer was moved up next to the windscreen, right under the pilot's eye.

The third test run went according to plan, so a further two runs were made at full throttle, producing speeds of 117.15 mph at 3100 rpm with a water temperature of 70°C and 120.6 mph at 3100 rpm, again with a water temperature at a perfect 70°C.

On 1 September 1937, the Water Speed Record fell at 126.32 mph, but Campbell felt that *Blue Bird* and her engine had been nowhere near stretched. On 2 September, the slipway was a hive of activity. The 12-inch diameter, 20-inch pitch propeller was replaced with a 13-inch diameter, 20-inch pitch steel prop, the ping-pong balls added for buoyancy were removed, and due to the R's easy starting, the extra compressed air bottles and brackets were removed, saving over 150 lbs. Finally, it was decided that the fuel tank, which was designed to carry 35 gallons, should only be half-filled. The first run produced 128.43 mph at 3100 rpm, water temp, 70°C; the second run was at 130.57 mph, again at 3100 rpm, giving an average speed 129.5 mph, and another record.

The following August, in a letter to Mr Hives, Campbell requested a special extractor exhaust, to try to gain a few more miles per hour from

R39. The reply, dated 30 August 1938, shows the kind of lengths Rolls-Royce went to on Campbell's behalf:

Dear Sir Malcolm

We are in receipt of your letter of the 26th instant, together with the copy of your letter to Mr Hives, and he has asked us to deal with your various questions.

We have examined the case of extractor manifolds to be fitted to your boat as replacement for the new ejector type recently fitted instead of the original Miss England type water cooled configuration. We find that you could expect no more than half of a mile an hour increase at a speed of 130 mph. The chances are the increase in back pressure would more than offset any advantage, and in practice very little improvement can be expected from this type of system below 200 mph, for this reason we strongly advise that you retain your existing ejector type manifolds.

With regards to your forth-coming attempts at Lake Halwillersee we can only foresee a small increase in available power.

The altitude of this lake is 380 metres above sea level, the resulting loss of power would be 4%. If you were to use the sprint fuel mix (i.e. 60% methanol, 20% alcohol, 10% acetone with 4.2cc tetra ethyl lead per gallon), you could expect an increase in power of 5½% – a net gain therefore of 1½%. This we would envisage would increase the record by about 1½ mph.

This prediction proved extremely accurate, for on 17 September 1938, the record was again raised to 130.94 mph. During this time, letters flew between Campbell and Hives at a great rate. On 15 April, Campbell wrote asking if Rolls-Royce would approach Eyston to swap the spare works R39 for his own anti-clockwise R17, but was informed on 21 December that Eyston would allow him continued use of R39, but would not allow him to purchase it from the factory. It is also interesting to note that in 1938 Campbell made references to a new challenger that was to use two R-types, and enquiring if the 1929 *Miss England III* motorboat engines, R17 and R19 had been brought up to the latest specification. A little later on, probably when Reid Railton had suggested the new Ventnor hull for *K3*'s successor, Campbell's requests changed, asking for either a racing Merlin (the Merlin being a development of the R-type design philosophy) or a new Griffon (the prototype of which was a modified R). In another letter dated 21 December 1937, Campbell asked Hives if it would be possible to convert R17 from counter-clock, to clockwise rotation. This is of interest, as all R-types were odd numbers, yet in many of Leo Villa's notes he makes reference to R18. Could it be that R17 was indeed converted and renumbered?

After Sir Malcolm raised the Water Speed Record in August 1939 (using R39), he put the second *Blue Bird* speedboat, the Ventnor *K4*, into storage until after the World War II. He then switched to the new jet engine and fitted a De Havilland Goblin II in *Blue Bird*. But before he could perfect this new combination, Sir Malcolm died after a series of strokes, at three minutes to midnight, on New Year's Eve 1948. This was not the end of the road for the R-type, however. When Donald took the plunge and followed his father's example, his first problem was replacing the Goblin jet with the original piston engines. Having obtained them from John Simpson, he went to check them at Thomson and Taylors at Brooklands. The R engines had been well looked after and Vospers were entrusted with rebuilding *Blue Bird K4* to her original pre-war form. Although he was not successful in raising the record, he did reach some high speeds. On 17 August 1949, Donald Campbell sent a telegram to Ernest Hives, which read:

> *Blue Bird* powered by R37 this morning attained photographic-recorded speed 152 mph before breakdown of gearbox during southward run STOP Cannot adequately express my praise for wonderful performance of this old unit so worthy of the name Rolls-Royce.
> Regards Donald Campbell.

On 10 June 1951, R39-powered *Blue Bird*, converted to a prop-rider, won the Oltranza Cup on Lake Garda, in northern Italy. The R engine had returned to its roots – that of racing around a circuit, albeit on water as opposed to above it. Donald Campbell kept the R-type at the forefront of record-breaking until 1951 when *K4*, travelling at about 170 mph, suffered a structural breakdown and sank. At the time, she was powered by R39.

The R-type engine went through what amounted to 10 years of technical development in less than a year, and most of this in the 6 months leading up to the 1931 Schneider Trophy. This alone gives it a unique position in record-breaking. The engine was a V12, with a 6 inch bore and a 6.6 inch stroke, and a bore/stroke ratio of 1.10 to 1. The swept volume per cylinder was 186.6 cubic inches or 36.7 litres. The clearance volume per cylinder was 37.32 cubic inches, giving a compression ratio of 6 to 1. The normal running speed was 3200 rpm at which the piston speed was in excess of 3,520 feet per minute. The supercharger rotated at an incredible 23,904 rpm, with 33lbs of boost available at an intake blast of 400 mph. The average power output was 2,300 bhp, although the highest ever recorded power output was 2783 bhp. The 'R' had a dry weight of 1,640 lbs giving a power to weight ratio of only 0.51 lbs per bhp, astounding even by today's standards. Quite simply the R-type engine was far ahead of its time, a marvel of British skill and ability.

There was very nearly a further chapter in the engine's history. As is known, the prototype Griffon was a modified R-type. After the scrapping of the remains of the old *Blue Bird*, a new craft was planned. At first, Ken and Lewis Norris were instructed that the craft they were designing would be to take the Harmsworth Trophy, as Donald Campbell was convinced that John Cobb and his *Crusader* jet boat would soon hold the Water Speed Record. After Cobb's fatal accident the plan changed, the Harmsworth Trophy was forgotten and the outright record became the goal once more. The new *Bluebird* was to be another prop-rider and the power plant selected, the 'son of R' – a type 65 Griffon. But this was not the only plan to change.

As the new *Bluebird*'s purpose returned to that of regaining the World Water Speed Record, the design philosophy changed from the proven piston engine to the so far unsuccessful jet propulsion and, in turn, the technology of construction for the hull also changed. As speeds increased, the strength of the craft also had to increase, and the traditional material of wood made way for all metal construction. The inherent rigidity of an aluminium-skinned steel frame was crucial to mounting the far more powerful pure thrust jet, a problem Sir Malcolm Campbell never solved, and without doubt *Bluebird K7* became the first boat to succeed in utilising both jet propulsion and all-metal construction. The last *Bluebird* of the line, the CN7 car created its own unique set of problems. Regardless of the fact that a wheel-driven record-breaker has no need to corner at speed, torsional strength is important to maintain traction. Added to this, the substitution of a piston aero engine with a free turbine also created problems with air containment and delivery. Of all land speed cars, CN7 has been by far the most technically advanced car ever built, predating the construction techniques of Grand Prix cars by some years. It can be argued that the two *Bluebirds* that originated from Ken and Lewis Norris, were not only the pinnacle of the *Bluebird* family tree, but outstanding designs in the field of record-breaking.

3.

Down from The Highlands

The origins of the Campbell family are in Tain, county Ross-shire, Scotland, a place known for having more than its fair share of brave, determined fighters. It was a quality that was to be passed down through many generations, and was still very evident in Donald during his life. Much of Mary Queen of Scots' army was comprised of members of the Campbell clan, which also had a large presence in the 17th-century battles with the Covenanters. Records of the rebellions of 1715 suggest that it was again the Campbell clan that fought for the 'Old Pretender' and Bonny Prince Charlie and that in the conflict of 1745 it was a Campbell who declared himself the 'Young Pretender' and who, alongside other Campbell clan members, fought at the battle of Culloden Moor. This 'pretender' had a son, David, who was the founder of the Campbell family from which both Malcolm and Donald are descended. The conflicts of 1715 and 1745 did not prevent the English Government disbanding the clan system, as was hoped, but still the Campbell family lost their lands and estates on the Isle of Arran. Today, the Campbell tartan, along with its name, is shared with a British army battalion also known for its bravery in battle, the Blackwatch. It is said that the sword used by David Campbell's father at the battle of Culloden Moor had been made by the renowned swordsmith, Andrea de Ferrara. It became a treasured family heirloom and it is known that a broadsword was bequeathed by Donald to 'such children of mine as shall be living at the time of my death'. However, although this historic weapon should be with his daughter Gina, its whereabouts are unknown.

David Campbell married Isabella MacGregor and had a son, Andrew and it is he who decided to make the journey south to seek his fortune. He arrived in London with what he had carried with him, but in time managed to establish himself as a jeweller and diamond merchant. The business prospered and on Andrew's retirement in 1838, it passed into the hands of his son, Joseph. The business flourished, and was in turn passed on to Joseph's son Andrew, who continued to develop, and prosper from it. Andrew's second child was a boy named William, who, on inheriting the same business, branched out into several new fields, all of which seem to have been successful as he died in 1920 leaving £250,000.

William married and lived in Chislehurst, Kent. He and his wife Ada had two children. The younger was Malcolm Donald – later to be Sir Malcolm – and he was born on 11 March 1885. His sister, Freda, had been born some five years earlier; she was probably more than aware of her parents' strict Victorian ways that are said surfaced in Malcolm years later.

Like Father, Like Son?

It is often said that a man is a child of his grandparents, rather than of his parents, and it certainly seemed to have been true in this case. One can only guess that human qualities are hereditary but if this is the case, it is not difficult to see where Malcolm and his son, Donald were to get their single-minded determination and business acumen, and for that matter their strict sense of morality and discipline. William Campbell was a strict disciplinarian who felt that in his own home, his word was law. He found great difficulty in understanding how anyone could question his authority, and often used the dictum 'to spare the rod is to spoil the child'. Perhaps it is worth mentioning that for all his hostile behaviour towards his son, Malcolm always said that he grew up with the very highest regard and loyalty for his father, something that was to be echoed by his own son Donald. It should be borne in mind that this parental attitude was the norm during the late 1800s and early 1900s, especially in the 'well to do' middle classes. It was felt very necessary to instil the correct set of morals from a very early age, and maybe this is responsible for the exaggerated stories of Malcolm's so-called cruelty and meanness in his later years. After all, it had been the way he had always been treated by his father and it had done him no harm.

The young Malcolm was packed off to a preparatory school near Guildford, where there was a strict pecking order in force, the bullying starting at teacher level and handed down from older to younger as a matter of course. Malcolm did not enjoy the experience, and it was to be a period of his life of which he rarely spoke. From here he was sent to Uppingham, where he, like his son in years to come, did not distinguish himself academically. Maybe it was the surroundings, or the system, but neither was it conducive to Goldie Gardner, another record-breaker. It was a place Gardner hated, not least for the cold baths the boys were forced to take, although it was a habit that he kept right up to his death. The only outlet all three of these men found at this extremely strict school, came through sport, especially that of a solo nature. Malcolm excelled at the more unorthodox such as ram riding, and proved an excellent cross-country runner. It seemed that even in his formative years the young Malcolm would excel as an individual, as opposed to a team player.

After his stay at Uppingham, he was dispatched to Germany to learn the business methods of that country, and became very friendly with a lad called Freido Geertz, who became known to Malcolm as 'Fritz'. The pair shared many youthful adventures, and many narrow scrapes. Malcolm and Fritz once managed to obtain a .22 pistol, which the young Englishman kept in his room. The pistol became the centrepiece to many of these young men's adventures, until one day, in circumstances that Malcolm never fully explained, a shot narrowly missed Fritz, and the gun became surplus to requirements. Malcolm's thoughts drifted to things mechanical, which in turn led to his first race on wheels, on his bicycle, in which he finished third. His memories of this time in Germany were very happy, in marked contrast to his feelings toward the 'Hun' in the years leading up the second world war. It was with more than a little sorrow that he returned to England, only to be dispatched to Caen in France with the instructions to learn both the language, and French business methods.

On his return, Malcolm was expected to tell his father what he had decided to do with his future. He had shared his infancy with the motor car, and ventured that perhaps his future lay in the motor business. Of course, he was right, but it was a subject his father refused to entertain and a position was soon found for him with a firm of insurance brokers, Messrs. Tyser and Co, in the City. In typical fashion, the experience was used to gain enough information to enable Malcolm to set out on his own venture. An uncle suggested that libel insurance for newspapers might be the thing, especially as there had recently been a spate of rash claims between newspapers and irate members of the public in courts around the country, and in less than seven months Malcolm Campbell and partner had their first client.

First Motorings

By this time Malcolm had left home and was living at a private 'hydro' (a private hotel, traditionally with 'hydropathic' facilities) in Sandridge Park. While living there, he purchased a Rex motorcycle, for the princely sum of £15. Keeping the machine running meant sacrificing many of the normal pursuits of a young man, as he later recalled:

> "I used to deny myself everything in order to find money with which to maintain the Rex. New clothes, visits to the theatre, midday lunches. Even when my business prospered I was ready to spend any amount that was necessary on cars, but things outside this seemed inessential."

He stuck with this philosophy for the rest of his life and it is easy to see how those that did not know him could see it as mean. But how many of us still hang on to feelings, actions or childhood habits that were born out of necessity? As far as Malcolm was concerned, then as in later life, he was simply sacrificing one thing for another. As his insurance business prospered, so the Rex made way for a newer, more powerful 3½ hp Quadrant, at a cost of £45. It was perhaps natural for a man of Malcolm's character to use his motorcycle to compete, entering the 1906 London – Land's End trial. Although it was only his second competition (after his bicycle race in Germany), Malcolm still managed to secure a gold medal. It was his first trophy, but his interest in motorcycles was soon to be exchanged for a new one.

Driving Ambition

In the early days of the motorcar, there was no such thing as a driving school. If you wanted to drive, you bought a car and tried to drive it. A young man, especially one of only 21, could rarely afford to buy a car of his own, but this did not stop Malcolm finding a way to drive. Staying at the hydro at the same time as the young Campbell was a gentleman by the name of Fraser, who was there with his wife and daughter. Malcolm suggested that a car would be a great advantage to the Fraser family, and it transpired that the only thing preventing Mr Fraser from buying one was his inability to drive. In spite of the fact that he had never sat in a car himself, Malcolm instantly offered to give him all the instruction he needed, and with that Mr Fraser placed himself completely in the young man's hands.

A short time later a 15-18 hp Germaine, fitted with a Phoenix engine, was duly purchased. It cost Fraser £250, and Malcolm was aching to drive the car, but not so keen to let on that he had no experience of driving. A five-minute road test with a mechanic at the controls was to be all the tuition Malcolm was to receive before the Germaine was trundled back to the hydro and put away for the night in a shed. Simply from taking mental notes of how the mechanic had driven, Malcolm decided that, if he could remember what was what, he would take the car out that evening. The plan fell to pieces when Mr Fraser asked him if, the very next morning, Malcolm would teach him how to drive on the way to Sevenoaks. The lack of sleep caused by Malcolm's worrying was probably a major contribution to his early arrival outside the shed, ready for the off. After starting the car first time, and a small hiccup with the parking brake, Malcolm preceded to do a few laps of the surrounding roads. A perfect drive to Sevenoaks followed, and Mr Fraser had his first driving lesson. In a comment echoed by his son many years later, Malcolm termed his crash course in driving as 'a piece of cake'. Another of the hydro's guests approached Malcolm with the suggestion that if he bought a car, Malcolm could drive it for him. A 1906 Panhard was found, and Malcolm and owner covered many hundreds of miles. Malcolm Campbell was now a motorist, but another challenge would soon present itself.

Campbell the High Flyer

Malcolm bought his first car, the Panhard that he had driven for his friend at the hydro. He often used to drive from his new home in Bromley, to the old Egyptian Hall, in Piccadilly, and it was there that he saw a newsreel film of Wilbur and Orville Wright, and their short first flight into history. In an instant, Malcolm was convinced that the future lay with the aeroplane, and a new passion was born. Campbell's quest for the air started with a thirst for information. Photographs were collected, drawings obtained, and many more visits to Piccadilly followed to see how others were trying to leave their earthly bonds. After constructing many models, Malcolm decided that building a full-size aeroplane would be relatively easy, and decided to build the 'Campbell Flyer'. At that time, Blériot and Latham were waiting on the French coast in readiness to become the first to fly the English Channel. Such was Malcolm's belief in the aeroplane that he arranged to have an insurance policy against the 'risk' of either man succeeding, what Malcolm would later call 'a sure bet'. Latham's attempt failed, but on 25 July 1909, Blériot landed in Dover, and the sure bet paid £750. The aircraft was put on display in an Oxford Street store, where Malcolm spent an entire day making notes and sketches, absorbing as much as he could about the frail little machine.

The driving force behind his quest for flight lay in the prize money being offered for pioneering flights, something which would surface in later life as he made a very handsome living first from racing, and then record-breaking in cars and boats. As he once said, "Where else can one earn £25,000 for two minutes' work?". It was not to be easy work however. Malcolm and a carpenter friend rented a barn on the edge of some strawberry fields in Orpington and construction preceded in earnest. Every spare moment went into building the flying machine, and it soon soaked up all of the insurance pay-out. Undeterred, both men forged on, until the day came for the maiden flight. It was hoped that this historic moment could be a quiet one, but news had spread, and by the time the twin cylinder JAP engine was started, a large, unfriendly crowd had gathered, blocking the planned runway. As with driving, Malcolm had learnt all he knew from watching others, and threw himself in at the deep end. The crowd had, by this time, become a good deal more obstinate, so Campbell decided that he would just have to get on with it, and hope that once approached by the fledgling 'plane, the crowd would disperse. The first flight amounted to a small hop, and later 'flights' became merely longer hops. A larger engine was bought, and work continued into 1910. It was not long before both men's resources were exhausted, at about the same time as the last big flying prize was won by Tommy Sopwith, and the difficult decision was made to sell the aeroplane. A large motor dealer by the name of Friswell convinced Malcolm that the best way of selling the aircraft would be to auction it. It would, after all, be the first time an aero-plane had ever been sold, and so, a short time later, the 'Campbell Flyer' was put under the hammer. Bidding started at £50 and rose steadily, but not quickly enough for Campbell, who joined in with his own bids in an effort to get the price he felt certain his craft was worth. Malcolm was suc-cessful in raising the bidding to £300, but he somehow managed to buy his own aeroplane! In desperation he offered it to the man who he had been bidding against, but was dismissed with the comment, "You brought it, you can keep it". It was a hard lesson to learn. Malcolm already owed the auctioneer £22-10-6, and was forced to put the machine in the next auction the following week in an effort to recover the further £300 he also owed him. It was sold successfully, and the excited ex-aeroplane owner was desperate to see how much he had made. "Yes", he was told, "it has sold, for £22-10-6." It had cost Malcolm about £800 to build and all he had succeeded in doing was covering the sales costs. The Campbell spirit was not dampened for long, however, and in an effort to forget the whole sorry episode Malcolm returned to the car – and to motor racing.

Back to Banking

The name of Campbell had appeared in the programme at Brooklands as early as 1908, when Malcolm had first raced a motorcycle and, later in the same year, a twin-cylinder Renault car, but on both occasions he had fin-ished well down. A 1908 Darracq, that had nearly won the 1908 Tourist Trophy, was bought and this took Malcolm to his first victory. With his insurance business thriving, he could afford to take his racing seriously, and the Darracq made way for a Peugeot and, as was the fashion of the time, the car was given a name, 'Flapper' after a successful race horse of the time. Success was not so easily come by with this car and it was soon replaced by another Darracq, logically named Flapper II, but this car was quickly sold when a faster Darracq became available. This was the car with which Victor Hemery had won the 1909 Vanderbilt Cup in America, and was easily capable of 100 mph. It has passed into legend that before this car could be named, Malcolm was invited by Maurice Maeterlinck to see his play, 'The Blue Bird'. In Malcolm's own words:

"Everyone liked the play, and the name sounded lucky, so I decided to christen the machine thoroughly and knocked up an oil chandler, from whom I brought brushes and every tin of blue paint he had. By morning the next day the body and wheels were blue to match its new name".

As Malcolm and his new mount prepared for their first race, the paint was still wet, and both driver and mechanic were covered with blue patches, but the all-blue outfit won its first race, regardless of the fact that it was not easy to handle and that before each race the wooden wheels had to be soaked with water to make the spokes expand so that they stopped rattling while the car was racing. *'Blue Bird'* won its second race as well, but the wheels were later to seal the car's fate.

Malcolm was very impressed by the power of his new mount, but felt that with a little more work she would be unbeatable, and a programme of tuning and modification started that would guarantee a top speed in excess of 100 mph. *Blue Bird* next appeared on the start line during the August Bank Holiday meeting at Brooklands, and a confident Malcolm Campbell decided to show that the heavy handicap given to him after his first wins would be no great penalty. Coming off the Byfleet banking on the final lap, he had *Blue Bird* well in front and gave her the gun toward the finishing line. Suddenly the front of the car seemed to fall away, as the offside front tyre exploded, and the car lurched toward the spectator railing. Malcolm kept his foot hard down, sensing that victory was still in sight, as *Blue Bird* was within striking distance of the finishing line. The huge car, still hard under power, drifted wider still and kept its inevitable appointment with the high concrete curbing. The back wheel took a tremendous impact, and also collapsed. *Blue Bird* heeled over, nearly to the point of rolling, just as the steering broke. Purely on reflex, Malcolm braked as hard as he could, and the rear of the car slew away from the curbing, coming to rest just short of the railings and the stunned spectators the other side. There the ashen-faced driver sat, unable to believe his luck: he had survived and finished fourth!

Malcolm was a deeply superstitious man, and after the turnaround in his racing luck, he was convinced that his survival had been in 'the lap of the Gods'. From now on, all his cars would be blue.

A friend of Malcolm's had seen the incident and rushed to the paddock to see how *Blue Bird*'s pilot was feeling. The friend, Major William Whitall, was well connected with the motoring press of the time, and admission was granted to him and his family. Major Whitall sought Malcolm out and on finding him in a surprisingly unconcerned frame of mind introduced his daughter, Dorothy. She later wrote, "I was barely a teenager but instantly saw a man quite out of the ordinary, and although young I had never met anyone I could idealise. But here was someone different, someone worthy to be installed in the gallery of heroes. And there in my young mind I placed him". Dorothy was not to encounter her new hero again for some years – but when she did, the meeting was to be of a completely different nature.

Malcolm's business prospered further, and he branched out, joining an underwriting syndicate whose dealings extended well beyond that of Malcolm's libel insurance, but it was by no means sufficient to support his five racing machines, and his small fleet of road cars. He had married a woman by the name of Marjorie Trott, a lady of some wealth, and it was she who supported Malcolm's pre-war racing. Unfortunately Malcolm

1928 – 1932

A rare shot of Capt. Malcolm Campbell at speed on Daytona Beach, Florida, 1928
(© Topical Press Agency; by kind permission of John Gould)

The genius of Frank Lockart – the Stutz *Black Hawk*. The car crashed twice, finally
killing her driver *(by kind permission of John Gould)*

The 1929 *Blue Bird* at the Arroll Astor premises – not the car's sleekist incarnation
(by kind permission of John Gould)

Daytona Beach, Florida, 1928. Capt. Malcolm Campbell and the *Blue Bird*
(© Leo Villa Collection)

1927: the first purpose-built *Blue Bird* at Pendine Sands, South Wales. Capt. Campbell
looks thoughtful as Leo Villa continues his preparations *(© Leo Villa Collection)*

Capt. Malcolm Campbell breaks the World Speed Record in 1928 at Daytona Beach,
Florida at 214mph *(© Topical Press Agency; by kind permission of John Gould)*

1929: 'R' engine being lowered onto the test-bed. On the right is George Parkin who became Head of Production Engine Test, and who retired in the 1960s (© *Rolls Royce plc*)

Capt. Campbell takes the new *Blue Bird* on a trial run on the wet sand of Pendine, South Wales in 1927 *(© Campbell Collection)*

Under the skin of the first purpose-built *Blue Bird*. The gearbox, designed by Joseph Maina, is clearly visible *(© Campbell Collection)*

Fuel being filtered into the float, which also acted as a fuel tank, of a Supermarine S6.
On the left is A.C. 'Cyril' Lovesey who was in charge for Rolls-Royce at Calshot.
In 1940 he was put in charge of Merlin development and remained so throughout the war.
Subsequently, he developed the Avon jet engine, and was called back from retirement
in 1971 to help with the RB211 *(© Rolls-Royce plc)*

The Supermarine S6 in profile. The pilot standing in the cockpit gives some idea of the compact
size of the aircraft *(© Rolls-Royce plc)*

Malcolm Campbell stands in front of the 1931 *Blue Bird*. The lump on top of the radiator cowl is a duplicate forward-mounted rev counter. To the left is the special Austin 7 with which Campbell set several class records. *(By kind permission of Dunlop Tyres plc)*

Daytona Beach, 1932. A casual Malcolm poses for the camera *(© Leo Villa Collection)*

Early 1932 and the new incarnation of *Blue Bird* is tested on the banked track of Brooklands
(by kind permission of Mrs Goldie Gardner)

had inherited much of his father's thinking, considering himself always to be in the right, and beyond reproach. He had been told by a close friend that "he was either the most perfect of gentlemen, or the most perfect son of a bitch", and indeed there seemed to be no halfway point. He had a supreme belief in his own abilities, something that any racing driver must have, but this had developed in him to the point were he had become so egotistical, that he become self-centred and selfish in the extreme. Of course, he had his better points – he could be generous to a fault, and very considerate, but it was dependent on his mood. It would be unfair to call him a Jekyll and Hyde character, but many people who only saw one facet of his ways could very often be extremely shocked at his self-satisfying attitude or charmed by his kindness and generosity. It is not difficult to see how the public at large had heard these stories filter down and had chosen either to love or to hate the man. Ultimately, it was this that ruined his first marriage, which lasted just short of two years.

Two Wheels and Wings

In 1914 the Campbell racing stable consisted of a Coupe de l'Auto Sunbeam, a Schneider, a Darracq, a Peugeot, and a Grégoire, with which Malcolm took a third place the day before war was declared in Europe. At the onset of war, he wasted no time, and volunteered as a dispatch rider, working with the King's Messenger Service. He was sent to France in September 1914, and while there applied for a commission, which led to his becoming a Second Lieutenant in the Royal West Kent Regiment. During his first leave, he sold his entire racing stable, the Coupe de l'Auto Sunbeam fetching all of £250 (it was sold at the end of the war for £2000!) and forgot about cars and racing, preferring instead to apply himself fully in his new position as Head of Transport. Having been a perfectionist in all he had done, he was shocked at the haphazard way things were run and set about knocking the whole operation into shape. He obviously succeeded as he was personally congratulated by Lord Kitchener. Late in 1915, the chance to reacquaint himself with the aeroplane led to a transfer to the Royal Flying Corp, and in 1916 Malcolm Donald Campbell, passed out of Gosport to become a ferry pilot. It was a job that was well suited to Malcolm in many ways. He left England in brand-new aircraft, and returned with machines marked, 'unfit for flying'. It meant that he got to fly a vast range of different craft, and it developed him as a pilot, as flying the 'basket cases' back over the Channel was never an easy task.

Malcolm's favourite war-time tale revolved around a young man who approached him, just as he was about to fly one of these sick machines home for refurbishment. Seeing the opportunity of arriving back in England at least three days before the next 'Leave Ship' could get him there, the young soldier asked if he could fly back with Malcolm, but only if a solemn promise was made that he would not try to scare him in any way during his first flight. Malcolm promised, permission for the 'lift' gained, and the two men prepared for their cross-Channel flight. The engine was warmed, but would not rev above 750 rpm, 250 short of the safe take-off limit.

After asking the mechanics to rectify the problem, the carburettor was cleaned, and the plugs changed, but the revs would still not climb above 750. The last possible cure was the magneto, but it was a long job, and the two would-be travellers were asked to come back the following day for another attempt. Promptly at six o'clock the next morning, both men returned to find the aircraft waiting, and after warming up the engine, Malcolm opened the throttle. Again, the engine failed to rev above 750. Malcolm gave the whole matter some thought, and decided to give it a try. As he later recalled:

> "The young chap's face was a picture, and fully aware that he had never flown before, and had absolutely no faith in the aircraft, I reminded him of my promise to get him home without a scare".

They had only been in the air for a minute when the engine cut, and Malcolm was forced to glide back to earth in a steep spiral. His passenger was beside himself. "I thought you promised not to do any stunts" he ranted, and it took a while before he could be convinced that it had in fact been a genuine failure, and even longer to get him to climb aboard again. Eventually the battered craft rose into the air and set off for England. Beneath, the Channel shipping was very busy, and barely five minutes into the flight the engine cut out completely. Nothing would persuade it to restart, and Malcolm looked around for a large ship to ditch near. Any pilot forced down was entitled to a week's leave, and if the ship that picked you up happened to be travelling somewhere far away, then you just had to wait until you got there before making your way back home, a thought that crossed Malcolm's mind several times as he selected a suitable ship. The altimeter was showing 200 feet as they crossed the bows of a ship that Malcolm hoped might be on its way to India. Just as both pilot and passenger braced themselves for impact, the engine coughed and started. Immediately, Malcolm applied full power, climbed to 5000 feet, and continued on his way. The rest of the flight went without a hitch. His passenger was so quiet, that it was not until the aircraft pulled up at the end of the runway that Malcolm even remembered he was there, for it was then that the young man, with a face as white as a sheet, vaulted out, and sprinted off, never to be seen again.

At this stage, it is worth making a note of another one of the many coincidences that seen to follow the Campbell story through the years. A young man of Italian descent had signed up at the outbreak of war in the Royal Flying Corp, travelling around many airfields as a mechanic, including some very near the front line. At about the same time as Malcolm was at Gosport, this same young man was also stationed there. His name was Leo Villa – later to be engineer and friend to both Malcolm and Donald.

Malcolm had learnt a lot from his flying and, as was his way, he felt that others should benefit from all that acquired knowledge. He wrote a book called 'Hints to Beginners on Flying', and paid from his own pocket to have 5000 copies published. He transferred to Denham, becoming a Captain just before the armistice and his return to Civvy Street. But he returned to his insurance business only to find that all of his pre-war clients had gone elsewhere, and so more through chance, than choice, he decided to go into the motor trade.

He managed to find and rent a showroom in Albermarle Street, in London and signed contracts with a chassis builder for the supply of 700 chassis over the next year. Taking deposits of between £50 and £100, Malcolm succeeded in pre-selling 580 cars, but as the weeks turned to months it became obvious that he had been let down. He did manage to sell on some of the orders, and recovered a sum of £10,000, plus interest from the manufacturer, which in turn was paid back to the dissatisfied customers. It was another lesson from the school of hard knocks, and as always, a lesson Malcolm was to remember. As he later told friends: "I was very fortunate to break even, and never again will anyone catch me with all my eggs in one basket. I shall be more than careful from now on".

He kept his word, and was more than careful for the rest of his life, never once risking more than was necessary, and wherever possible not even his own money. He was convinced that the 'sure bet' did not exist, and to that end kept his own money very safe. It was one of the many things that would later label him as a man mean with money but, as he pointed out, "I have to be careful you know, all this might end tomorrow".

He had been fairly successful with his racing before the war, and thought that with a little more application, motor racing could bring not only fame, but possibly financial gain as well. The deciding factor was again to be the hand of fate.

Malcolm had made several trips to Paris, in an effort to try and import a Gregoire car. Most of the problems had been ironed out, but the whole project started to drag its heels. Although not an impatient man, Malcolm liked things to be done quickly and efficiently so, as the negotiations drew out, it did not take much to distract him. He was told of a Lorraine-Dietrich in which Victor Hemery had won the 1912 French Grand Prix. In Malcolm's already-superstitious mind it was too much. His first successful car had been a Lorraine-Dietrich, which had been raced by Victor Hemery, and so he had to have this new car, regardless of the difficulties arising from exporting it from France. Ignoring the fact the car had only two bucket seats, a large rear-mounted fuel tank, and the traces of a racing number on the bonnet, Malcolm convinced customs officials that the Lorraine had been a staff car during the war and, without hindrance, the car was shipped back to England. Within weeks, the engine had been rebuilt and tuned ready for racing.

With the wheels and body given two coats of blue and the name 'The Blue Bird' neatly sign-written on the bonnet, all was ready for the return of Captain Malcolm Campbell on Easter Monday, 5 April 1920. The Essex Motor Club had arranged the meeting, but because of torrential rain the organising committee decided that they would postpone the event until the following Saturday. After a brief discussion the competitors who had made the trip arranged for a series of match races, and 'Blue Bird' was duly drawn against a Matchless motorcycle, ridden by a Major Woodhouse. In Malcolm's first race after the war, in the first meeting to be held since peace had been declared, the 'Blue Bird' luck had returned and Malcolm Campbell won the first post-war race at Brooklands.

A short time after, Malcolm returned to Brooklands to compete in the 100 mph Long Handicap. His new 'Blue Bird' Schneider was drawn next to his old Lorraine-Dietrich, driven by a Mr Hawkes, the car's new owner (This car was later resold and named 'Vieux Charles Troix III'). Behind Malcolm was Henry Birkin in his first race, driving a Peugeot and, next to him, Henry Segrave in an Opel. The new *Blue Bird* fell from contention soon after A.V. Ebblewhite dropped the Union Flag, and the contest was between Segrave and the old *Blue Bird*. Unfortunately, the little Opel had a tyre burst at almost top speed, Segrave being extremely lucky to be able to bring the car back to the pits. Hawkes eventually finished first, but it was Segrave who earned the respect of not only the crowd but of Malcolm as well, by taking the Opel out in a later race, and winning.

During the next week Malcolm was to encounter the new 350 hp Sunbeam at close quarters at Brooklands. The desire to own the car was instant, it was what Malcolm described as a 'real racing machine'.

Captain Malcolm Campbell took part in all of the 1920 season of races at the famed concrete 'bowl' of Brooklands, and branched out to compete in many other events the following year, including hill climbs, sand racing and seaside speed trials. 1920 also saw his marriage to Dorothy Whitall, the young girl who he had meet after his lucky escape in the first *Blue Bird* at Brooklands some years earlier.

In 1921 another vital component of the Campbell saga was fitted into place, the ex-RFC mechanic, Leo Villa. During the early part of 1921, not only did Leo Villa become part of the Campbell furniture, but so did the 350 hp Sunbeam. Malcolm's conviction about the car's racing ability was reinforced by its absolute speed. During runs on the sands of Saltburn and Southport, the Sunbeam had hit speeds that were, in Malcolm's mind, far in excess of the then Land Speed Record. Indeed, at speed trials held in Skegness the 350 hp Sunbeam, with both Malcolm and Leo Villa aboard, recorded a timed speed of 150.869 mph, far in excess of the current record held by Campbell's friend, Kennelm Lee Guinness in the same car, at 133.75 mph. As was often the case at this time, the use of non-sanctioned timing equipment, meant that these runs would not be officially accepted. As the 350 hp was developed, further attempts were made. In Denmark, on the sands at Fanoe, timed runs proved the car, and the driver, were more than capable of setting the record. On both occasions, the attempts ended in disappointment. Malcolm had won the speed contest, but had been robbed of setting a new world record, again by dint of non-sanctioned timing equipment. The last Fanoe contest was also marred by the death of a thirteen-year old boy, called Clausen, who was struck by a tyre that had separated from the *Blue Bird*'s front wheel. Malcolm had beseeched the organisers, not only to ensure that the timing equipment would be of an accepted type, but also to improve upon safety measures. They had failed on both counts, and it seems that this became one of the catalysts that spurred him to prove that the Land Speed Record was his for the taking. He also became convinced that safety should be a major issue, and started to campaign for better measures, not only on the race track, but on the public highways as well, culminating in his books, 'The Key To Motoring' and 'The Roads, And The Problems Of Their Safety'.

On returning to England, Malcolm considered the Sunbeam a failure. He had spent a lot of time and money on a new body and mechanical modifications, and still did not hold the official Land Speed Record. Leo Villa was put to the task of preparing for the next attempt, while his employer set about finding a suitable course somewhere in the British Isles, so that the newly approved RAC timing apparatus could be used. During this time, Malcolm entered into discussions with Amherst Villiers, an inspired engineer who specialised in racing engines and, moreover, in superchargers. Villiers suggested that new camshafts should see the 350 Sunbeam well over the current record, and further discussions were made about a purpose-built car, solely for attempts on the record.

Pendine Sands in Carmarthenshire, North Wales became the chosen venue, offering a full seven miles of relatively firm sand at low tide. It became the British venue for Land Speed Record attempts. After Malcolm's first successful attempt at Pendine, he became aware of the opportunities that were opening up to him. News coverage was far in excess of what Malcolm had expected, and well above that for 'normal' motoring. He had received financial support from Esso and from KLG spark plugs (owned by Kennelm Lee Guinness, who would later join Malcolm on treasure hunting expeditions) and made a handsome bonus when the record was won. Malcolm saw the chance to earn a 'reasonable' living, as well as attracting attention to both himself, and his country. Since his early successes, Malcolm had been genuinely surprised by the media attention that he was receiving, and the more so by the way that fame brought more money by way of more sponsorship.

Toward the end of 1925 Malcolm became more and more engrossed in the idea of buried treasure – see also page 100. He was a romantic at heart, and he became fascinated by stories of pirates, and their buried booty. He visited several islands, and on more than one occasion buried some of his Brooklands trophies in the grounds of his home, in order to test various means and devices for locating valuable metals. Needless to say, there are many stories that around Povey Cross, his home in Sussex, it might still be possible to find several items of motoring history.

It seems strange that a person so well known for his level-headed thinking, should be so drawn. The thought of going off to the far side of the world, with only a supposed 'treasure map' as evidence, and the extremely high cost of travel in the 1920s, can really only be described as whimsical. But here was a man who, by his own admission, felt that whatever he was doing was the right and only thing to do. There simply was no argument against it. In his youth, his favourite book had been *King Solomon's Mines* and, once hooked, treasure hunting was no different from any other of Malcolm's earlier obsessions, simply reinforcing the single-minded application that went into everything he did. Once his mind was applied, everything, his motor trade activities, even record-breaking, would become a side issue – so much so that his 1926 expedition nearly brought an end to his fledgling garage business, as it was left completely in the hands of Malcolm's staff, some of whom he would later describe as completely incompetent. As was often the case, it was a lesson learned and not repeated.

By 1927, the first purpose-built *Blue Bird*, appearing not unlike an over-sized Bugatti, had been built. After initial problems with the construction, the chassis was taken to Malcolm's home at Povey Cross to be finished by his own team, under his own supervision. At the time the car arrived, Malcolm was dabbling in one of his periodic, but all consuming hobbies. Living in a purpose-built kennel, right next to Malcolm's very well equipped workshop, were the dogs that Malcolm had started to breed. Quite how Malcolm decided that dog breeding was the thing to be doing, one can only guess, but as always the application was total. Unfortunately, the proximity of the kennels to the workshop led to problems, as Leo Villa recalled: "The chassis had been put in the Skipper's workshop so that the team that he had got together could finish the job, which he felt had been dragging its heels. For some time he had been breeding dogs, and next door were over twenty Alsatians, nearly twenty Airedales, plus sundry household pets. The trouble was that, although the Skipper had bred the dogs, he hadn't yet got around to training them. What you have to remember was that the bulk of the work was being done by panel beaters, with its attendant hammering. Each blow was greeted by constant, and deafening barking. The other thing was that we were working a shift system, nearly twenty hours a day, and the barking went along with it. The locals were convinced that Captain Campbell was working on a secret project, and the dogs were there to guard that project. I think the Skipper was secretly quite keen to keep up the pretence. Anyway, not long after, the old man started to build a model train lay-out for young Donald, so the dogs dwindled in number, until only the favourites were left. By the time the railway was finished, it was decided it was too good to let the lad play with, so Don and Jean were merely allowed to watch."

Blue Bird proved ineffective on initial trials at Pendine, and Malcolm returned to Povey Cross thoroughly depressed, complaining that after all of the problems that the team had overcome in Fanoe, and on other previous attempts, it seemed that his luck had still not changed. Malcolm's make up was not that of an ordinary man, however, and after several days' thought, these same drawbacks became the impetus for renewed vigour in the work required to ensure success. Where others would simply given up, Malcolm became even more fixed on his goal; failure simply did not exist in the Campbells' book.

"The team had arrived back at base just before the Skipper," recalled Leo Villa years later, "and we knew he would be in a foul mood, but when he did arrive he was staggered to find that we had not unloaded the car, 'come on you lot' he shouted, 'let's get the bloody thing inside and knock some sense into it, I'll be buggered if I'm going to be beaten after all this. Villa, get on with it". I think we were all surprised, but we got used to it, it seemed that any setback just spurred him on even harder."

Indeed, it did seem that with the years Malcolm's resolve was considerably strengthened by setbacks, the philosophy of his earlier life gaining strength through failure. He had once said: "You can't just give up on things, it was more than just my time and money, but the efforts of all of the team. I had to succeed, my consideration was the least important".

The urge to go on with the first *Blue Bird* gained momentum with the entry of Henry Segrave and Parry Thomas into the record-breaking arena. At first, it had not occurred to Malcolm to develop the *Blue Bird*; after all, it had already cost nearly four times the original estimate, but Malcolm saw what he thought were important barriers to be broken, and the financial rewards were becoming a valuable addition to his earnings from his showrooms in London.

In the following years, the Land Speed Record became almost his own personal property. But the high point of this period was his knighthood in

1931, of which he was justifiably proud. Malcolm also felt that his exploits were giving Britain a new-found prestige. As one newspaper exclaimed, "Our two greatest ambassadors of commerce, the Prince of Wales, and Captain Malcolm Campbell". The die was well and truly cast. Malcolm would not be satisfied until he had topped 300 mph on land, after which he promised those close to him he would 'pack it all in'. In order to achieve this goal, a Schneider Trophy Rolls-Royce R-type was secured for the 1933 season, boosting Malcolm's confidence that the 300 was at last within his grasp. On this attempt, Malcolm took his entire family, and his long-time friend Goldie Gardner, who was to act as team manager, to Daytona Beach, Florida, USA. The problems of running on seaside sands again raised themselves, and held the new record down to 272.1 mph, well short of the hoped for 300.

During 1934 *Blue Bird* yet again took on a different guise, being completely re-bodied to house a new Rolls-Royce R-type that Malcolm had managed to buy from the manufacturer. By early 1935, the *Blue Bird* entourage was again on the beach of Daytona, but soft sand and wheel spin kept the speed down yet again, even though a new record was set. Finally, on the advice of John Cobb, the team moved onto the dry salt flats at Bonneville, in Utah. Cobb had used the flats to set numerous class records, but on first sight, Malcolm was convinced that his tyres would be ripped to shreds, especially when one considers that the thickness of rubber used on the canvas casings was in the region of 0.0025 of an inch, to alleviate problems with balance at high revolutions. Malcolm was certain that on this attempt, his life was seriously at risk. Eventually, but far from easily, the three hundred barrier was broken, and Malcolm was good to his word, retiring from record-breaking, but only on land. For some time before his final runs in the *Blue Bird* car, plans were being made for an assault on the Water Speed Record. In his early twenties, Malcolm had been told by a gypsy woman that he would meet his end on water. Maybe she was right, for the Campbell legend did end on water, but this was in the future. Malcolm felt he had to wrest the record from America, but confided that the gypsy's premonition was disturbing him, and that the Water Speed Record would be the end of him.

As early as 1935, Saunders Roe had been in the process of testing Fred Cooper's design for what was to become the first *Blue Bird* record-breaking boat. With the help of Reid Railton, the design was to incorporate as much of the mechanics of the *Blue Bird* car as possible, especially the engine. By mid-1936, the hull had been transported to Brooklands where the final fitting-out would take place. The new *Blue Bird* was duly registered at Lloyds of London as unlimited racing boat *K3*. Initial trials took place on Loch Lomond, but the actual record attempt, much to Malcolm's chagrin, was to take place on the Swiss, Italian border on Lago Maggiore. As with his most recent attempts, Malcolm took his entire family, as well as the usual team, and succeeded in raising the record, not once, but twice in two days. *K3* proved to be an unstable craft, and Malcolm confessed that he did not like the way the boat handled. Discussions between Malcolm and Railton, and then between Railton and Cooper, steered toward a new craft, but not before an invitation to try and raise the record at the Geneva International Speed Trials had been made. The close company of hundreds of spectator boats, and strange underwater currents put paid to any official try at the record, although a speed of 120 mph was timed. Malcolm, feeling that such a long trip should not be for nothing, then moved camp to Lake Halwyll (Hallwiler See) high in the mountains, where the promise of a purpose-built boat house and free accommodation at a local hotel proved too much of a draw to even consider going home without a record.

K3, with her new bodywork, and improved cooling, increased the record again, but proved to be even more of a handful than the previous year. Vosper's Commander Peter du Cane was allowed to take the helm, and although not surprised by the unpredictable handling, which he considered normal for that type of hull, he did feel that perhaps a new design may be more suitable for high-speed work. Railton had brought with him a revolutionary new hull from America, which Malcolm tried and was impressed enough to decide that *K3* was to be instantly retired. On his return to England work commenced in earnest, and by August 1939 the new *Blue Bird*, *K4*, was ready for her attack on the record. In only a matter of days, Malcolm was on his way home with yet another record under his belt – but sadly, a record that was to be his last.

To Politics and War

In Europe, Hitler had been building his armed forces at an alarming rate, and as early as 1935, Malcolm had warned that England was in danger of attack from the air. Indeed during 1936 Malcolm had ordered the construction of the first ever privately owned air raid bunker, which had four rooms, kitchen, and bathroom. After his knighthood, he was in great demand as a public speaker, something that he came to enjoy a great deal. During this time, he was persuaded to assist in a local by-election by a Conservative candidate who, with or without Malcolm's help, lost. Then, in October 1935 he was invited to attend the annual dinner of the Navy League, and was considerably impressed by a speech made by Lord Jellicoe, who had publicly voiced the opinions the Malcolm had harboured for some time. Malcolm knew in his heart that the Third Reich was a serious threat to world peace, but up until then had found no-one willing to listen. He became increasingly concerned that the opposition of the day had voted against proposed measures that would have strengthened the Services. Added to this, Malcolm was also at odds with the Government policy of keeping the truth from the British people, for fear of offending those in Germany. He had already published two books, 'Drifting To War' and 'The Peril From The Air', warning both public and government that war was imminent. Cartoons of the day showed *Blue Bird* fitted with torpedo launchers, Campbell was a warmonger to some. But he felt that he had not had a fair hearing, nor had the public heard all that they should have, so Malcolm decided to stand as a Conservative candidate, and was accepted for the Deptford seat. Sadly, although held at the time by a Conservative, it was expected that the Labour party would take not only the Deptford seat, but also the election. Malcolm, in complete contrast to party policy, fought his entire campaign on the need to be prepared for the expected conflict. But, without the support of his party it was unlikely that Malcolm would ever have stood a chance of victory, even in a normally Conservative stronghold.

Many years after the election the Prime Minister, Mr Baldwin, finally explained why he had not told the Nation the truth about the relative strength of the British and German forces and therefore had not supported Malcolm in his bid to become an MP. It was simply because if he had, his party would not have won the election. Although Malcolm was right, his failure to follow the party line left him out on a limb, and cost him his victory, and the end of a short foray into politics. Just after the war, Malcolm and his wife were driven through the borough of Deptford, which had been devastated by the nightly attacks of the Luftwaffe. He could have been forgiven for taking an 'I told you so' attitude.

At the outset of war Malcolm offered his services to the British Government and set up, with the help of Goldie Gardner, a motorcycle mounted police force, and helped a great deal with setting up the communication lines that became vital to the services still based in England, but always felt that he had more to offer his country in its time of strife than he was allowed to show.

Private Lives

So much for the public Malcolm Campbell. As has been mentioned before, most people had seen only one side of the Campbell persona, that of the press or the 'Chinese Whisper' syndrome and, depending on what it was they had seen or heard, the decision to love or hate the man had been made. Few had first-hand experience with which to decide, and it is probably more this, than anything else that has led to the enigma that is Malcolm Campbell. Everyone has many facets to their personality, but those in the 'celebrity' bracket, especially those that keep the private parts of their lives just that, tend to be seen in only one light.

But the scales have to be balanced, no one can be sweetness and light all of the time. Malcolm Campbell could be generous to a fault, or seemingly the meanest man that ever lived. He was a great fan of slapstick comedy, and would laugh at the antics of the Crazy Gang until tears ran down his face but, if seen, his demeanour would change, and he would instantly refer to the on-stage behaviour as, 'scandalous, simply scandalous', and then proceed to start laughing again. It is behaviour more easily understood today than then. He was seen as the perfect family man, yet it is suggested that he would subject his son to ridicule for the sake of it. He could be the consummate sportsman, but would turn his back on an interest when another, newer interest came to the fore as easily as others take off a coat. He is supposed to have actively attempted to obstruct his own son from following his career, but why should he be so against his son going into the record-breaking game? Some suggest that he felt that Donald was incapable of actually handling the 'sport'. Malcolm it is said, was often heard to say, "If Donald ever tries this, he'll kill himself", yet Sir Malcolm's own daughter, and the widow of Goldie Gardner, have both said that they never heard him voice such an opnion. Leo Villa had difficulty remembering if Donald ever actually expressed an interest in taking over from his father while the 'Old Man' was alive and even less memory of the Skipper protesting his son's interest in 'having ago'. Mrs Gardner remains convinced that Donald Campbell simply decided to try for the record because, after his father's death, the means just happened to be in the workshop, and then came the spur of the American challenge.

Jean Wales (nee Campbell), Mrs Goldie Gardner, Colonel Bowser (who spent many a boyhood day being driven around by his 'uncle' Malcolm) and the few people who have personal memories are all of the same belief, that with the passing of time it is easier to remember the bad, than the good. It is like describing somebody 'warts and all', and then only describing the warts. Sir Malcolm spent much of his spare time talking at boys' clubs, raising money for charity, promoting good causes, campaigning for road safety (as early as 1933 he had suggested the use of seat belts in cars, and special restraining seating for babies and small children). It is difficult to think of many people who have given a fully furnished house as a wedding present, but not only did Sir Malcolm do this on two occasions, but also to Leo Villa, who was, after all, 'only' an employee. One can only surmise that as these facts were not common knowledge, as they are never normally given consideration in the whole jigsaw that is Sir Malcolm Campbell.

We have all, on occasion, made decisions whether we like someone on the most basic of information, sometimes barely even a glance. Yet here we have a man labelled because of what was thought about him by others. Malcolm Campbell was one of the first sportsmen to concentrate so firmly on what to others was merely a sport. Today, we admire those that can show such unwavering concentration, but in Campbell it has been seen as meanness, cruelty, or arrogance. Take the more recent example of Ayrton Senna, considered by many as one of the best racing drivers of recent times. His application to the task of winning was admired by many, even used as a shining example of the dedication needed to succeed. Yet, early in his Formula One career, Senna had told his young wife that he had no time for her in his plan for the World Championship. His ultimatum was such that the marriage ended. Nobody in the racing world, let alone the public at large, saw it as anything other than total application. Still admirable, but a shame for the ex-Mrs Senna.

Campbell kept his marriage intact and led a near-normal life, regardless of his sacrifices – how times change, and how the opinions of a few can influence the majority. Even in our modern age of communication, those of celebrity status can keep their private lives away from the prying eyes of the press and public and, because of this, some can gain a reputation that may have no basis in reality yet, once reported, once read, it is as good as the truth to those that do not know. In the 1930s, with communications in its infancy, things were no different; an offending article was a good article, and nothing sticks like mud once it has been thrown. That Malcolm Campbell never rose to, or retaliated against any of his detractors is not too surprising, bearing in mind his upbringing, and that he could never know that his state of mind would be of such conjecture after his death.

As any member of his family will tell you to this day, he was happy knowing that those close to him knew what sort of person he was, saying of those that he did not know, "I have nothing to do with anyone outside of my closest circle. If those outside that circle do not like, or understand what I am about, then hang them, hang them all". In his later life, Sir Malcolm had to face failure for perhaps the first time in his seemingly charmed lifetime. He had once said, "When I have to confess to myself that I can no longer carry on as I was able to do, say twenty years ago, then I want to die". A statement of this kind would indicate a mind to which failure was unacceptable. His last attempt at the Water Speed Record in the jet-engined *Blue Bird K4*, had been fated from its first days. Campbell had received press coverage ranging from sparse, through indifferent to blatantly personal, something which had never happened before.

Compared with the pre-war success of the *K4* hydroplane, which took only a matter of days to capture the record, Campbell's final effort seemed thwarted as soon as it had begun. Even the weather, which always seemed to be perfect for the Skipper, decided to bite back. All the high-speed runs proved to be highly uncomfortable, and on occasion Campbell actually seemed to be totally disinterested in receiving a further physical battering at the helm. Here was a man of sixty-eight attempting to raise his own Water Speed Record for no other reason than he already had the means. His health was rapidly failing, as was his eyesight, indeed his team had to arrange huge rolls of white cloth at each end of Coniston for the Skipper to 'aim' at through his glaucoma-affected eyes. There was no possible way he would be seen in public with glasses. He had collapsed several times before Christmas 1948, but had kept it very quiet, even from his immediate family until he found himself partially paralysed on the steps of a London Hotel where he was attending a conference. Not for the first time, he was told to take it easy in order to recover, but anything other than 'full speed ahead' was, "simply not on, old boy". Nothing seemed to slow him down, and as he carried on as normal, he seemed to have made a full recovery. Nevertheless his doctors, including his racing friend Dr Benjafield, were adamant that he should retire and lead a quiet life.

On his last visit to Coniston, he appeared weary of the whole thing, causing those present to wonder why he had bothered at all. On one occasion, the team had assembled ready for four timed runs, but after an hour of waiting, du Cane became restless and told Leo Villa that if Campbell was not going to bother, he himself would take *Blue Bird* out for the required runs. Leo went at once to Goffy Thwaites' boathouse, where he was surprised to find his boss sitting in a chair, reading a newspaper. No amount of encouragement would prise Campbell from his apathy, until he was informed of du Cane's eagerness to make the runs. Instantly Campbell appeared to return to his old self, making two runs at very high speed, but well below the record. *Blue Bird* was returned to Vosper for further modification and Sir Malcolm considered his options. He could return to the old R-type engine, persevere with the experimental jet engine, or commission a new challenger. His death decided for him.

4.

Leopoldo Alfonso Villa

Publisher's note: the name of Leo Villa is inextricably linked with both Sir Malcolm and Donald Campbell. This chapter has been researched, to a substantial degree, from Leo's personal notes and diaries and is an attempt to present both his personality and the important part he played as chief mechanic for the *Blue Bird* and *Bluebird* cars and boats.

At 2 am, on 30 November 1899, Leopoldo Alfonso Villa was born. His birthplace, his mother and father's flat, overlooked Shaftesbury Avenue, Soho, within earshot of the sound of Bow Bells – so Leo was technically a cockney. His father, Leopoldo Mauritzio and his Uncle, Ferdinando, were Swiss by birth, having been born in Lugano, but their family had moved over the border into Italy prior to their move to London. On their arrival, both brothers found jobs in London's busy restaurant trade, and eventually Leo senior married Adelaide Florence Hawkins, a Scots girl from Greenock. They had three children, Amelia, Leo junior and Ferdinando. Soho, although not as poor as other parts of London, was not affluent, but the young Leo was lucky in that his father had secured a well-paid job in one of the top restaurants in the city.

Leo was not unlike many children of the time, and had very little time for education, although he soon developed a keen interest in things mechanical. This had come through his uncle Ferdie, who owned a Globe motorcycle, which, with its 'hot tube ignition', was a very poor starter indeed. Leo and friends often had to push the machine around Soho Square in order to send Uncle Ferdie on his way.

The place to see machinery of the type that interested the young Leo was of course, Brooklands, and he often made the trek to the Surrey track. It is quite probable he saw Malcolm Campbell race there, but his first hero was Ralph Palmer, who was well known in the early years of the track. Although still only 15, Leo had left his school at St Martins in The Fields, and was just the right age to start work with his father at Ramano's Restaurant in the Strand, as a pageboy. Leo took an instant dislike to the 'bowing and scraping' and the 'silly uniform'. His father had worked for Alfonso

Ramano for a couple of years, but Leo's job was an unpaid position, being looked on as a sort of apprenticeship

Leo's most notable talent at the time was for drawing, and he won a scholarship to the Castle Street Art School. Ramano's was already beginning to wear thin and after an argument with the restaurant manager, in which a bottle of ink was deposited on the manager's head, Leo left. The turn of events meant that he lost his chance to develop his art, but fate was to take a hand.

Leo's uncle Ferdie had become manager at Paganini's, a restaurant frequented by the upper-class English, as well as some Italians living in London. One of the regulars was a racing driver by the name of Giulio Foresti and, after chatting with the young tear away, Foresti offered Leo a job in his car workshop on a wage of 15 shillings a week. These were happy times for Leo, learning directly from the man Leo came to know as the 'maestro', in a little workshop in Bryanston Square, off the Edgeware Road. As was to be the case with many young men, these happy times were to be interrupted by the spectre of war.

The Cockney goes to War

By 1917, the third year of the First World War, Leo was old enough to sign up and, after a short bus ride to the army offices in Lambeth, the boy became the man, as he was accepted into the army. He reported to a temporary barracks at Hampton Court and, after a couple of uncomfortable nights, he was transferred to Talavera Barracks, Aldershot, and on again to Halton Camp, Wendover Bucks. Leo's assessment must have been accurate as he was asked to do a trade test and was transferred to Kenley Aircraft Acceptance Park, near Caterham as 'Air Mechanic 2nd Class Leo Villa, Royal Flying Corps'. This was to serve as the perfect apprenticeship for Leo's time with Malcolm Campbell in the years to come, for his tasks were centred around the installation and repair of aero engines. His first job was fitting 160 hp Beardmore six-cylinder engines to Armstrong Whitworth airframes. Although young, his abilities were obvious and because of his natural aptitude for repairing engines he was sent to airfields quite close to the front line. On the occasions he was in England, he worked at Gosport, where Malcolm Campbell took his flying course, and for a second time these two men's paths so nearly crossed.

Leo was de-mobbed in 1919, whereupon he immediately rejoined Foresti in his racing workshop in London. By then the young Cockney was no mere apprentice, and the 'maestro' had no second thoughts about throwing Leo in at the deep end and to the task of rebuilding a 90,266cc Astro-Daimler on his own. The car had been entered by Foresti in the 100-mile Short Handicap at Brooklands, a race that Foresti wanted to win as an advertisement for his workshop's skill and ability. With Leo riding as mechanic, Foresti was beaten into second place, by Captain Malcolm Campbell. Some weeks later, Leo was at Brooklands again while his boss was testing a car and, as he rounded the corner of the clubhouse, his attention was drawn to the far side of the paddock.

Leo recalled "Foresti had sent me back to fetch some different spark plugs, we were having quite a bit of trouble with them oiling up at the time, but I forgot all about them when I heard the most terrible slanging match going on. Some poor chap was kneeling down with his hands stuck up inside the engine of this car looking very fed up. Leaning over him was this man, about five foot tall, ranting and raving about how he had been told to change the plugs and 'why the bloody hell didn't you change them when you were told to?'. The poor mechanic could not defend himself. It was impossible to get a word in edgeways. I thought I knew how he felt, but my last thought was that I hoped that I'd never have to work for a boss like that. It was only later on I found out who he was, Captain Malcolm Campbell."

Foresti at this time held the franchises for Itala, Diatto and Isotta cars, but business had not been good for anyone after the war and when the chance to race in his home country was offered, Foresti revoked all the dealerships in one go.

"I knew Foresti was having trouble, and thought I'd better start looking for another job, but one day I heard the old greeting, ''allo ole sporty' as the boss strolled in. He was very fair and explained about the offer to race abroad. It came as quite a shock when he looked me straight in the eye and said 'Veela, you want come a race de cars with me?'. It only took a little thinking about and, after getting a passport we were off."

Racing Abroad

The 'maestro' and his mechanic left England on 9 March 1921 on their way to take part in their first race, the twelfth Targa Florio. The car they were to use was a standard production 3 litre Itala, which kept Leo happy, as he had worked on them before, plus it meant that it should be reliable, which was even more of a comfort as those breaking down in the mountains could fall victim to bandits. Foresti took no chances, though, and left the start with a loaded revolver under his seat. Leo's concern was for his own safety should the gun go off when they hit a bump! The event itself was an anticlimax and after one very hectic, over-staffed pit-stop, Foresti and Villa cruised home in first place in the 3-litre class. For Leo's part, he won 1000 lire and a silver medal. For the following year the pair were offered a works drive by the French Ballot concern. Foresti and his mechanic had so impressed the Ballot brothers, that a very lucrative offer was made which Foresti could not refuse. So it was that Foresti and Villa were to take part in the 2-litre class, driving a works sports-racing Ballot

1932 – 1940

The finished *Blue Bird* on Daytona Beach, 1932. The chase plane in the background was unable to keep up with the car at speed *(© Campbell Collection)*

Brooklands, 1933: Sir Malcolm Campbell inspects the Rolls-Royce R33 installed in the *Blue Bird* chassis. Note the duplicated steering arms *(© Leo Villa Collection)*

The 1935 *Blue Bird* is revealed to the press at Brooklands. In his school cap, the young Donald Campbell looks on *(© Campbell Collection)*

Sir Malcolm Campbell examines the course marker line on the salts of Bonneville, 1935. On his arrival, Campbell was convinced that his tyres would be shredded on the rough salt *(© Leo Villa Collection)*

Sir Malcolm Campbell in the cockpit of the 1935 *Blue Bird* about to set off on a lap of Brooklands to celebrate achieving 300 mph at Bonneville. Outside the circuit, road signs had been changed from "30" mph to "300"! *(© Leo Villa Collection)*

Sir Malcolm Campbell's *Blue Bird* being shipped onto the *Gudrun Maersk* in February 1935 for an attempt on the World Land Speed Record *(© Fox Photos)*

Edward Spurr in the tiny boat *Empire Day,* originally built for Lawrence of Arabia *(by kind permission of John Gould)*

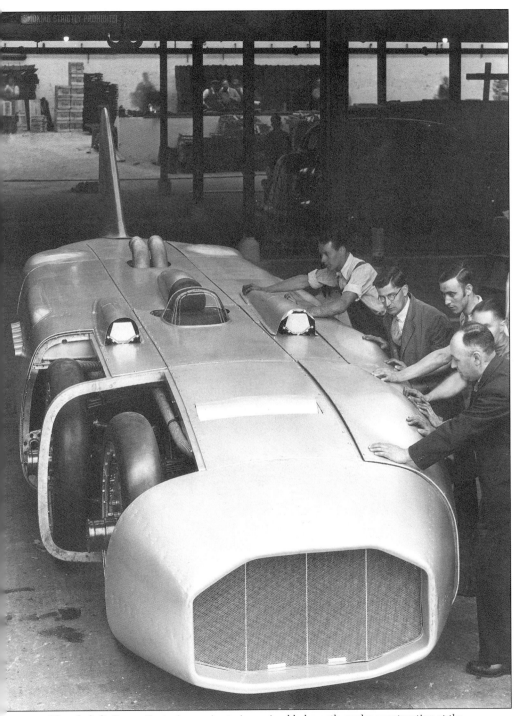

Thunderbolt, George Eyston's massive twin-engined behemoth, under construction at the Bean Cars works in Tipton *(by kind permission of Bert Denly)*

Kaye Don at the helm of *Miss England II* after her rebuild at Rolls-Royce, Derby
(© Rolls-Royce plc)

A close-up of the dashboard of *Blue Bird K3* in 1937, taken after the water temperature gauge had been moved into Sir Malcolm's line of sight. Along with the instruments, warning light and magneto switch, there are no less than four lucky charms: two St Christophers, a framed lock of elephant hair, and the *Blue Bird* plaque *(© Campbell Collection)*

Blue Bird K3 gets under way on Lago Maggiore. Underneath it is possible to make out the stabilising fin, while on the foredeck the cooling scoop made from Sir Malcolm's Rolls-Royce horn is clearly visible *(© Rolls-Royce plc)*

Celebrating the record, Lago Maggiore, 1937. The team stands on board K3, with Leo looking by far the happiest! *(© Leo Villa Collection)*

The entrance to the Bonneville Salt Flats *(by kind permission of Mrs Goldie Gardner)*

John Cobb's refurbished *Railton Mobil Special*, outside Thomson and Taylor's at Brooklands *(by kind permission of John Gould)*

in the 1922 Targa, and a visit to the Paris workshops of the brothers Ballot was arranged.

The car surprised Leo, for it was far more advanced than any car he had yet seen. Leo was 'shown around' Foresti's car by Jules Goux's racing mechanic, Pierre du Cros. Ballot were entering two cars, one for Goux, and the other for Foresti, and so du Cros and Villa were to work side by side preparing the cars.

"The engine was a four cylinder 2 litre, with inverted overhead valves operated by a vertical shaft and bevel gears, and developed about 72 hp," recalled Leo. "Everything looked so clean. The crankcase, gearbox and rear axle cases were all aluminium, and had been highly polished. I remember that only one car a week was built, and that each one had a solid silver radiator cap in the form of a nude nymph. The whole car was very smartly turned out, and I think my hopes as well as the maestro's were very high."

In order that the pit-stop debacle was not repeated for the second year, Foresti arranged to have spare wheels and petrol hidden around the course. Foresti felt even more certain that he needed some form of insurance, and again departed from the start with a revolver tucked under his seat. As the race progressed, Foresti signalled toward a clearing beside the track, and Leo prepared to conduct his roadside pit-stop. Unfortunately Foresti had decided that most of the refuelling could be done on the move, but he had not informed Leo, who recalled, "I remember that none of the new wheels was properly secured, and that I'd only just managed to fit the funnel in the tank. I was just lifting up the petrol bidon *(a large container)*, when Foresti dropped the clutch. With no warning I could only do one thing, and dropped the fuel overboard. The funnel snapped off and the remains dropped inside the tank, plus we lost two of our spare wheels, the other one I was holding!"

After a few scares, Foresti managed to bring his car home second, behind Goux, and the order came through that both cars were to be cleaned and driven in formation back to the factory in Paris. On their return, the Ballot brothers announced that success had brought a huge interest from abroad, that a new dealer had been appointed in England, and the second-place car had been bought by the new franchise holder. Foresti was to drive his old Targa Itala, and Leo, the Ballot, over to England, where they were both to stay on to help the new owner tune both cars before returning to France, and the Ballot factory. As the cars were unloaded in Folkestone Leo met the cars' new owner, one Captain Malcolm Campbell.

The Return to England

Leo sat with Campbell as the Captain drove the pair back to Povey Cross,

Campbell's house near Horley. When they arrived Leo was given a guided tour of the immaculate workshop and was shown the room where he would sleep that night. It had a four-poster bed, which to young Leo was absolute luxury. The next morning, Campbell left for his showroom in Albermarle Street, London and left Leo to start work on the two cars. Foresti was stunned by the spotless workshop. Everything had its place, and there was a tool for every job.

Leo was forced to agree with the maestro when he said "You know Veela, dis a man must have a plenty solido". During the next few days, Campbell spent much time looking over Leo's shoulder, and started to make a few hints that there might be a job there for him if he wanted it. Campbell was exacting in the extreme, and Leo thought long and hard before making a decision. He had to admit that he was fed up living out of a suitcase in hotels and, given the relative luxury of Povey Cross, maybe it was not such a difficult decision after all.

"Foresti was not very upset when I told him what Campbell had suggested, and that made telling him a little easier. Foresti had a happy-go-lucky outlook, and was very patient, Campbell on the other hand was a very exacting person to whom nothing was impossible. I'd made my choice, and there was no going back. All dear old Foresti said was, 'My God Veela, you gonna have some kinda job ere, old sporty'."

Leo Villa had arrived as resident mechanic as Campbell's interests were being drawn toward the Land Speed Record and the car Malcolm had described as 'a real racing machine', the 350 hp Sunbeam. This car held the Land Speed Record at 129.7 mph, driven by Kennelm Lee Guinness. Campbell had borrowed the car for racing on the sands at Saltburn, and had beaten the speed Guinness had recorded. He had approached the car's designer, Louis Coatalen with an offer to buy it, but had been turned down.

"I remember," Leo later recalled "Campbell walking into the workshop when he had returned from the sand races with the 350 hp (Sunbeam), and he was convinced that his speed had been far greater than Guinness had recorded. His expression was fixed and his tone changed in a way I was to become used to; he wanted something, and he was going to get it. 'Villa,' he said 'that car is bloody fast, and I intend to get it'. I knew then that he would."

Soon after. Campbell instructed Leo to drive him down to Horley station. When they arrived there the 350 hp Sunbeam was being unloaded. Leo opened the boot of his car, ready to tow the Sunbeam back, but Campbell had other ideas, and drove it to Burtenshaws', the coachbuilders, where it was to receive a coat of blue paint.

A Life's Work

Leo's life became firmly linked with the names Campbell and *Blue Bird*, and although he still worked on racing cars, record-breaking was to become his forte. Campbell had rented two lock-up garages in Rodmarten Mews, behind Baker Street, where his newly imported Itala chassis were being delivered. While not working on *Blue Bird*, Leo worked here, preparing the chassis before they went off to the coachbuilders for bodies to be fitted. Campbell had requested some assistance from Sunbeam, and a man called Harry Leech was sent to join him. Leech worked for Sunbeam on a freelance basis, and was an expert in aero engines. In his long association with the Campbells, he returned to work on various Government-backed, highly secret jobs, including work on the diesel engines used on the ill-fated airship, the R101, from which Leech was one of the very few survivors.

This was the return of happy times for Leo, for while in the lock-ups, he was in charge. His work had always been of a high standard, but with the likes of Malcolm Campbell watching, he could never be certain that his work was going to be up to the Captain's standard. In the lock-up, with his new friend Harry, he felt relaxed and able to work. One day, Leo was working with Leech on Campbell's four-litre 'Indy' Sunbeam, when he was distracted by a young lady. "I had never really had time for the opposite sex, but something drew me to this girl." recalled Leo. "Conversation was easy, and she became a frequent visitor. Fortunately, she was very interested in motor racing, and I wasted no time telling her I was Captain Malcolm Campbell's mechanic. Her name was Emily Jane Proctor, but neither of us thought it suited her. To me she became Joan."

Leo was able to spend more time with Joan when he bought himself a 16H Norton motorcycle, and the more time he spent with her, the more the romance blossomed.

Leo recalled that "At the time he had asked me to work for him, Campbell had said to me that I should never marry. 'Racing and romance don't mix, stay single if you can, it has never done me any good.'. He had told me about his first wife, and had always said that it was her affair with his business partner that had caused the split. He always maintained that it was not the adultery that bothered him, 'You know Villa' he told me, 'the thing I could not stand was the lack of loyalty, you can't buy loyalty, not at any price'. I think he was worried that if I got married, it would divide my loyalty, so I never told him about Joan. He went off with Lee Guinness on his yacht, looking for treasure in the Cocas Islands, and while he was gone, Joan and I went off to Brixton Registry office, and married. After a two-day honeymoon, I went back to work. Campbell was quite annoyed when he found out, but he got used to the idea, and even gave me a wage rise as I was then earning for two."

A Loyalty you can't buy

It didn't take long for Leo to develop a loyalty for Campbell, but even Leo had not realised it until the French Grand Prix. Campbell had entered a Bugatti, as had his main rival Sabipa. The race was flagged off in pouring rain with Sabipa and Campbell leaving the rest of the field behind. Try as he might ,Campbell could not get close enough to Sabipa to overtake, and so he was going to have to rely on quick pit work to get into the lead.

"I watched Sabipa come into the pits shouting at the top of his voice that his clutch was slipping. None of his crew realised that, although I was standing in the English pit, I could understand everything they were saying. The French were frantically looking for 'Une broche' (a small tommy bar), and all I could do was look blankly back, biting my lip at the names I was called because I didn't want to give the game away. Eventually Campbell came past, just as the French got Sabipa back out on the track. Under my foot was a small tommy bar that had fallen over 'our' side of the pit counter. I surprised myself. At first I wasn't proud of what I had done, but then I became aware that I had done it out of loyalty, I really quite liked the boss by now!"

By this time Leo and his wife had been joined in their new house in Surbiton by Leo junior, who became known to one and all as Tim. Campbell was paying his chief mechanic £5 a week, but this never managed to take into account the very late evenings, and sometimes nights, that Leo was required to work as the various *Blue Birds* were built.

By the time Leo was preparing for his first trip to America, he was already spending much of his day 'accompanied' by Captain Campbell's young son, Donald, whom he had been introduced to when the tot was just months old, and one of Leo's unofficial tasks was to look after the seven-year-old master Campbell, and sometimes his sister Jean as well. More than once Leo 'carried the can' for the two, but as he once observed, "It went a long way to making up for missing young Tim during those long all-nighters".

Leo had been in two minds about his first trip across the Atlantic – it was an adventure, but he would be leaving his family behind yet again. The team arrived in Daytona at the height of prohibition, which did not perturb Leo one bit as he was almost completely tee-total, in fact the rest of the team had nick-named him 'cissie'. Strangely though, when the Land Speed Record was successfully beaten, the local police force held a celebration party for Campbell and crew, at which some very fine Scotch was served!

Each year seemed to be the preparation for what was becoming the annual attempt at the record, racing taking up less and less of Campbell's time. This preparation was to be 90% of Leo's life. His home life was only what could be snatched between record attempts, working on racing cars or fixing the estate machinery at Povey Cross, and 1929 was going to be no different.

Leo remembered the time that they went to South Africa: "Campbell bounced into the workshop early one morning and announced he was flying down to South Africa to survey a new venue for his next crack at the record. He had brought a Gypsy Moth aeroplane (christened *Blue Bird* of course), which yours truly had to bring up to fettle. It was the usual thing, Campbell would walk in and say 'Be a good chap Villa, just take a look at this would you, see if you can do anything with it', which usually meant a rebuild. Anyway, with that I knew, when we had finished rebuilding the *Blue Bird* car I was going to be away for sometime."

The *Blue Bird* team arrived at Vernuek Pan (a place that Leo always referred to as Vernikity Pan) in South Africa, while Segrave was taking out his new car, the *Golden Arrow* to Daytona Beach. The attempt at the Pan was going to be fraught with setbacks, the biggest of which came with the news that Segrave, after only one test run, had upped the record to 231 mph, an increase of 23 mph, and well above the design speed of the newly modified *Blue Bird*.

"It came as quite a shock that we had travelled all that way, to have no chance at all of succeeding. That evening was one of the few that Campbell didn't fly back to the city, and he looked as unhappy as the rest of us felt. He looked me in the eye and said, 'I'll be buggered if I'm going back with nothing, we'll have a crack at some distance stuff'. It raised the spirits until next morning, when we had a good long chat with Steve 'Dunlop Mac' MacDonald, the tyre man. The Dunlops we had with us were purely 'sprint' tyres and should only have been used for one mile at top speed. I don't suppose Dunlops were any happier than me, but Campbell was adamant, he was going to have a go at the five-mile and five kilometre records.

"Campbell nearly always called me 'Villa', I suppose it was 'employer and employee', but as he climbed into the car he let his guard slip, and for a brief instant I saw the real man for the first time. 'You know Leo' he said, 'I'm getting too bloody old for this sort of thing'. His gaze swung around, along the great, long, white line up the centre of the course, and I'm glad he did, because I always got emotional at times like that, but this was the first time there had been a chance of something going wrong, and I realised how I might feel if anything should happen to the Skipper. But Campbell, for all his stern aloofness, had a soft side, which you only saw when he let it show. I was choked enough to have a last go at trying to get him to think about pushing the tyres beyond what they had been designed for when he snapped back to his old self. 'Come on you bloody clot, start the bloody thing up', and I knew what I had to do."

Both of the longer distance records fell, but far from easily. After this, the 350hp Sunbeam was sold to Jack Field for £250, a lot less than the £1500 Parry Thomas had offered Campbell in 1923. Field raced it a few times and sold it on for £10 to the bandleader Billy Cotton (the car is now on display at the National Motor Museum, Beaulieu, England). Campbell's turnaround in his racing stable was quite phenomenal, and Leo was hard pressed at times keeping up with it all. It was not always plain sailing, and Leo was to find out that on occasions Campbell could be quite unscrupulous.

Leo recalled a particular event that was so characteristic of his boss: "Campbell had been selling Bugattis from his sheds at Brooklands, and had sold one of the 2 litre cars that were guaranteed for 100 mph, to Brian Lewis. Anyway, we were testing something or another when in comes Lewis complaining that his car would only pull 80. 'Come on Villa, we'll get the thing up to a 100' said Campbell and gestured over to Lewis' car. I went straight for the bonnet straps, just to have a quick look, but Campbell invited me into the car in his usual polite way, and we were away. About half way around the lap I realised that the bonnet straps were still undone. I struggled forward to try and catch the rear one and stop it flapping when the bonnet flew open, catching Campbell on the head. It knocked him cold. I leant over, flicked the kill switch on the magnetos, and grabbed the steering wheel, pulling up about half way along the finishing straight. I probably saved both of us, but Campbell gave me a sound ticking off. Later I found out that he had told people how it had been he who had cut the ignition and brought the car to rest, saving both of us.

"Each time he told the story it was decorated a little more, sometimes I got the impression that he had forgotten I was with him when it happened, but I can tell you, he was out like a light. I know, I was there. Funnily enough he did that sort of thing often. He got so used to blowing himself up that he forgot who it was he was taking advantage of. I remember he once gave Donald a book for Christmas. Typically, it was a book about himself, called 'The Romance of Motor Racing'. On the spine was Sir Malcolm Campbell, in big gold letters. Don was very proud and later showed it to one of his father's guests. 'Look' Donald said proudly 'this is the book my father has just written'. The guest was John Wentworth Day, the man who had actually written the book, and he was not best pleased, but kept politely quiet. I don't think Don ever found out, and I never did find out what, if anything happened between Wentworth Day and Campbell about it but it was a good example of how Campbell got a reputation for using people to bolster himself. He just didn't seem to care."

It is interesting to compare this version of the Bugatti bonnet story, with the one that appears on page 112 in Campbell's book, 'My Thirty Years of Speed'. In this, Campbell claims to have been stunned, and pulled the car to a halt in a half daze. There is no mention of a passenger until the very end and, even then, there are no names mentioned. He then goes on to claim that having halted the car, he collapsed back into unconsciousness, and only came to again in the clubhouse, and could not remember a thing, claiming that it took weeks to recall the whole incident. According to Leo's diaries, this is about the time that Leo told 'the Skipper' what had happened. Yet, in the 'BP Book of the Racing Campbells' the incident is recalled in the paddock in an exchange between a fellow racer and the 'Skipper'. Campbell, caught with a damp towel around his head is asked, What's up Rajah, how did you do that?", to which Campbell is quoted in response as saying, "Ask my mechanic, he knows!"

Leo got used to receiving little, if any credit for whatever he did for his employer, but it became very difficult to bear when on occasion Campbell, who had no background in engineering whatsoever, would actually question Leo's ability. At Daytona in 1935, Campbell had complained that he was not getting full revs from the Rolls-Royce R-type engine, and informed Leo that he might, "find the bloody reason Villa, I'm so close". Leo suggested that it might be the air escaping from the radiator disturbing the supercharger intake, Campbell's answer was typical: "Don't be a bloody fool Villa, the boffins at Rolls have spent years getting that to work, why should you know any better?"

The whole team returned to England, happy that they had raised the record, but disappointed that it had been by such a small margin. Leo sought out the car's designer, Reid Railton. "I went off and had a chat with Reid, who stood sucking on a pencil. He thought for a while and said that I might have something. I think it was only a matter of hours at the wind tunnel at Vickers, and he came back with the advice I should extend the supercharger intake beyond the radiator outlet, and with a pat on my shoulder left the sheds. You can imagine I wasn't very impressed by Campbell's reaction: 'All that time and effort Villa, I could have told you that!'"

Campbell had made it clear during 1934-35 that, having once achieved his ambition to be the first man to exceed 300 mph on land, he intended to retire. This ambition was fulfilled in September 1935, and Campbell stood by his word, but only it seemed from record-breaking on land. Unknown to Leo, Campbell had commissioned Thomson and Taylors, at Brooklands, to start design work on a gearbox for a *Blue Bird* boat in September 1936, when work on the hull was well advanced. Indeed, the idea of a water-borne *Blue Bird* must have been in Campbell's mind for some time, as initial design proposals for the craft were carried out as early as 1934.

During the latter part of 1935, and early 1936, Leo was occupied in

moving his workshop to Campbell's new house, Headley Grove, at the top
of Pebble-Combe Hill, in Surrey. For the first time in years it looked as if
both Campbell and Leo, were going to slow up and enjoy life a little. Leo
was delighted. "Campbell had suggested that we market some of my
inventions, like a diver's torch, and an electric grass trimmer *(now called
a 'strimmer')* that I had come up with. I was happier than I had been for
some time, and was even trying to buy our house in Surbiton. Campbell
told me his new estate had two houses in its grounds, and invited my
family to move in. Tim was nine at the time and the thought of having my
family so close swung it for me. Campbell laid on gas and electricity and
had a bathroom installed. I was even happier. The first clue I had about
the boat was when Sir Malcolm's 1935 car came back to us, and I was
instructed to remove the engine. Alf Poyser, the Rolls engineer turned up
one morning, saying that he and I had to take the unit down to Saunders
Roe, on the Isle of Wight. Campbell came along and before we entered the
building he stopped Alf and me and said, "Now you chaps, everything
you see today, you're to keep completely under your hats".

I was very impressed, until we were told that the engine would not be
required. The boat, *Blue Bird K3*, eventually arrived at Brooklands, and
my first job was to sling the hull from the ceiling, to work out the centre of
gravity. It was a task I didn't enjoy at all. The rafters were creaking, and
the ropes banged every so often as they pulled tighter and tighter. I never
really liked the first boat, it always gave us trouble and seemed to be
always beyond its limit.'

After trials on Loch Lomond, Leo was sent to Northern Italy to survey
Lago Maggiore, the venue chosen for Campbell's first attempt on the
Water Speed Record. His Italian came in useful, and cheered him up a bit,
since he was worried about the boat project from the minute he had seen
the hull under construction.

"I was never really very happy in the early days of the water record.
The only thing I knew about the boat was the engine, our trusty
Rolls-Royce R-type. At least I had one up on Campbell in that I spoke the
lingo, which meant for the first time he would have to ask me what was
what, because he couldn't bluff me otherwise!"

The second *Blue Bird* hydroplane, *K4*, proved a far easier proposition.
Campbell had made the decision to take his new mount to Coniston
Water, in the English Lake District, as he was worried that the accelerat-
ing threat of war would maroon him abroad should the balloon go up.
With a new record under his belt, Campbell and Leo set off to Hythe Pier,
in Southampton where his latest *Blue Bird* yacht was moored. With Leo
working the engines and Campbell steering the course, they moved *Blue
Bird IV* up the River Dart, to where Campbell thought she would be safe.
Campbell had written two books in the years leading up to the war, warn-

ing a complacent Britain about the threat, first of war and then the danger of air raids once it had started. He was accused of being a warmonger, but of course was proved all too correct. On the way back from the River Dart, both he and Leo heard the news that war had been declared.

Leo's main task during the war years involved looking after *Blue Bird K4*, and the spare R-type engines. Unknown to Leo, they had been sold, along with the original *Blue Bird* boat, but had yet to be delivered. He was also in charge of looking after Campbell's air raid shelter, which had been built just before the war had started. Eventually, Leo took the three R engines to Thomson and Taylors, for long-term storage. After the armistice, Campbell returned to record-breaking, but his health was already failing. Leo had one of the first jet engines to contend with. Although De Havillands had sent along some technicians to assist with the new Goblin jet engine, he had to learn a lot, which was to be of great value in the years to come.

Campbell's eyesight had started to fail, he had already had one operation for glaucoma and his other eye was beginning to show signs of failing completely. Suddenly Leo had the unusual task of driving the Skipper to functions, something that very rarely happened. By this time Headley Grove had been sold to the Maharajah of Baroda, and Campbell had moved to a new home called Little Gatton, where all of his staff were fitted out in blue blazers with brass '*Blue Bird*' buttons.

"Don used to tease the footman terrible, but I think he stood it in good humour. Sir Malcolm had remarried, after his second divorce, but it only lasted a few months. I had found a house in Lower Kingswood, near Reigate, and spent the next few weeks moving *Blue Bird K4*, and all of her gear to Little Gatton. I remember that Lady Dorothy, Campbell's second wife, had moved into the old gatehouse, and quite often I saw them walking around the grounds as if they had never been apart. Late one evening, I was on my way out, and I stopped to have a quick chat with Lady Campbell. Just then a car swept in, driven I think by Goldie Gardner. In the back was another racing friend of Campbell's, Dr Benjafield, and slumped next to him a very grey Sir Malcolm. He had been having terrible trouble trying to get the jet-engined *Blue Bird* to work, and I thought that maybe he was exhausted, he was, after all, 63 years old and had been receiving a terrible pounding in the boat. Lady Dorothy curtly dismissed me, and rushed off up the drive. The next day the doctor called again, and told me that Campbell had suffered a stroke. Fortunately, Dr Benjafield and Goldie Gardner had been on hand to bring him home and he was confined to bed for at least a month. Two days later, there he was in the workshop looking very bored. It was one of those times when his guard was down, I think he was feeling that maybe he wasn't as immortal as he liked to think. He looked worried. For the first time that I can remember, he actually stopped me from what I was doing and I think it was the first time he had sought me out to talk to. 'Leo' he said, 'this isn't the first time you know. Benjy has told me I have had my share of warnings . I want to die at the wheel of a racing car at the age of seventy'. Then he gave me a firm punch on the upper arm and said, 'Good old Leo'."

Normally Leo could find a way around Campbell, but after his second stroke he became even more impossible. His temper was getting shorter and fiercer, and he became extremely irritable.

Just before Christmas 1948, Campbell's old butler, Reg Whiteman, reappeared, lending a hand with the festive preparations. It was a bit of a shock to Leo:

"On the Wednesday before Christmas, the 22nd, Reg came and dug me out saying the 'Old Man' wanted a hand delivering some Christmas presents to the staff at Tilgate. I always found it funny that up front was the owner, driving his car, with his mechanic beside him, and the butler sitting in the back. Campbell was always a good driver so when he started to 'muff' the odd gear change I looked across. He looked terribly unwell, and I was just about to suggest we stop when the car veered across the road. It was just like the day at Brooklands as I lent across to try and control the car. Reg and I managed to get him into the passenger seat and as we did so I said that we should turn back. He had great difficulty even talking, but made it quite clear we would complete the task we had set out to do. It was one of the very few times I drove him anywhere. His speech worsened but occasionally I heard him mutter 'good old Leo', but as he grabbed at my leg there was no strength. We finally arrived back at Little Gatton, where Reg and I had to carry him up to his room. I don't think I saw him again. I spoke to Don on the following Friday, but he did not really know what was going to happen. Later that night the Skipper died." It was New Years Eve, 1948.

On Friday, 7 January 1949, a Memorial Service was held to the life of Sir Malcolm Campbell, MBE. It was attended by people from all walks of life, not just from motor racing. St Margaret's, in Westminster, simply did not have the capacity to hold all those that arrived, and outside the streets were full, but oddly still.

In the weeks that followed, Leo spent all his working day, thinking not only of what had been, but also of what was to be. "It wasn't only that sad phase that follows the loss of someone, but also the worry of what on Earth was I going to do next".

Much has been made of the contents of Campbell's will, which had been written in February 1948, especially with regard to the accusations of meanness and the deliberate prevention of his son ever following in the family 'business'. Apart from the usual declarations the main bequests were listed in section three as:

a] To my former wife Lady Dorothy Campbell the sum of five hundred pounds.

b] To my old friend Leo Villa the sum of one thousand pounds in appreciation of his loyal and devoted services.

c] To Reg Whiteman (his former butler) the sum of two hundred and fifty pounds in appreciation of his services to me during the long period of years he was in my employment.

d] To Edgar Charles Harvey (his footman) the sum of one hundred pounds, also in appreciation of his services to me.

e] To my old friend William Erlam Garden (Campbell's longest standing business partner) of the North British and Mercantile Insurance Company, the sum of two hundred and fifty pounds.

f] To my old friend Major John G. Lepper of the Bridge House, Bisham Marlow in the county of Buckingham, the sum of two hundred and fifty pounds.

I give and bequeath free of all duty all of my silver cups and other trophies won by me, and all my trinkets watches and jewellery to my said former wife Lady Dorothy Campbell, my son Donald Malcolm, my daughter Jean Hulme and my sister Winifred Mather, to be divided between them in equal shares, and that my trophies shall be kept in my family and as far as possible treated as heirlooms.

In addition to this, Campbell left his former wife an annual income of £400 and to his long serving mechanic Leo Villa, a house in Reigate. The only other instruction was that his properties, Little Gatton, 51 Meadow Way Woodhatch, Reigate, 68 Prince Albert Square Earlswood, Surrey, and Tilgate lakes in Sussex, as well as his books, silver plate, china, pictures, furniture, motor cars, household and personal effects and belongings were to be sold and converted into money to set up trust funds for his children and in turn, his grandchildren. There was absolutely no provision preventing Donald using any of the *Blue Bird* record-breaking equipment; indeed it appears that anything to do with Campbell's career was totally forgotten about, from scrap books to the *Blue Birds* themselves.

Leo Villa later said "It always struck me as odd that the Old Man's will never mentioned the *Blue Bird* car, or boat. I was left £1000, and allowed to select a keepsake from his effects. I must admit that I did rescue quite a few things from the rubbish that someone had obviously decided weren't worth keeping, but as for the *Blue Birds*, it seemed like they were just considered as part of the workshop, and to be disposed of the same as the rest of the contents. Anyway Don said that as the money was to go to his sister, and eventually to both his sister's and his own children, he would just arrange to buy the equipment from the estate, but no, I cannot remember any instruction to stop Don buying anything that could lead to him going record-breaking."

Donald purchased his father's 1935 car and the latest *Blue Bird* boat, *K4*, which was actually at the Vosper premises complete with the experimental jet engine and undergoing modifications. Leo recalled:

"I remember Goldie Gardner visiting Don just after the sale. I think we all felt worse after that. Gardner waved to me on his way to his car, and left. I remember Don went around the grounds for about three hours, and finally came into the workshop as dusk fell. 'Leo', he said, 'Goldie has just told me that some American called Kaiser is building a boat to have a go at the old man's record. I've thought about it, and I simply can't let that happen. What say you we bump up the record out of their reach, who knows it may put them off, and we'll have it for ever. I wasn't so certain. I didn't answer straight away, and went to see Don the next morning. I hadn't got that much sleep the night before. Secretly I was pleased that I might still have a chance to do a job I knew, but Don's safety worried me. I told him I was with him, but added 'you're taking on a man's job, don't ever underestimate the difficulty of what you'll be trying to do. Once you start you'll never be able to stop, and you'll never get used to the atmosphere'. Don went quiet, pulled his chin, and winked – it was like going back all over again. 'Good old Leo' he said, and punched me on the shoulder. I do remember it was a good deal harder than his father."

After the problems encountered by Malcolm Campbell with the new jet engine, and De Havilland's concern over letting Donald take over the development of a new propulsion system, the decision was made to convert *Blue Bird K4* to its pre-war aero-engined form. Leo's son, "Tim" had been working for Kine Engineering, of which Donald was a major shareholder and director, but as work progressed on the *Blue Bird*, Tim ended up working more and more with his father as part of the *Blue Bird* team.

"Don kept saying that all he wanted to do was put the record out of the Yanks' reach, but the nearer the boat came to being finished, the more I started to worry. I mean Don was a better engineer than his father, but I don't think I'd seen him drive a car at over 80, let alone driving a boat to over 140 mph."

The 'new' *Blue Bird* arrived at Coniston during 1949. The crew was familiar but there was a new pilot, Donald Malcolm Campbell and there to support him his wife, Daphne. The attempt was typical of the way Donald's later attempts would go. Bad weather, mechanical difficulties and a sniping press, but after a couple of 'moments' while running on the slower 'soft' plugs, Campbell had shown his mettle.

"Don had shot off down the lake the first time, well over the 100, and done a beautiful turn. He arrived back at the jetty with a huge grin on his face, really excited. I shall never forget his words, just like his father had said to me before: 'it's a piece of cake Leo'. It was only later that I started to worry again. On the Friday night, Don found me in the bar, and very casually mentioned that tomorrow was going to be the day he was going to run on the 'hard' plugs. I tried everything to persuade him otherwise, but it was no good."

The next day, Saturday, August 19th, Leo showed his new boss all the loyalty he had shown his old one: "When the Skipper had told me to do something, I had always done it. Don was new to the game, but in the end I did as I was told and fitted the hard plugs."

After two very difficult runs, *Blue Bird* returned to the slipway.

"Donald was as white as a sheet. We had seen the boat swerve violently on both runs, once nearly going over. Don fixed me with a look I was going to see often, 'That' he said, 'frightened the life out of me. You could get bloody killed doing this.' Then a few seconds later, we looked at each other and laughed. It wasn't such a piece of cake after all."

During the 1950 'season', *Blue Bird* and her crew had encountered a problem with cooling of the trusty R-type engine. Both Leo and Harry Leech had told Donald to keep his eye on the dials, but it always proved difficult to 'spare them the time' as Donald once put it. After a long discussion, it was decided that the best and simplest solution would be to carry an observer. The right-hand fuel tank was removed and a seat installed, confronted by a replica of the dashboard that faced the pilot. The most obvious candidate to observe this replica would be someone who knew the boat as well as the pilot, but the team had someone who knew the craft even better. "Unfortunately" said Leo, "I was picked as the most qualified. I didn't try to get out of it, but I wasn't happy at all."

By now the name of Leo Villa was firmly linked with those of both Campbell and *Blue Bird*. Try as one might to find some form of history outside of record-breaking, for the most loyal of mechanics, it is impossible. It was nearly all that Leo did, and as he said: "If I wasn't at home asleep, I was in the workshop, or at Coniston, and usually with my sleeves rolled up until late."

On 2 July 1950, *Blue Bird*, with her new observer unhappily ensconced, was towed out ready for a run. The engine had been warmed, and the hard plugs fitted, this was going to be something new. "Don pressed down with his foot, to operate the valve for the compressed air, and once that had the 'R' turning over he spun the starting magneto. There was an almighty crash, and all of a sudden all I could see was the sky, as the prop dug into the water and we performed a water-borne 'wheely'. I was so scared, I can remember a great deal about those first runs, especially that it was bloody cold and I didn't enjoy it in the slightest."

As far back as 1939, the wind tunnel model of *K4* had shown an alarming tendency to do back flips at anything over a scale speed of 150 mph. But far from being worried about how they were going to combat this as their speed approached this figure, it appeared that they were going to have trouble keeping the bow from diving under the water.

"All through Don's first attempts, we were cursed with cooling troubles, and we actually managed to 'boil' the faithful old R37 engine, Sir Malcolm's favourite from his attempt at Bonneville. Both Don and I were convinced the stern was rising, lifting the cooling scoop out of the water and forcing the bow down. Harry produced all these graphs to prove otherwise, but we were certain. Eventually Reid Railton proved that Don and I were right and I think it was the same afternoon we heard that the American Stan Sayres had beaten the record. We had reached 150, with great difficulty, but Sayres had set the target at 160.32. We were dumbfounded. Railton found out that Sayres had used a technique called 'prop riding' in which the aft planing surface is the hub of the prop. This meant that only one blade was submerged at any one time. The problem we had encountered was *Blue Bird* trying to prop-ride. Don and I felt happy knowing we were right, but depressed that we had been beaten to it. Don contacted Sayres in the States and he proved very helpful. The decision was made, *Blue Bird* was going to become a prop-rider. Reid did some of the early calculations but Don couldn't afford to pay to have the work done."

By then, Donald's first marriage to Daphne Harvey, was over, and he was living at the Reigate Hill Hotel, with his daughter Gina. The hotel owner, Margaret Parkes, allowed him to store *Blue Bird* in the garages at the rear of the building and, with this in mind, Donald decided to carry out the conversion work himself. The *Blue Bird* team consisted of Don, Leo and his son "Tim", Harry Leech, Len Coles, Doug Floyd, Lewis Norris and, to some extent, his brother, Ken.

Between them, Railton and Lewis Norris had decided that the major modification was to move the centre of gravity forward to encourage the stern to rise. To do this the engine was moved forward some six feet, more or less where the single central cockpit used to be. The twin cockpit concept was to be kept, and the cockpits were installed directly above the planing shoes. These shoes were modified to have a steeper angle of attack, and the position of the seats above these led to a considerable compromise in comfort as Leo was to find out later in Italy.

An invitation from a Gabriel d'Annuzio arrived just as work started on the conversion during January 1951, which led to some soul-searching on behalf of the team. Leo recalled, "Don told us that we had got this invitation from Italy. He did say he'd like to do it, but said it would a be rush to have the boat ready on time. But it did take a while to find out that it wasn't to be a straight record attempt, and longer to find out it was a race around a circuit! Funnily, working to a deadline is quite helpful, it certainly stops dawdling in the workshop! I was very happy, after all it wouldn't be the first time I had been to Italy with *Blue Bird*, and I had enjoyed the first trip no end. But the course at Lake Garda, was a triangular circuit, and *Blue Bird*'s ability to corner was an unknown quantity. The thing that swung it for Don was that the trophy had been put up in memory of Sir Henry Segrave, and even though Kaye Don had tried, no Englishman had ever won it, but he was still very concerned about getting the boat around the corner markers."

The Oltranza Cup meeting was organised by the Club Motonautico Gabriel D'Annuzio. Count D'Annuzio had been a great admirer of Segrave, even to the point of obtaining the twisted steering wheel from *Miss England II*, and installing it in a shrine-like display, where it is to this day. He had donated the Oltranza Cup, for the fastest two consecutive laps, and the Grand Prix, for the overall winner. D'Annuzio was an eccentric who lived in a huge villa overlooking Lake Garda in northern Italy, and could often be seen on his motor cruiser, patrolling the lake, dressed in full military uniform.

Regardless of what Donald Campbell considered a patriotic duty, Leo was very concerned, especially as *Blue Bird* had been conceived to travel as fast as possible, but in a straight line. Leo had one thought that made him feel a little better about the prospect. "My view was that Sayres boat, Slo-Mo Shun, had taken the record, but was a prop-rider built for circuit racing and so *Blue Bird* should be able to cope fairly easily. Don took quite a bit of convincing, but in the end the entry was confirmed. This led to the usual seven days a week work with more than its fair share of all-nighters. We only had four months before the competition. It was at times like this that the differences between the Old Man and the new Skipper showed themselves. I was in the workshop stitching the old R37 back together and had the long job of lapping in all 48 valves. It was a terrible job because the engine was two monoblocs, which meant that you couldn't just lift of the heads, you had to lift what amounted to two separate engines and even then getting the valves in was no easy task. But old Don just rolled up his sleeves and mucked in".

It is interesting that, while going through Leo's notes and diaries, very rarely does he refer to Sir Malcolm Campbell in any other way than Campbell, the Skipper, the 'old Man', and only very occasionally as Sir Malcolm. He had only really known him as an employer, and a difficult one at that. One can only surmise that because Leo knew Donald Campbell from the age of four months that they were more like friends that had ended working with each other. Leo always called him, the Skipper, Donald or more often Don.

During practice for the Oltranza Cup meeting, it became apparent to both pilot, and co-pilot that it was going to be a very rough ride. Even on glass-like water, the feeling induced by sitting directly above the planing shoes was one of extreme vibration. Running flat out in the wake of other craft must have been beyond description. On race day, *Blue Bird*, and her opposition prepared for the off. "Just before the start we sat very quietly waiting the signal to start. Harry and I had already warmed the engine on the soft plugs and the hard racing plugs were in. Before I had time to think I heard the R revolving on the compressed air, which meant Don had already stamped on the air cock on the floor, and was furiously spinning the hand-starting magneto, but the engine did not start. We had a merry bloody ride as the other boats all set off because the ruddy cannon had gone off. I knew Harry had already jumped on deck and was tugging on the engine cover. I followed suit, and I think we managed to change all twenty-four plugs in a little under three minutes, which is no mean feat. Don spun the engine again and the thing coughed into life. Somehow, Harry and I managed to get the engine cover back on without frying our ankles in the exhausts. Harry leapt off, and just as I was settling back into my seat Don killed the engine, engaged the dog clutch, stamped on the air valve, spun the hand magneto, and we were away. I caught my shin on the cockpit surround. I looked across at Don to express my feelings shall we say, and I saw a different man. His face was grim with concentration, and if we had been running on willpower we would have been going about two hundred."

Blue Bird soon started to catch the trailing boats, and the ride started to become even more precarious. For the first time *Blue Bird* had to negotiate a corner, and in rough water at that, as Leo later recalled: "I saw the buoy coming and felt certain we couldn't do it, but Don hardly lifted his foot. We were going over the wakes of all the boats in front, I was convinced we were going to turn over. Don's driving was beyond what I thought he was capable of, and we were soon chasing off down the next straight. It was then that I heard him shouting something, but in all the noise I couldn't make it out. I lent across and heard something to the effect of, 'what are our revs'. I believe my answer is now well documented, but it was on the lines of, to hell with the revs, to hell with the boat, and to hell with you too. I was merely a passenger, but at the end of it all a very impressed passenger. I gained a awful lot of respect for Don that day."

The team returned to England with renewed confidence, as well as the Oltranza Cup, and by the end of September 1951 *Blue Bird* was again on the slipway at Coniston. Dr Ian Corlett had designed, with the help of Lewis Norris, four new propellers, and Campbell was anxious to try them out. *Blue Bird K4* was fourteen years old and had been through no less than four major refits, some of which were not that well funded. She was still suffering from a tendency to corkscrew, and late in that September, Campbell and Leo were out on Coniston Water trying out yet another modification.

"We set off down the lake and at around 90 mph we started to suffer a

1940 – 1950

John Rhodes Cobb in the driver's seat of the *Napier Railton*. This shot clearly shows the car's 'crab' track and unusual engine layout *(by kind permission of John Gould)*

German officials congratulate Major Gardner on his 200mph record, achieved on the Dassau Reichs Autobahn *(by kind permission of Mrs Goldie Gardner)*

Goldie Gardner lifts his goggles after his 200mph record run in his small MG *(by kind permission of Mrs Goldie Gardner)*

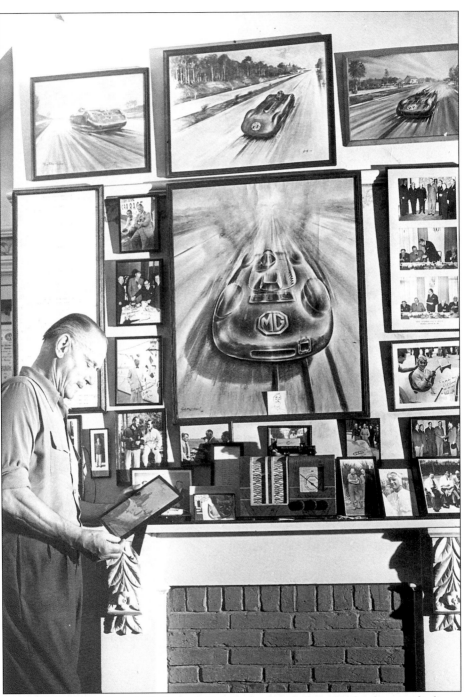

Goldie Gardner at home in Eastbourne. Sir Malcolm Campbell was his daughter Rosalind's godfather, and she later went to school with Gina Campbell. Goldie, a record breaker *par excellence*, was Sir Malcolm's project manager for many years
(by kind permission of Mrs Goldie Gardner)

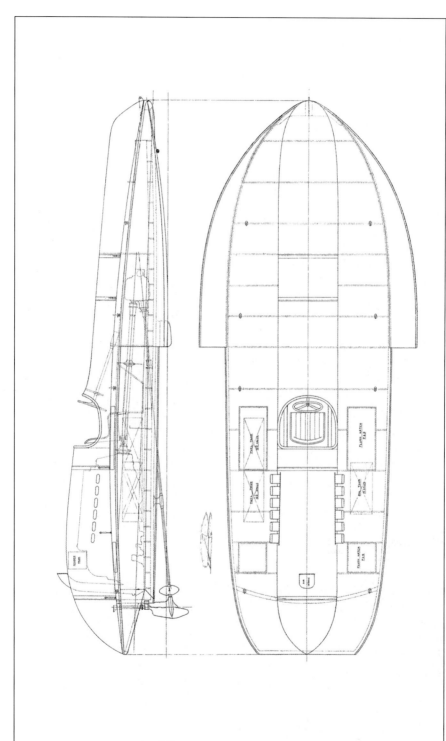

The original general arrangement drawing of *Blue Bird K4*, showing the distinctive 'v' drive from engine to propeller (© *Vosper Thornycroft plc*)

Blue Bird K4 running in perfect conditions, 1939 (© Campbell Collection)

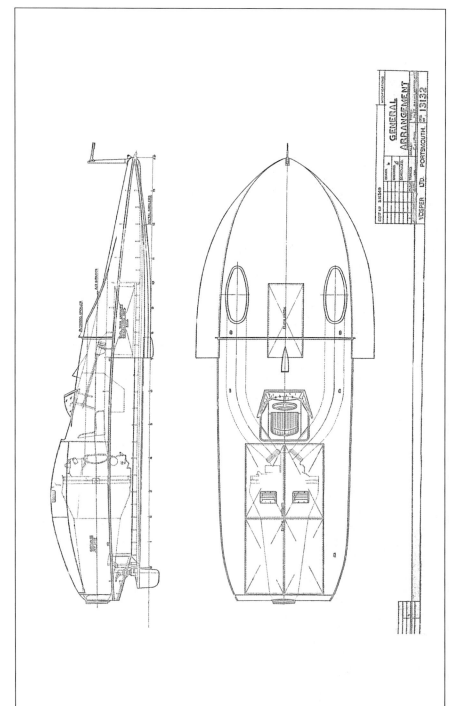

The original general arrangement drawing for the Goblin jet-conversion for *Blue Bird K4* (by kind permission of *Vosper Thornycroft*)

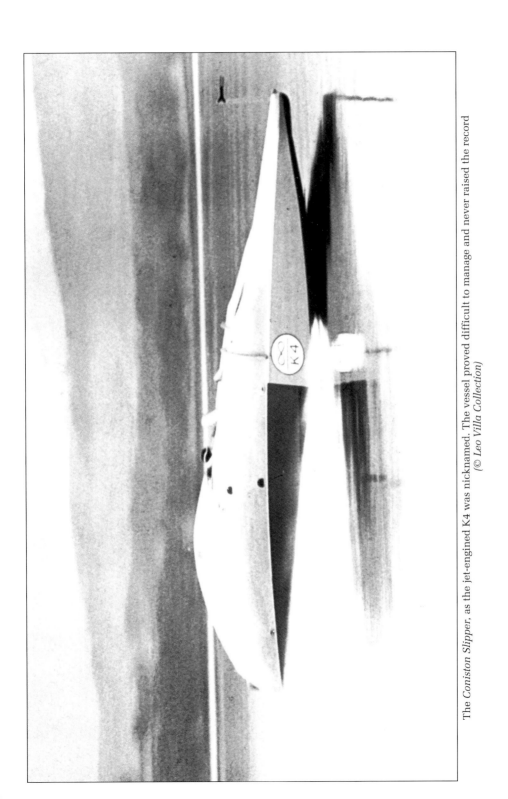

The *Coniston Slipper*, as the jet-engined K4 was nicknamed. The vessel proved difficult to manage and never raised the record
(© *Leo Villa Collection*)

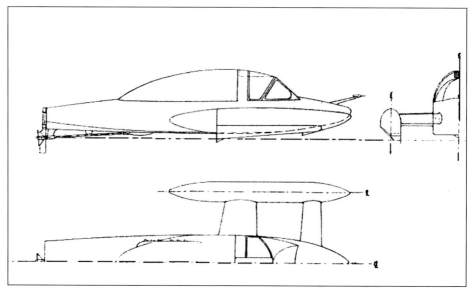

Original concept design for the *Bluebird* "prop-rider". This was to have been the Harmsworth Trophy boat, until John Cobb's death and the goal of the project then changed *(by kind permission of K.W. Norris)*

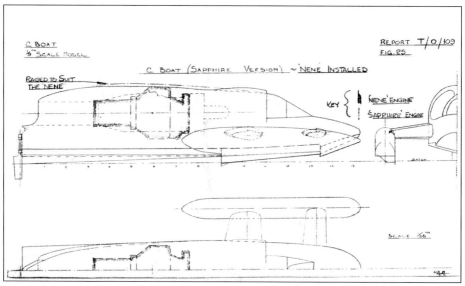

An early concept drawing of *Bluebird K7*, showing two alternative engine installations *(by kind permission of K.W. Norris)*

violent bouncing, but all Don did was to keep his foot well and truly down. Suddenly, it all went calm and we shot off, accelerating at a terrific rate. We swung around at the southern end and down went the Skipper's foot. Suddenly we were hitting speeds of 160 to 170 mph, and on a calm surface. I remember looking across at Don who seemed to be grinning from ear to ear. Then there was a terrific bang."

It is widely stated that *Blue Bird K4* hit a submerged railway sleeper, although none was ever recovered. More interesting are the comments of those that had the sad task of breaking up the remains of the hull. It would appear that the fabricated gearbox mounts were found to have ripped, and the gearbox was only attached by the gearbox input shaft. Although it is now impossible to prove, it seems more likely that metal fatigue had seriously weakened the strength of these mounts. *K4* had been built in less than eight months, with a proposed life span of about two years. Sir Malcolm Campbell was more than aware of this, contacting Rolls-Royce as early as 1945 to try to obtain two engines for his new Water Speed Record contender. Fourteen years later *Blue Bird K4* was being pushed to much higher limits than was ever intended. The drive shaft from the 2750hp Rolls-Royce R-type was only five feet long, and was directly connected to the gearbox. On the other hand, the prop shaft was much longer than originally intended, and prone to flexing. The evidence suggests that when travelling at nearly 170 mph the mounts simply gave way, allowing the propeller shaft to shear. The gearbox was now free to spin out of its mounts, tearing a huge hole in the bottom of the hull. The damage was confined to a 6ft by 7ft hole, situated between the planing shoes.

In Leo's words, "We were all very down when we lost the 'Old Man's' boat, Don especially. All we had to show was three scrap engines, sundry metalwork, and a written-off hull. Reid Railton had told us he was engaged in work on a new jet-powered boat for John Cobb (the then current holder of the Land Speed Record), and we were pretty certain that if Vosper, Railton, Peter du Cane, and Big John were involved it was bound to succeed, which was little consolation to Don, but at least the record would remain British. Don spent a great deal of time at home (Abbots, near Betchworth, Surrey) with the usual assortment of visitors. Bob Coley, who had helped Don with his attempts financially, mentioned to me that Don seemed lost without *Blue Bird*, and asked me what I thought Don's reaction would be to the suggestion of building a new prop-rider to challenge for the Harmsworth Trophy. I thought it was worth having a go at, I mean we knew an awful lot about prop-riding by now so we put it to him and Lew and Ken (Norris)".

Leo was at home a little more by this time, working what some would describe as a 'normal life', at Kine engineering on a nine to five basis. Weekends were spent motoring in his Talbot Sunbeam, with his wife, but it was a sudden and dramatic change. "I must admit to feeling a bit lost myself. It was nice to suddenly have so much time at home, but I had spent so long in the atmosphere of record-breaking, it seemed very strange to be separated from it, it is nearly all I have ever done."

For a while after the demise of Sir Malcolm's old K4, Donald seemed at a loose end. He was bitterly disappointed having wrecked his father's old boat, and with John Cobb set to capture the water speed record, there seemed little point in planning a successor. But Bill Coley suggested building a boat for the Harmsworth Trophy, which gave a much-needed sense of direction to both Donald, and his team. Donald decided to change the name of his craft, as it would be his own, and "Blue Bird" became "Bluebird".

As soon as design work started on the replacement for *K4*, Leo started to spend time away from home and, as the work progressed, commuting between Campbell's house and the Norris Bros, became more frequent. But the 29th of September 1952 was to change everything.

Leo remembered the event vividly: "I was at Abbots, going over some paperwork with Maurice, when Don walked in. I never did find out if Don got it from the radio, or if George Eyston phoned. I heard Don mention both at different times, but he came into the room looking very ashen faced. 'It's bloody awful Leo' he said, 'John's boat has crashed and he's dead'. I could see the hurt on his face, he'd known Cobb since his childhood, he was a very old friend and Don was deeply shocked."

For a few weeks after Cobb's accident the new *Bluebird* was put on hold, and Campbell considered his options. Leo was convinced he knew what would happen. "Every time I saw Don he was miles away, deep in thought. Then I heard he was selling his shares in Kine Engineering, so I asked what was going on, but I knew before he even said it. I suppose I was a bit miffed, but in all honesty it was really only a decision Don could make. Anyway we were after the record again."

Design work for the new prop-rider was well advanced, but now the speed target had increased so much that doubts started to surface about the potential of an 'old-fashioned' piston engine, let alone getting a propeller to rotate efficiently at over 18,000 rpm.

The Norris brothers were convinced that the jet engine was the only way forward, especially after comparing notes with Reid Railton. Campbell himself wanted the project to be at the forefront of technology, and was anxious to succeed where his father had failed, taming the jet engine in a boat. Finally, the decision was made for him when Saunders Roe, who were heavily involved in the project, made it clear that they did not wish to be involved if the jet option was taken. Campbell, never a man to be put in a corner, was determined. He would, with his team, build a jet-engined challenger for the World Water Speed Record. Leo Villa remembered it thus, "I was again spending a lot of time away from home, either at Abbots, with the Norris brothers, or with Don going around trying to raise the funds. I was very concerned about the whole thing, with what Don was taking on. In the Old Man's day money was quite easy to come by, and big companies were only too happy to be seen to be associated with record-breaking, but here was Don trying to convince people, not long after a war, that they should be giving him money. Trouble is, and much to my surprise, he started to succeed, but it was always going to be uphill, I mean the first estimates were for around £25,000."

Leo was joined full-time by Maurice Parfitt, who not only became assistant, but also a close friend, and both were going to have to learn an awful lot about jet engines very quickly. As the project gathered speed, the major components started to arrive at Leo's workshop. Commander Rod Banks, an expert in fuel mixes who had done much for the performance of the Rolls-Royce R-type and record-breaking in general, had suggested the Metropolitan-Vickers *Beryl* as a suitable engine, and even organised that the project received two units on loan. By the summer of 1954, one of these units was bolted down on the workshop floor at Abbots, and Leo had read enough manuals to feel confident enough to try to start it.

"Don and I had been through the manuals that had come with the Beryl, and we knew sooner or later we were going to have to start the thing, but it wasn't going to be like the Goblin jet that the Old Man had used. That had come with its own team of technicians, and they always did the necessary. Anyway we rigged up a dashboard and controls, and used a very small can of kerosene, just in case we couldn't stop it. It was nothing like the old R, it only had two plugs, which stopped working once the engine was running. I shall never forget the din as the Beryl started to turn over, then there was a yellow flame, and she was running. We took the revs right up, because I remember looking at the bolts holding the engine cradle down, thinking, 'what happens if they let go, do we chase it?'. We shut it down, and even with the cotton wool stuffed in our ears, mine were ringing. Don and I walked out of the workshop generally very pleased with ourselves, and then we looked at the drive. We had blown every scrap of cinder off it leaving just a dirt track were the cinder drive had once been."

During the building of the hull, Leo was given the *Blue Bird* mascot, and the silver St Christopher that had been mounted on the dashboard of all of Sir Malcolm Campbell's *Blue Bird* cars and boats. Leo knew that the next job was to fit them to the new *Bluebird* dashboard, although he thought that it was about time the new Skipper had something of his own. Leo organised the design, manufacture, engraving, and presentation of

Donald's own St Christopher. One has to wonder if Leo would have ever done this for Sir Malcolm.

The *Bluebird* team was strengthened further with the addition of Ken Ritchie, who left Norris Brothers to join the team, and he, Maurice Parfitt and Leo moved up to Blackburn to start installing the engine and systems to the hull that was under construction at Samlesbury Engineering, better known for the construction of bus bodies.

Leo Villa recalled the times at Blackburn: "Don visited occasionally between trying to find yet more money. But unlike his father, when he was there he spent every minute making sure everyone was happy and we were making good progress. Other than that it was just like the old days, late nights, and being away from home. I don't think I got home much that autumn. Don was making a lot of noise about what he was calling the 'Water Barrier'. We all knew that quite a few aircraft had met with accidents when attempting to break the sound barrier, but I was sceptical that we would actually encounter anything with the boat. Having said that, the Italian, Mario Verga, and John Cobb had met their end at speeds around two hundred mph, so if nothing else it kept the press interested, and I am sure that for whatever reason Don kept the thing going. It must have helped him find the few extra quid he needed."

Leo was uneasy about the new *Bluebird*. His only experience with jet engines had been with Sir Malcolm's Goblin jet just after the Second World War, or the brief runs made with the Metropolitan-Vickers Beryl in the workshop at Abbots.

A New *Bluebird* Takes to the Water

The Beryl was taken to Blackburn and under Leo's guidance installed in the new, all metal *Bluebird*, a craft of which the like had never been seen before. Once the handing over ceremony had been held, Donald was desperate to get the craft to the Lake District, where he could start learning about the new *Bluebird*.

Against what had been discussed within the team, Campbell was persuaded to make his first jet-powered attempt at Ullswater. This new venue was smaller than Coniston and included a nasty 'dog leg' toward one end. It was to this background that the team arrived on the shores of Ullswater. Not long after the launch of the new *Bluebird*, when the craft was named by Campbell's second wife Dorothy, it became very clear that Donald Campbell wanted to get on with the task at hand. Leo recalled, "I had to hand it to Don, here we had a new boat, the like of which had never been seen before. We had a totally different type of engine, and we were at a new venue, and yet he couldn't wait to get stuck in".

However, it soon became apparent that all was not well with the new craft, as Campbell failed to get beyond a lowly 15 mph. Water was rushing into the jet intakes, causing the engine to flame out, and then it would restart instantly as the solenoid in the starting system had stuck. It was obvious that the main problem was the intake of water, and Leo, free from the scathing dismissals of Sir Malcolm, ventured that perhaps they could temporarily cover the space between the spar arms, blocking the flow of water. After consulting the Norris brothers, and only on the understanding that any test runs did not exceed 150 mph, the plan was accepted. Campbell took the craft out the next day, and for the first time *Bluebird* planed perfectly. Leo Villa had come to the rescue again, but it was to put him in a position he didn't want to be in, the driver's seat!

"We could all see that the water rushing into the engine was preventing any sort of run, so after a chat with Ken and Lew, we decided to fix two sheets of 'Ali' (aluminium), blocking the water. We towed Don out to the middle of the lake and we heard the familiar whine as the Beryl started up. There was the usual upheaval, spray going everywhere, and then all of a sudden *Bluebird* shot off down the lake looking very good indeed. At least we were on the right track. Don was obviously getting more confident because he brought the boat very close to the jetty in a beautiful manoeuvre, but I was surprised to hear he still wasn't happy. He told me that when he started to accelerate it felt like the bows were trying to dive under. Then, as they started to lift and plane, they seemed to dive back in again. None of us on the course boats could see this, and all of a sudden Don looked at me and said 'I know old boy, you give her a squirt tomorrow, and I'll have a look myself'. I thought he was joking, but he was bloody serious. I didn't sleep much that night because I was nervous. Not only because I wasn't certain what on earth I was doing, but I really didn't want to be the one to stuff the thing into the shore."

Leo's 'trial by water' went without a hitch, and eventually he was to admit to having quite enjoyed the whole experience. But further tests were no better, *Bluebird* still suffered from the 'flame out' problem as well as having a good deal of trouble becoming 'unstuck' from the water and planing, and so the new craft was left locked in a boathouse while the team travelled south to plan the next stage. While Ken and Lewis Norris tried to find a solution by mathematics, Leo and the team would try to find the solution by modifying the various models that had been used in the development stages.

"I suppose we looked a bit like Fred Karno's circus, testing the models. Don had a largish pond at Abbots, and I rigged up a pulley system to pull the scale models of *Bluebird* across. I would be on one side ready to set the pulley system going, and on the other side Tim (my son) and his mate Don Woolley (then a full-time team member) were holding the model ready to let her go. And then there was Don. He was perched up on a stepladder set up in the middle of the course, which you could only get to by wading out.

Anyway there he was, ciné camera in hand, ready to film it all. It sounds ridiculous , but it worked very well, and it certainly wasn't a game. We were very careful in reproducing the thrust line etc., and once we had rushed up to the 'dark room', Don's bathroom, the film was very useful indeed."

The two teams both reached the same conclusion at more or less the same time. Cliff Polley, a member of the Norris Brothers design team also became a full-time member of the *Bluebird* team, and had suggested that raising the front spars could solve the problem, which fitted in with what Ken and Lewis Norris had come up with. A Glaswegian panel beater was drafted in to live on-site to carry out the modifications, which were completed in double-quick time, and then the team returned to Ullswater.

Early on the morning of 21 July 1955, *Bluebird* was ready to try for the record, Leo Villa resuming his position as linchpin of the whole operation. He had been with the Campbells, father and son, for 34 years, and it is difficult to believe that any of the attempts would have taken place, let alone succeeded, without him. Leo was crucial to the team. He was chief engineer, chief mechanic, in charge of all radio communications, hotel arrangements, transport for crew and equipment, ever-present at wind tunnels, tank tests, design meetings, and – other than Donald Campbell himself – probably the only face the public recognised in the *Bluebird* team. Therefore, it was no surprise to find Leo Villa first at the jetty on 21 July, and later in the day in a small boat in the middle of the measured mile, co-ordinating the record attempt by radio. By the afternoon, the new Water Speed Record stood at 202.32 mph.

"Don was stunned when he finally took the record. I think it took him a good week for it to sink in. The team and the boat arrived home, and Joan and I were invited to Abbots for a 'family' get-together. Don was, as always, the life and soul of the evening, involved in every conversation. At some stage, he appeared at my side, with rather a large Scotch in his hand, and the talk drifted over an invite to take *Bluebird* to the USA, the planned modifications to the boat, even his father's successes and, more surprisingly, his few failures. Then all of a sudden Don suggested a walk outside. I wasn't aware of it at the time, but Don carefully steered me towards the old barn, and as we stopped outside he said, 'I've got something for you Unc, you're not to say anything, just accept it as my thanks for all you have done for me, both in the past, and now', and with that we go in and there is a bright red Triumph, not any old Triumph, but the very one that Don had caught me admiring months before. I was speechless."

Since 1921, the names of Campbell, *Bluebird* and Leo Villa, had been as one. Leo was a very keen gardener, and even used the old splashguards from *Bluebird* as cloches, under which he grew some exceptional cucumbers, but most of his life was conducted in the Campbell workshops, building or modifying the *Bluebirds* of both Sir Malcolm and Donald Campbell. In private he was just that, spending as much time with his beloved Joan, and driving his Triumph sports car simply for the pleasure of it. He kept records of every job he undertook, either in written form or as photographs, hundreds of them. As far back as the early thirties, he was using colour film and stereoscopic cameras to produce a unique record of the most astounding quality, all kept in a carefully indexed filing system, from his early childhood, right up to the very latest *Bluebird*. But from this point on, it would not be any old *Bluebird*, but the new, jet-age *K7 Bluebird* that would ensure that his association would be set in stone, not only in the minds of the public, but in the history books as well.

5.

Of Mice and Men

To some, life itself is the greatest challenge of all. There are others to whom 'normal' life is merely an interruption to their ambitions or challenges. There are those who go hang-gliding or pot-holing, and only they know why they do what they do. There is a smaller group whose ambition is to surpass another, even if that person is a personal hero. But there cannot be many who throw themselves into a challenge where the target is not only a public hero, but also their father. A target such as that is by far the hardest to attain, let alone surpass.

Three months before Leo Villa started his full-time employment with Captain Malcolm Campbell there had been another arrival at Povey Cross. On 23 March 1921, while Malcolm was in his grounds, building a dog kennel, his son Donald Malcolm was born. There had been a nanny in the house for some months before the birth, preparing for the event, and Donald's early life centred around his mother and the young Scottish lass. Later still, if Donald was with neither of these two, he could be found with Leo Villa in his father's workshop. Even as a five-year-old Donald showed a natural aptitude for taking things to pieces, and with Leo's help, putting them back together again.

By the time Donald was six he had been involved in enough workshop mishaps, that his parents felt he would benefit from the regime of preparatory school life, which soon saw the young Campbell enrolled for the Manor House, near Horsham in Sussex. The school was run by a Mr H. Layton and his sister, who acted as the school matron. Discipline was extremely strict, but regardless of the regime, Donald was remembered by Miss Layton many years later as 'a loveable little boy, who loved to play, but not work'. Donald always said that he was never happy at Horsham, which must have been very evident as his mother started to make plans to find him a new school after only a year. Donald's health began to suffer, and a family friend and Brooklands Bentley racer, Dr Benjafield, suggested finding somewhere near the coast for the sea air. And so, at the age of nine, Donald started at St Peter's school, Seaford, also in Sussex, during the Easter of 1932. He was remembered by the then headmaster,

Mr Knox-Shaw, as "a buoyant little chap, but someone who didn't take to team events, although he always did well at whatever he did, to the point where he was chosen to play for the Rugby first eleven, the first team at soccer, and the second eleven for cricket, and he excelled at individual pursuits especially boxing and shooting".

From his early school days Donald had a lucrative business, selling his father's signature to the other boys, and it was during his time at St Peter's that his father received the KBE, the knighthood increasing the value of the signatures no end – though not enough to prevent Donald from flooding the market, and doing himself out of business. His early school life very much mirrored that of his father's as, in 1934, Donald moved on to Uppingham, an extremely hard school founded by Archdeacon Johnson in 1584. Donald was put into the same 'house', West Deyne, as his father had been in some twenty-three years earlier. Discipline was considered by some as extreme, starting in the morning with cold baths, and carried on through the day with a strict pecking order handed down from the older boys to the younger. New boys were expected to pass a test on school geography with a severe beating as punishment for failure. Likewise to let down one's team in any sport was considered a great failing and, bearing in mind Donald's earlier sporting achievements, it is no surprise that again he excelled at solo pastimes such as boxing, shooting, fishing and golf. During school holidays and the odd weekend, Donald would return home where Leo Villa became his protector as well as teacher. While keeping the mischievous boy away from an easily annoyed father, he also helped Donald with his early forays into engineering. At the age of twelve, Master Campbell could strip and rebuild a motorcycle, and was also driving, using a bull-nose Morris to tour the family estate.

Academically things had not improved, Donald staying in the same form for three years. At sixteen he contracted German Measles, but unfortunately for him it developed into rheumatic fever. The treatment for such an ailment in the 1930s was very much as it is today, involving many weeks' rest in bed. Young Donald was sent to the school sanatorium, but it was not very long before boredom set in and he took to wondering around the hospital wing. The last straw was when he was found out of bed, shooting rabbits out of an open window with a .22 rifle. On his father's advice, Donald was sent to the Cote D'Azur and Cannes to recuperate. Campbell family history was again to repeat itself as Donald purchased himself a .22 pistol as his father had done in Germany many years before, although the problems he encountered were of a slightly more serious nature, having neither a licence, nor the sense to fire the gun out of public gaze.

Donald returned to England in 1938, convinced that the world was drifting toward an inevitable war. In fact, what with his father's views, reinforced by the construction of a huge underground bunker at his home, Headley Grove, and the publishing of no less than two books on the subject of his country's defence by Sir Malcolm, it would have been a great surprise had he not agreed with his father. More than anything, Donald Campbell wanted to be a pilot, preferably a fighter pilot, but the medicals were strict, and it was certain that Donald's rheumatic fever would preclude any flying activity.

Sir Malcolm had other ideas for his son, securing Donald a job as an office boy in a London insurance broker's, on a salary of £1 per week. Donald objected to the position on two counts. One that he had not found the job for himself, and the other that it prevented him from following his own path, although he couldn't say what that path was. His father argued that it was how he had started out, but the young Campbell was disappointed, especially as he had got used to accompanying his father abroad on record attempts. During June 1939, while riding his motorbike on a photographic excursion, Donald fell off while adjusting his bag. He fractured his skull and hurt his back and was laid up for well over a month.

By the end of September 1939, war had been declared, and Donald, still suffering from acute back pain and headaches, went to enlist in the Royal Air Force. He passed his first medical at the Croydon recruitment station, and was sent to RAF Cardington, near Bedford, for a further medical and flight aptitude tests. Somehow, he managed to pull the wool over the eyes of the examining board, and was drafted into the RAF with the number ACH 964147, but within a month Donald, after further tests at RAF Halton Hospital, was given a discharge from service because of his history of rheumatic fever, which can cause permanent damage to the heart valves, something not ideal for anything that entails working at altitude.

Some weeks after returning home Donald, while riding his recently repaired motorcycle, drove into a Canadian army truck, and fractured his skull for a second time. With the injuries he had sustained in his first accident, now compounded by a second, more serious mishap, he was hors de combat for a considerable time. Feeling as though he was letting his country down, he joined Briggs Motor Panels, of Greys, Essex, in 1942 as an assistant in aircraft sales, and later as a maintenance engineer in Dagenham. During weekends and evenings he joined his father's Mobile Special Constabulary, along with Sir Malcolm's friend, Major Goldie Gardner, patrolling areas of likely invasion on their motorcycles. Toward the end of the war, he again tried to enter the RAF, this time succeeding in becoming a ferry pilot, again much like his father before him. But, after gaining twelve hours on Lysanders at RAF St Athan, in South Wales, the war ended.

Peacetime and Business

Donald had enjoyed the engineering experience he had gained, both with Leo Villa, and with Briggs during the war. After hostilities had ceased, Donald and the brothers Edward and Richard Duncan, started their own engineering works, producing wood-working equipment. Sales in England went better than expected, and Donald and his partners decided on a European sales drive. With typical ingenuity, Donald persuaded the brothers to purchase a sixty-foot, ex-Royal Naval recovery vessel, which was converted into a floating showroom. The boat was moored off several ports on the Portuguese coast, while Donald spent much time flying between London and Lisbon. Sadly, while making for a new port, the vessel caught fire after a major engine room explosion, and eventually sank. Fire, and the destruction it can cause appeared to form a central theme in the early life of Donald Campbell. Along with his sister Jean, many childhood games took the form of firefighting, in which Donald would light something in the grounds, a haystack or a pile of rubbish, and then both children would run to their own aid with buckets or hoses.

Donald also got into trouble while with his father on record attempts. While travelling to South Africa in 1929, a passenger complained about Donald's habit of rushing around the decks. His father, on hearing the complaint, severely admonished his son, who in turn sought revenge by attempting to ignite the complaining passenger's trousers. It was also on this trip that Donald encountered his father's stringent budgeting at first hand. While left alone in his hotel, the young Campbell found that he could cool himself with a selection of soft drinks, all of which could be charged to his father's room number, although it is said that all of the extra 'expenses' were paid back in full!

Donald inherited much from his father, including the ability to learn by observation, for this was how his father had learnt to drive. According to Leo Villa, much of the knowledge that Donald took with him into his own record-breaking attempts was garnered from what he saw during the 1935 land speed attempt on the salt flats at Bonneville. Although not taking an active part in the trials, he visited, watched, and enquired at every opportunity, in every department, learning about the gas starters, timing strips, clocks, tyre pressures and tools, and writing it all up in a daily journal which he referred to on many occasions in the years and attempts to come. During August of 1939, Donald became an active member of the *Blue Bird* team, keeping logs on both the hull of *Blue Bird* and the R-type engines, as well as handling one of the launches. By the time he stepped into *Blue Bird* himself in 1949, he was already well versed in the processes of a record-breaking attempt in all but actually driving the vehicles. Simply because of his inquiring nature, he cannot have failed to sense the atmosphere that surrounded his father's attempts at both the land and water speed records. He had thoroughly enjoyed bathing in his father's reflected glory while at school, and in the days of the last pre war attempts he had undoubtedly come to actively be part of the 'show'. His father was at ease with the sight of newsreel cameras and microphones. But the young Campbell was less at ease than Sir Malcolm with the trappings of fame: in 1939 he accompanied his father on the first of many trips to Coniston Water, an area he said that he fell in love with from the first moment he saw it. On this first visit, film footage showed Donald to be very nervous when christening his father's boat and some say that, even in later life, he never actively sought the fame that came with his chosen profession. Yet he really came to life when a camera was in the offing, or if there was a chance of getting a quote into print – but like so many in the public eye, he failed to keep his private life separate from the public one.

During the war years, Donald would see his father only occasionally, and it came as quite a shock to Sir Malcolm when Donald introduced his wife, Daphne Harvey, whom he had married in 1945. Yet again, Campbell family history was repeating itself as Malcolm had married his first wife (see page 54) without the prior knowledge of his father, which might explain why Sir Malcolm only refused to speak to his son for just under a day. In September 1946, Georgina was born, and the family set up home in Reigate Hill. Donald spent most of the following two years pursuing his business interests which centred around Kine Engineering, a small concern in which Donald had invested £1200, becoming a director.

It is uncertain where Donald was when he heard of his father's death but, according to those that knew him, he was inconsolable for weeks after and would drive everyday to his father's last home, Little Gatton, where he would sit alone in his father's study. Eventually, it fell to Donald to go through all of his father's paperwork and tie up any loose ends so that Sir Malcolm's trustees could begin to finalise the will. Donald was astounded how meticulous his father had been, finding diaries, journals, notes and reports written up on all his projects and business interests. Donald found himself doing far more reading than tidying up. Contrary to popular belief, Donald felt his father's will a little too generous, especially to those outside of the family. It also allowed for his mother, sister and himself to receive an income for life from the estate, as well as a trust for any of Sir Malcolm's grandchildren. In modern terms, the estate was worth in the region of £4.2 million.

It has often been written that Donald had decided very early in his life that he would follow his father's footsteps, but his family and others close to him are not so certain. In the oft-written story, it fell to Sir Malcolm's friend and project manager, Major Goldie Gardner to convince Donald that perhaps he should protect his father's record from the Americans, but Gardner's widow, Una, is adamant that with very little to do outside of his engineering business, his idea was simply to try it as he had access to the required equipment. On the other hand, Donald's sister, Jean, is certain that he had decided to follow his father many years before. Leo Villa's opinion was that he wanted to succeed with his engineering business and saw an attempt on the Water Speed Record as a superb promotion vehicle, but his desire to succeed completely took over after his initial failure to increase the record on his first attempt.

Whatever the spark that ignited Donald, the fire was to become all-consuming. During the weekdays, he concentrated on Kine Engineering, but evenings and weekends were spent at his father's old sheds at Brooklands. Donald's preparations for his attempt on his father's record were kept quiet until work on the old pre-war *Blue Bird* K4 was finished. A press day was arranged at Adams Brothers' yard in New Malden. It was Donald's first solo encounter with the press, and although he appeared nervous, he handled the situation with great aplomb, indeed by the end of the day he seemed to be enjoying the whole thing more and more.

The 'new' *Blue Bird* team arrived at Coniston to find the same loyalty that had been shown to Sir Malcolm during his visits, but Donald was at what he would always describe as the 'point of no return'. The team arrived to find a large press presence, and numerous onlookers. If Donald was doing this simply for the prestige, he had prove himself. Leo later commented that after a very short time 'Don' started to revel in the press and local interest in his endeavours, and this must have played a major part in the manner in which he attacked his first runs. There were no slow passes, no gradual build-up of speed, as Leo later put it, 'he jumped in and put his bloody foot right down'. It became obvious that Donald was not to be fêted to the same extent as his father for, even during his first runs, it looked like anything that could go wrong, would do, and Donald Campbell was going to have to overcome many obstacles if he was to succeed. Perhaps it would have been a different story if, after only a few runs, Donald had lifted the record, and had returned south triumphant.

Perhaps there never would have been any further attempts. As it was, the timekeepers made a miscalculation and at first confirmed a new record, but later retracted it. Donald had hot gearbox oil sprayed into his face, he had two narrow escapes when *Blue Bird*'s stability was compromised, and, as was to become a feature at nearly all of his following attempts, there was bad weather. The team returned home to Surrey with their leader depressed at having got so near to a record.

Campbell was not used to failure. To compound his depression, the team had suffered several accidents and it appeared that perhaps *Blue Bird* was beyond her limits. But as was to be the case on many occasions in the future, the failures became the spur to succeed. Donald Campbell was into record-breaking up to the hilt. But although he had the advantage of having all the necessary equipment, these first trials were not cheap. Some say the first attempt was looked on as 'a bit of a lark', much as in later life there were those who suggested that Donald did not have the required 'bottle'. It is inconceivable that Donald, having seen how meticulous his father had been and, having been involved first-hand with several successful record attempts, would have risked his neck, or even his family reputation in such a light-hearted way. Again, it was typical of how most of Donald's attempts, and even his successes, were treated. After the demise of the *Blue Bird K4* (see page 87) and the death of his friend John Cobb, Donald went for the record 110%, and started work on *Bluebird* K7. He had become totally engrossed in the speed record, to the point where it had already cost him his first marriage.

By April 1952, he had married again, to New Zealand-born music student, Dorothy McKegg. As the *Bluebird* K7 project developed, and took more of his time, Donald sold his half share in Kine Engineering, which he confessed was not an easy decision for him to make. The company had flourished, and Donald had been extremely happy there, but his application to record-breaking had become total. As his father had always done before him, he simply knew he had to sacrifice one thing for another. Record-breaking itself was not the only spur that drove Donald, however, especially when the decision had been made to use a jet engine in the new craft. Cobb had paid the ultimate price in trying to harness the jet engine, and Sir Malcolm's only real failure had been with this new form of propulsion.

Donald's desire to succeed where his father had failed became almost obsessive. Added to this was Donald's deep interest in engineering, the new *Bluebird* was to be as advanced as it could be, with all-metal construction and its futuristic appearance. To finance the project, Donald approached many of his father's sponsors, some of whom jumped at the chance of being involved. Donald proved himself to be a very persuasive negotiator in his own right, by also getting the support of many new sponsors. The project had absorbed over £18,000 of his own money, as well as re-mortgaging his home, Abbotts, which can only have added to the stress he was under. This was a time when he was often heard to say, "I am in this thing up to my neck".

On 23 July 23 1955, Donald finally succeeded in annexing the World Water Speed Record. Publicly he was elated, but privately he viewed it as a bit of an anti-climax. Like his father before him, Donald started to show an interest in treasure-hunting. He had studied a vast tomb of documents his father had left regarding his trips to the Cocas Islands. It has never been clear how successful or otherwise Sir Malcolm's trips had been. It was claimed that he had a large biscuit tin containing gold, emeralds, and rubies, and that Leo once sold a gold Byzantine crucifix – which would fit in rather well, as the treasure on the Cocas was the booty from raids on the churches of South America. In a letter to Ken Norris, Donald quite calmly stated that a friend, an RAF captain, had recently returned from the islands some £30,000 the richer, and mentioned that according to his father's papers, there was a large quantity of gold lying just off a small bay in the islands, protected by ever-present sharks. The motive behind the letter is summed up in one paragraph, which states, 'It seems a shame to leave it all there, especially as it is only down some fifteen feet. I wondered if the boffins at Norris Brothers could come up with a detector that could locate such precious metals?' It is not known if Donald ever went on any treasure hunts of his own, nor if Norris Brothers produced the "treasure detector".

Later that same year, Donald was awarded the CBE, but yet again his private life was beginning to falter, his second marriage failed and Dorothy returned to New Zealand. His comments at the time go a long way to explaining not only his, but also his father's philosophy. This was the same philosophy that labelled Sir Malcolm as mean and selfish, and Donald as weak and obsessive. "Any man who is going to succeed in his chosen job," he had said "and I don't give a damn what job he chooses, is going to have to sacrifice his own comfort, pleasure and family considerations."

He became a victim of the 'This is Your Life' television programme on which he appeared uncomfortable and ill at ease with the gaze of the cameras. Many of his friends state that he was really only at his best publicly when fully prepared, and on the odd occasions when he was caught on the hop, he could become quite irritable. Yet, when invited to speak after dinner, or with warning, he was fluid, informed and confident. Perhaps the best examples of this are the interviews recorded during the fateful last attempt at Coniston in 1966/67. Unexpected questions were greeted with curt, stilted answers, proffered in tones bordering on annoyance, quite out of character with the usual polite, authoritative Donald Campbell that the public was used to. He grew to relish the public attention, but only when it was wanted, and reacted badly when he felt that his private life was being pried into.

One can be in no doubt that Donald genuinely wanted to promote Britain and her industry, craftsmanship, innovation and technology, and he was an indubitable patriot. Since succeeding in raising the Water Speed Record in America in 1955, the *Bluebird* team had been engaged in the idea of a new *Bluebird* car for an attempt on the Land Speed Record. Donald yet again proved to be the reflection of his father, and applied himself fully to the project, centring his life on the car that was to be 'British, and the best in the World'. Donald had learnt another valuable lesson from his father, that of using his celebrity status to acquire the necessary backing. He became a director of several companies, as well as developing several ideas of his own and of Leo Villa, to whom it must have seemed like an attack of *dejá vu* after the 1930s marketing scheme for inventions. Without doubt, the bond between Donald and Leo was much stronger than had existed between Leo and Malcolm, and in complete contrast to how things used to be, during the planning of the CN7 car, Donald sought the sage advice of Leo on ever-increasing occasions. To keep public interest, it was announced that the *Bluebird* team would be attempting to break the 250 mph barrier on water, which met with a lukewarm response. It mattered not to Donald and his analytical mind, which revelled in the experimentation that a new attempt required. The CN7 car, however, was to become another of the public misfortunes that would affect not only Donald's standing, but also his mental state.

In 1958, Donald married for the third time, to Belgian-born cabaret singer, Tonia Bern. In today's world, people are harder to impress, and even then Donald Campbell and record-breaking were beginning to appear out of time, but still he appeared as a man on a mission. Some saw that mission as promoting Britain, others as self-glorification of the man himself. If Donald succeeded, it had been done to promote himself; if he failed, he was letting down his team, and worse still his country. One can only guess why Donald Campbell continued to try to break records when men were attacking the very boundaries of space at speeds far in excess of what he was achieving. But it is very apparent that he was convinced that his endeavours were of great use in both research and promotion for his country.

To the public, especially the British public, the risks seemed to be very small indeed. Relatively few people had been killed attempting either the land or water speed records and, even then, not in recent years. Perhaps only Donald really knew what he was risking, for only he was 'at the sharp end'. But as he was often quoted as saying, "If you don't take risks, you simply don't live". There are millions of people in the world who indulge in motor-racing, power-boating, rock-climbing, sky-diving, and the like who know the sentiment behind such a comment.

Against the general trend of the day, Donald got over eighty companies to contribute not only financial support, but also expertise and personnel to his *Bluebird* car project. But, unlike the days of his father, with such generous sponsorship came the pressure to perform – and quickly. Although at ease with everyday trials, Donald did not perform well under pressure, especially in public. 'The old girl', as Donald referred to the K7 hydroplane had her share of public misfortune, not least being sunk on Lake Mead in the USA, but the new *Bluebird* car was to bring more pressure than most normal men are capable of enduring.

1950 – 1960

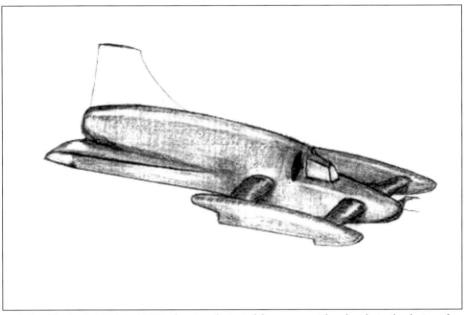

A Ken Norris sketch dated 1952, showing that a tail fin was considered early in the design of *Bluebird K7 (by kind permission of K.W. Norris)*

A 1954 sketch by Ken Norris, again confirming the early possibility of a tail fin *(author's collection)*

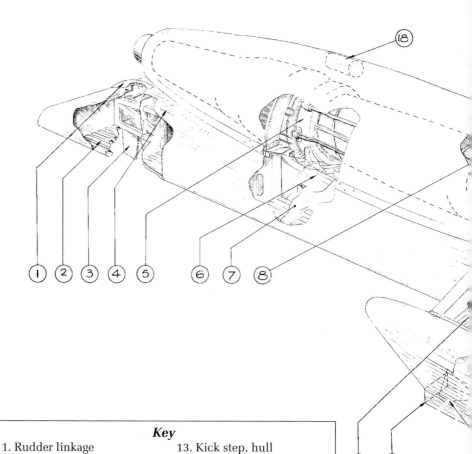

Key

1. Rudder linkage	13. Kick step, hull
2. Corrugated lower skin	14. Oxygen bottle
3. Rudder	15. Throttle pedal
4. Upper body panel	16. Pitot tube
5. Metropolitan-Vickers Beryl	17. Pitot head
6. Frame tube	18. Parachute pod
7. Bulkhead for water tank	19. Aerial
8. Fuel tank	20. Air intake duct
9. Rear sponson arm	21. Air intake
10. Planing shoe	22. Electric splash shield
11. Stability fin	23. Pilot
12. Kick step, sponson	24. Hinged cockpit cover

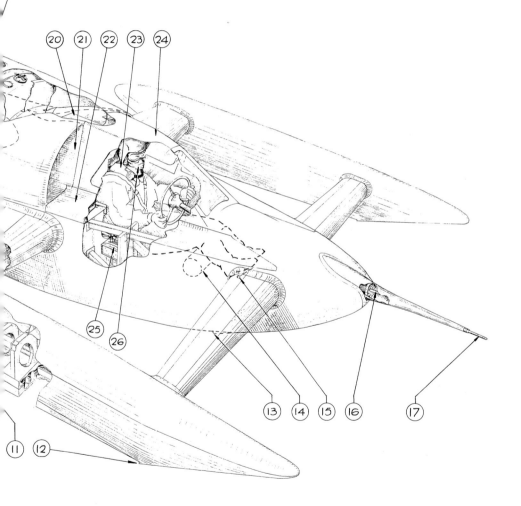

Cutaway of K7, prepared from the original design drawings but before construction had begun
(reproduced with permission, L. Funnell)

A rare photograph of *Bluebird K7*'s frame under construction *(author's collection)*

The Bristol-Siddeley Proteus under test for the project *(by kind permission of BP plc)*

K7 on her return from Lake Mead. Donald Campbell's gardener looks bemused by it all! (© *Leo Villa Collection*)

Donald Campbell in the cockpit of K7 at Lake Mead, prior to the record run (© *Leo Villa Collection*)

Family portrait. From left to right: Lady Dorothy Campbell, Donald, and his sister Jean. In the background, Maurice Parfitt and – extreme left, in her flying jacket – Donald's "assistant", Dory Swann *(© Campbell Collection)*

Donald Campbell and Tony James outside the wooden building where K7 received the Orpheus engine. Note the "old" curved splash shields *(by kind permission of Tony James)*

Donald checking his new "office". To his left, Bill Izatt is still working as K7 is loaded onto the transport lorry! *(by kind permission of Tony James)*

K7 on Consiton, shortly after her return from America. At speed, and planing perfectly, all three planing shoes are clearly visible *(© Campbell Collection)*

An early concept for CN7 in the wind tunnel displays twin rear fins. However, the car was built without any *(by kind permission of K.W. Norris)*

Bluebird CN7 revealed to the world's press at Goodwood, the project showing its BP backing *(by kind permission of Ray Govier)*

On 16 November 1955, Donald, in the *Bluebird* K7 hydroplane, increased the World Water Speed Record to 216.25 mph, on Lake Mead, Nevada, USA, despite the boat having to be salvaged from an embarrassing public sinking. The atmosphere prior to the project's final success was strained to say the least; a mischievous toast made over lunch one day by the boat's co-designer, Ken Norris, to try and alleviate the tension was greeted with a chuckle from around the table. His remark of "Here's to the Land Speed Record", was greeted by Donald with the reply of, "Well, let's think about it". Perhaps if he had known what the CN7 car would cost him, both in financial terms as well as emotionally, he might never have followed up on such an innocuous remark.

First estimates for the car suggested that the whole design process would take 25,000 man-hours (£25,000 at £1 per hour), and cost £12,500 to build. Added to this were costs for administration (£6,000), consultancy (£3,500) and aerodynamic and research work (£2,500), making a grand total of £50,000. (The *Bluebird* K7 boat had taken 8,000 hours and 100 drawings to produce. When the Land Speed Record finally fell to Donald and the CN7 it had taken over 36,000 hours and 800 drawings to produce.)

The Norris brothers' first aim was to find an aerodynamically neutral body shape that would avoid the problem of lift, as well as reducing the drag caused by excessive down-force. After extensive wind-tunnel testing, a distinctive flattened-lozenge shape evolved. The concept for CN7 began with sketches produced by both Ken and Lewis Norris, who started with not only clean sheets of paper, but open minds. To each of them, the whole project was to be treated as any other engineering problem. Next on the agenda was the power plant. Because of its ideal torque/speed characteristics, a free turbine became the obvious choice, and as the main consideration was not purely top speed, but more importantly acceleration, four-wheel drive was deemed an absolute necessity. Again, the free turbine scored heavily; because of its natural 'fluid drive', no form of gearbox would be needed. Next came the problem of attaining four-wheel drive, and here again, there was one further advantage with the free turbine. Six different four-wheel drive layouts were proposed, but all would have proved extremely complex as well as expensive to produce. The solution was easy to arrive at on paper, but would require some very specialist backing. Ken Norris recalls:

"Brother Lew and I formulated that the ideal way of splitting the drive front to rear would be to continue the main compressor shaft right through the engine and simply take the drive off each end into the differentials. We were mere 'boys' when we went cap-in-hand to see Sir Stanley Hooker (the chairman of Bristol Siddeley) and asked, 'Please sir, we'd like a Proteus with a straight-through drive shaft'. To our surprise he said yes".

By January 1956, the project had the promise of two modified versions of the Bristol Siddeley Proteus 705 engine, as used in the Britannia airliner.

The car's construction method became the next problem. Although a spaceframe was initially considered (much like the frame of the K7 hydroplane), an 'egg box' or monocoque construction technique was chosen because of the necessity for air confinement and because of its inherent strength. Wind tunnel results led to a few adjustments to the final shape, and although several types of stabilising tail fins were tried, it was thought an unnecessary appendage. The deciding factor was the similarity to the successful, and tail-less, Railton of John Cobb. Contrary to the opinion of some 'experts' in the Land Speed Record field, no provision was made for the later installation of a tail fin.

Construction began in August 1959 by Motor Panels Ltd of Coventry. The main frame was built along aircraft principles, with two main longitudinal beams of high-duty, non-corrosive BA 27-1/2H alloy supplied by British Aluminium. Sandwiched between these was an extremely light honeycomb of corrugated alloy foil. These and the similar lateral members, or bulkheads, were bonded under pressure with a form of 'Araldite' epoxy adhesive. Meanwhile, Dunlop was developing special 52-inch wheels and tyres that were to be mounted on four identical hubs. These in turn were fitted to equal-length wishbones which had a controlled movement of just two inches, governed by oleo-pneumatic spring damper units.

Calculations showed that the braking system would have to dissipate as much as 76 million foot/pounds of energy in just sixty seconds. Obviously, a lot of thought was going to have to be put into the system. Primarily the system was controlled by built-in pneumatically operated air brakes. These were backed up by all-wheel discs, operated by compressed air, the system being completed by a hand brake which operated on all four discs but by a completely separate actuation method using a different set of high-pressure cylinders. Not only could these hold *Bluebird* back against the engine for starting, but they could also be used for an emergency back-up should the primary system fail. A Burman re-circulating ball steering box with connecting chains eliminated the need for a rack or track-rods, which gave a maximum of four degrees of movement either side of centre on the steering wheels. Ideal for minute adjustments at 400 mph, but very trying for the turn-around crew at the end of each run. Between each pair of wheels there were separate differentials with a ratio of 3.6 to 1, the front differing in that it incorporated a free-wheel device to solve the problem of 'shaft wind up'. The latter is caused by the shifting loads during acceleration and deceleration in a four-wheel-drive vehicle with only one engine, which would be the Proteus 705 (engine number 427). Behind the scenes, the team was deciding on the venue for the attempt, as well as procedures to be followed. There were also two reserve drivers – Peter Carr (responsible for the *Bluebird* hydroplane's refit after the sinking at Lake Mead, and whose yellow-checkered helmet Campbell was then using) and Neville Duke – both successful test pilots, and friends of Donald Campbell. One other name mentioned as a likely back-up, if only in the boy's comic *The Eagle*, was that of Stirling Moss.

On completion, friends, sponsors and the press were invited to the Goodwood motor racing circuit in Sussex, where the car was given her first runs, and the press offered every chance for a photo-opportunity. While Raymond Baxter interviewed the team and sponsors, Donald took his first turn at the wheel, first at the end of a tow rope, and then under power. This proved very difficult because, even with the engine idling, *Bluebird* was reaching 80 mph with the brakes on!

The only other problems encountered during these first trials centred around heat distortion of the panels around the exhaust, and difficulty of getting into the cockpit, past the large, round steering wheel. By August 1960, *Bluebird* CN7 was on its way to the chosen venue, Bonneville salt flats, USA, carrying with it the hopes of over eighty sponsors from British industry. The American hot-rodders were agog when Donald's team arrived on the salt. There was a fleet of back-up vehicles, and twenty members of crew, each with a specific task at all times, in an operation to be run like a military exercise. Donald arrived on 4 September, and by mid-day on 5 September, *Bluebird* was uncrated and ready for her first run on the salt flats of Utah. With little fuss she reached 120 mph, but Donald was unhappy with the nervous steering (the car was now fitted with a yoke-type steering wheel), and only one further run was completed before the steering ratio was altered from 25:1 to 100:1.

On 16 September, after successful runs of 240 and 300 mph, Donald calmly announced that on the next run he intended to accelerate, from a stand still to 300 in two miles, something which he would have to do in order to get the record. Ken Norris was against the idea, while Don Badger, the Dunlop tyre technician had to forcibly remind the team that 300 was the upper limit of the test tyres fitted. All the same, as the cockpit clicked shut for what was to be the car's eighth run, Donald smiled and winked as he gave Leo Villa the thumbs up, and started the engine. It was obvious to the chasing pursuit car, that *Bluebird* had got away very quickly indeed, and even though Leo had his Rover up to 90 mph, his passenger, Ken Norris had all but lost sight of her. The condition of the salt was appalling, and as *Bluebird* accelerated hard the wheels began to spin on the oily black line that marked the centre of the course. The car slewed sideways and began to barrel roll, travelling nearly 280 yards on its first bounce, followed by a further four bounces and a long, long skid, before the remains of the car ground to a halt.

The chasing duo of Norris and Villa arrived to find the battered hulk lying right side up with the engine idling. As Leo ran around to open the cockpit his legs were sucked into the gaping maw of the air intake, one leg each side of the air splitter panel. Fortunately, Ken Norris switched the engine off very quickly before they set about opening the cockpit canopy. When they finally succeeded, both men stared in disbelief at Donald, who incredibly was not only alive, but still conscious. As they lifted the injured driver out, his wife Tonia and Peter Carr arrived on the scene,

Donald managed to whisper, "I seem to have clouted my ear", a considerable understatement as he had suffered a severe fracture to the base of his skull, burst an ear drum, ruptured his right middle ear and had several cuts and scrapes. Even so, he managed to walk into Toulle Hospital later that day. As he lay in hospital, he announced that he intended to have another try and, in response Sir Alfred Owen, owner of Coventry Motor Panels, offered to build a replacement car. Ken Norris, however, was more concerned with finding out what had happened to the first one. Analysis of the telemetry read-out showed what Ken Norris had already worked out for himself, that the accident had been caused by loss of traction on a less-than-perfect surface, compounded by the fierce acceleration of Donald's 'drag' start. The car's black-box recorder was destroyed in the crash, but had recorded 360 mph before its demise. Quick calculations showed that this speed had been reached in only 1.6 miles, encountering over 16G in acceleration. At this point, tyre marks showed Donald had started to stray from the black guide line stretched out across the salt and, once the car had gone beyond the critical degree of slip, it literally tripped over, and went into its death throes. Donald blamed the use of pure oxygen in his breathing mask, commenting that, "It had the effect of nitrous oxide. Once you knew you were in a bit of bother, it was too late, you could see the accident coming, but you were already five cycles behind the game, and you thought, 'too bad'".

If this was the case, it might explain why he had made no attempt to regain the course. The *Bluebird* was a total wreck. Only the engine, one differential box, sundry components and instruments were undamaged. It was obvious that the damage was the result of the car rolling, rather than the initial spin, which in turn was heavily influenced by the gyroscopic effect of the large-diameter wheels. Ken Norris made some comparisons with Mickey Thompson's *Challenger*, which was on the salt at the time, and with information on Cobb's *Railton Mobil Special*, which confirmed that the spin-off rate of the larger wheels employed by *Bluebird* was much greater. There were only two ways to change this: the use of smaller wheels (which was impossible) or an aerodynamic fin. The original wind tunnel tests were simply to establish if a fin was needed, but at that time the investigation was solely for aerodynamic stability. A tailfin would serve two purposes, but Ken Norris still asserts:

"It doesn't suggest, however, that a fully finned vehicle is the optimum as far as record-breaking is concerned, as the fin imposes penalties of increased aerodynamic drag and side force. Had the salt of Bonneville been in better condition in 1960, the record would have been broken, without the need for a tailfin".

CN7 rebuilt

By the end of November 1961, *Bluebird* had been completely rebuilt. The original cockpit cover was modified, first by covering the Perspex with a thin layer of fibreglass, and then replaced with a completely new canopy, made from very thick fibreglass that could withstand a load of fifty tons. It also incorporated a new flat glass screen. The original onboard telemetry was replaced with a Hussenot System, that could measure pitch, roll, yaw, linear acceleration, power, speed and degree and rate of movement in the suspension and steering to a very fine degree. The Proteus engine was retained, but a more powerful type 755 unit (engine number 425) was installed.

The undamaged diff-box was refitted and a new David Brown unit installed to replace the one that had been written-off, along with all-new Birfield constant-velocity couplings. The only other modifications were a change from the original Irvin safety harness to one of a newer design, and the inclusion of a tailfin. It is little known that the fin on *Bluebird* CN7 had removable sections, which could be removed section-by-section from the top downwards, to produce a tail fin of several different heights and areas, right back to its original 1960 tail-less specification.

CN7 runs again

On 9 July 1962 Donald gave the new *Bluebird* CN7/62 a shake-down run at RAF Tangmere, and five days later further runs were made at Goodwood. By April 1963, the *Bluebird* team had started to assemble in Australia for what was to be the longest part of the whole saga.

After the construction of a special causeway to allow access to Lake Eyre, the chosen site, it took two days to grade a nine-mile course. Rain had not fallen in the area for seven years, but as the camp readied itself for the first runs, it started to pour. The new track was ruined, and already a replacement needed. With the help of the army and a government working party, an alternative course was graded, but all did not bode well. On several occasions all hands were needed to pull vehicles out of pot holes caused when the wheels had encountered thin patches of salt, and broken through to the water and gypsum below (which was ninety feet deep in places). What would the four-ton *Bluebird* make of this new, shorter track?

By Monday, 13 May 1963, Campbell had reached 175 mph in under a mile, an acceleration rate that was going to have to be beaten by a considerable margin if the record was to fall. After every run, the whole car had to be meticulously cleaned of the emulsified salt that thrown up by the still wet track. As the track dried, reserve driver, Campbell's pilot friend Ken Burville, was allowed a couple of runs in the car, unlike any of the previous nominees. Leo Villa, the Campbells' long-serving friend and mechanic, and the car's co-designer, Ken Norris were also allowed to try the car for themselves. Leo went away first, but spent most of his run with his foot hard on the brake pedal, trying to cancel out the effect of an over-exuberant get-away. When Campbell and Ken Norris arrived, Leo jumped out and claimed to have found the whole thing quite enjoyable, if a little bumpy. It would be a different experience for Ken Norris:

"I was peering into the cockpit, wondering if it was all such a good idea, when I heard Donald shout out something to the effect of 'cheerio', and the team all disappeared. I was about eleven miles from camp with only one obvious means of transport. I remembered the start-up drill and set off along the course marker line. I remember thinking something like, 'this doesn't seem so bad, I'm only pootling along', when I noticed the tents of base camp along the horizon. In the seconds I had thought about easing up and braking I'd zoomed past it, and was going off in the other direction. Donald thought it was hilarious".

Campbell's system was to build up slowly, learning more about the car and the course as time went on. On this occasion, the course was so bad that progress was painfully slow, and feedback from the car negligible. This led observers to the conclusion that perhaps the effects of his 1960 crash were holding him back – what is known today as 'fighter pilot syndrome'. The runs had been disappointingly slow and had consumed months, waiting for conditions suitable for running the car. It was seen as a failure. Sir Alfred Owen announced that he personally blamed Campbell, accusing him of mismanagement. Stirling Moss, who himself had broken speed records on the Bonneville salt flats in the MG E.X 181, publicly stated that he felt Donald Campbell lacked the split-second timing needed to drive *Bluebird* to the record.

Again the rains came, and again the team aborted running on the wet salt. Eventually, the inevitable decision was made, and the project was abandoned, at least for 1963. A lot of 'dirt' had been thrown and dirt has a tendency to stick.

During planning for the 1964 attempt, it became obvious to the team that this new endeavour was going to be no cakewalk. Although several major sponsors such as Dunlop, Lucas and Girling all stayed on board, others, most notably BP, decided that it was time to call it a day. The only modifications to the car were the removal of the tail-mounted camera pod (installed by BP to gain footage for the film 'How Long A Mile') and the installation of a braking parachute. Any others were either deemed unnecessary, or too expensive – 1964, by necessity, was going to be a shoestring affair.

During February, the team set out for Lake Eyre once more, and by March the car had been prepared and was ready to go. Then, on 9 March, it started to rain again. By 20 April, the course had dried out enough for the convoy taking *Bluebird* out onto the Lake to start its journey. It was not until 30 April that the engine was started in anger for the first time. This had followed a journey fraught with mishap, as the lorry carrying CN7 had yet again broken through the salt crust. During the first day of May, *Bluebird* was prepared for her first run of 1964, and for once everything seemed to be going to plan. Then, during the night it rained and the lake flooded to a depth of 4 inches. By the 5 May, it had dried out enough to give *Bluebird* a run on a short five-mile course, and a speed of 200 mph was reached. On the 9 May, Campbell drove his car on the side of the main 20-mile course, to see if it had dried out sufficiently, but the conclusion was that the track, which had cost Campbell £6,000, was a complete write-off. The search was on again for a suitable stretch of salt.

During the next few days, heavy steel girders were towed over the salt to speed up the grading process and by 19 May the new track was up to twelve miles but far from perfect. *Bluebird*'s electrics were beginning to suffer from salt corrosion but, after yet another thorough strip and clean, everything started to function properly again. Things were looking up. By 24 May, the course had dried out considerably, and *Bluebird* CN7 was driven up to 300 mph, only to suffer from an appalling vibration, so severe that it affected Campbell's vision. Yet again Leo Villa and his team stripped and cleaned the pneumatic suspension system, suspecting that the salt, which was still very wet, was somehow affecting the car's performance. *Bluebird*'s electronic 'black box', confirmed the vibration, but could not throw any light as to the cause. On 27 May, a speed of 307 mph was recorded, but again on the return run the vibration reappeared, and forced Campbell to back off. For obvious reasons, wheel balance was suspected, but Dunlop's representative, Andrew Mustard, was adamant it could not be the case. All four wheels were changed, and a further run of 286 mph was made without problem. Again the murmuring started that Donald Campbell was losing his nerve. After all, every time he made a run at a speed approaching that of his 1960 crash, he was unable to improve on it on the return. It fell to the car's co-designer, Ken Norris to discover the cause:

"After one run, I went around the car to check the wheels. Running my finger around the rim I was surprised to find a thick gluey blob of salt forming in the rim where centrifugal force had thrown it, and where it was running around the outside of the wheel to the bottom".

The salt was still so wet, that when it was thrown onto the wheels, it ran down into the rim. When the car went through its turn-around procedure, the salt solidified in a lump weighing as much as half a pound at the bottom of the rim, putting the wheel out of balance. From then on, either the wheels would have to be changed after every run, or cleaned thoroughly. Even so, no apologies were offered by those who had doubted him yet again, and Campbell had nothing to say in response to his detractors.

The next day *Bluebird* hit 352 mph and on the 29th, preparations began for what were certain to be the record runs, but the infamous Campbell 'luck' was to strike again. The weather began to worsen again, and the course had started to suffer deep ruts, caused by the tyres. These were so deep that they were scuffing the sidewalls of the rear tyres as they ran through the trench left by the fronts as the salt collapsed. The car became uncontrollable as it rose out of, then fell back into the tramlines it left after each run, and it became impossible to use the same stretch of salt twice. As Ken Norris said just after his return home: "Largely, all we did on those trials at Lake Eyre, was to use the car as a salt tester. Really we weren't testing the car, because its potential was far greater than what happened eventually, we were using the car as a salt tester, to see if the salt was good enough to take the car".

After yet another delay Campbell made a run on 85 % power, but again the car lurched and slid so badly that he was unable to go any faster than 360 mph. Donald was convinced that the car was not able to push its way out of the ruts that it was cutting in the soft salt. It was later found, however, that a fault in the hydraulic throttle linkage was preventing anything like full power being used. An inspection of the track was made, and after a long chat with Leo Villa and Ken Norris, Campbell conceded that he had been taking 'a bit of a risk', and postponed any further runs.

Lake Eyre had been dry for seven years until Donald Campbell had arrived in 1963 to near-perfect conditions. Then, a year later, after nearly two years of on-and-off rainfall he was trying to force *Bluebird* through, rather than over the sodden salt.

Andrew Mustard, who was using a modified Elfin racing car to test scale versions of *Bluebird's* tyres, had been nominated as reserve driver on the 1964 attempt, and was determined to have his turn at the wheel. Indeed, he once publicly stated that he would sacrifice a very personal part of his lower anatomy for the chance. Again, the murmuring started to circulate, the more so after Campbell called an osteopath to the salt to treat his recurring back problem. Mustard wasted no time in announcing he felt Campbell was physically unfit to attempt the record. He was soon relieved of his post of reserve driver and project manager. Ken Norris managed to pour oil on troubled waters, and Campbell agreed to take an independent medical test, which proved he was indeed fit, and eventually Mustard was reinstated. Sadly, the whole episode was very public, and cannot have helped the already tense atmosphere, or Campbell's press back home in England.

By 13 July, Campbell was determined that his next runs were to be for the record. Ken Norris felt that more trials were needed but 'the Skipper' was adamant. He flew off with his wife, Tonia to collect the timekeepers from Adelaide but before he could return, it rained yet again. The news was 'phoned through, and the timekeepers were put on stand by. Campbell returned, and with Leo Villa and Ken Norris, walked the course. The last three miles were under water, the rest of the track was very soft. The trio kept kicking the salt with their heels. Eventually the silence was broken. "How long do you think it will take (to dry out)?" asked Campbell. The consensus was about three days. Villa recalled being shocked by the response: "The salt was so soft you could pick it up in great dollops with your hand, like dough. Don asked what we thought, and both Ken and I thought it would be a least three days. Don's face went grey as he pulled on his chin, 'Get the boys ready, we've been messing about long enough. I think it's worth a try'. I was amazed, the conditions were terrible, but he was set on it".

The Double

One test run was made at 320 mph, and again Campbell set off to collect the timekeepers. He returned on the 16 July, only to find the wind too strong for any runs. The following day was a Friday, a day of the week that Campbell never ordinarily ran on, but the weather was passable and the 'Skipper' ordered that the car should be prepared for a run. The team members were at their stations by 7.10 am and, not long after, Campbell was aboard and harnessed in. As he fastened his silver-blue fighter pilot's helmet, his wife, Tonia handed him Mr Whoppit, his teddy bear mascot, while she kept a firm grip on Whoppit's 'wife', Mrs Whacko (a slightly larger teddy!). The canopy was pushed firmly home and Campbell given the thumbs up. Within seconds, the huge car was away, and accelerating hard. By the time Leo Villa and Ken Norris had caught up with *Bluebird* she had already turned around, and was awaiting her new set of wheels. In the cockpit, Campbell appeared tense and stone-faced, but Villa and the team left him with his thoughts. Leo later recalled the event in his book 'The Record-breakers':

"Very little was said as the various checks were made; then *Bluebird* was raised on her jacks and the wheels were changed. Within thirty-eight minutes she was ready to go again. I remember noticing Donald sitting in the cockpit, staring vacantly at the open canopy. Only when I shouted, 'OK Skipper, ready when you are', did he seem to shake himself out of this uncanny lethargy. Later, he claimed that he had seen his father reflected in the windscreen and that his father had assured him that everything would be all right. I've always been inclined to take stories like this with a very substantial pinch of salt, but there is no doubt that he looked very strange for a few moments."

Minutes later, Leo Villa and Ken Norris were again chasing *Bluebird* down the salt on the return run. Like nearly all of the return runs before, this one too was a nightmare. All along the course, huge ruts had been cut into the soft salt, and on either side, ribbons of rubber and tyre casing lay strewn all over the measured mile. The effort needed to hold the car on course must have been super-human as it bucked and jumped over the disturbed salt. By a strange quirk, Campbell's speed in both directions was 403.1 mph, the record therefore being set at 403.10. Calculations showed that *Bluebird* CN7 left the measured kilometre at 445 mph and there can be little doubt that had the run-up not been shortened by nearly three and a half miles, due to rain, then Craig Breedlove's 407.45 mph would also have been beaten. As it was, the record had been hard won.

There were still five months remaining of 1964, and Campbell was determined to become the first man to set both land and water speed records in the same year. As if to underline Campbell's abysmal luck, the first lake he and his team looked at for the Water Speed Record, seemed ideal. Then when he returned some weeks later, it had dried up! Finally, the *Bluebird* team settled on Dumbleyung, about 140 miles from Perth. After yet more bad weather Campbell finally achieved his ambition, when he set a new Water Speed Record of 276.3 mph, on the last day of the year.

The cost of building and running *Bluebird* CN7 had exceeded £2 million, and she had not even been close to her true potential. Sadly for Donald Campbell, though, the die was well and truly cast. Earlier delays when he started to challenge for the Water Speed Record, as well as the 'failures' in reaching record speeds, were compounded by the apparent failures of the CN7 project. It seemed inconceivable that the wonder car of British industry should have taken three years to succeed. Only one man could be blamed, but it is debatable if his shoulders were ever going to be wide enough to bear the criticism. For Donald Campbell, the stigma of failure was very public and must have surely damaged the man both emotionally and mentally. As further record attempts swung the same way, he spent much of his public time on trial. Even as a child while supporting his father's attempts, he had put himself, to a lesser degree, in the firing line. As the years rolled by, and Donald took centre stage, he not only had his own sniping press to contend with, but also the 'he isn't his father' syndrome that has destroyed many others. He may have tried to counteract it, but to those close to him, it was evident that he had only partially succeeded.

His mood would swing from extreme to extreme, and he would make rash comments or decisions. He would allow himself to be forced into premature action with false bravado, such as his crash in the *Bluebird* car at Bonneville in 1960. No one that was close to Donald failed to notice that he had changed considerably after the Utah crash. His temper was shorter, his patience fragile, and he began to feel and react to the pressures of his position. He became irascible, unreasonable and prickly. He had always been one of the boys, a good party animal, at ease with those outside of his circle of friends as well as those close to him, and always receptive to advice. But after 1960 he could relax only with his very close friends, and was unwilling to act upon, or at the very least listen to the advice of others. He remained a staunch patriot but he, like many others, failed to understand why he never received the official recognition his achievements deserved, not least for his unique double of 1964. One can only assume that he must have upset someone of high position at some time, and that this was held against him until the end. Some of the most graphic displays of Donald Campbell under pressure are the interviews held during his 1966/67 attempt. One could argue that these are the hazards of public life, where one's personal frailties, shortcomings, and idiosyncrasies tend to come under far more scrutiny than normal traits. One only has to witness the output of today's political cartoonists, impressionists and satirists.

The CN7 saga can only have added to Donald's insecurities. Privately, many thought that his marriage to Tonia was too fragile to last, and there was public speculation as to its state. Donald was desperate to father a son to continue the family name but sadly, on the four occasions Tonia had produced a son, the infant died within hours. One can only speculate on the cumulative effect of these events on the brittle Campbell persona.

Donald's superstitions are legendary, but one has to wonder how genuine they were. They could, of course, been part of the elaborate 'act' that was put on for the world at large, to maintain interest in his projects. Or they could have been a manifestation of his insecurity. Although Donald admired his father as any other son does, he was also in awe of him, and probably to some extent in fear also. That is not to say he feared for his safety, but feared failure and thereby tarnishing the family name. Malcolm clung to the Victorian ideals of his own father, and Donald had always known the same strict discipline that went with them. In all but physical stature, Donald's father was a big man, who cast an even bigger shadow. Superstitious or not, Donald encountered the most dismal of luck. From his very first attempts, he suffered at the hands of bad weather, the untimely breakdown of mechanical equipment and general misfortune. He arrived in Australia in 1963 for the first trials on the dry salt of Lake Eyre after seven years of drought to be confronted with rain. This was repeated the following year, the year that Donald decided to attempt both the Land and Water Speed Records. On the last day of 1964, Donald succeeded in beating his own Water Speed Record, but never received the expected knighthood that many felt should have gone with it.

Dreams of the Future

During the next couple of years, he became further involved in the development of the *Jetstar* speedboat that his Bluebird Marine company had been working on. In addition to his other business activities, Donald was instrumental in forming Stewart Smith Associates, an insurance broking business of which he was a director and with whom he insured *Bluebird*.

Along with the faithful team of Leo, Ken and Lew Norris many projects were discussed, with added impetus being supplied by American announcements of proposed attempts on both the land and water speed records. Drawings were made for the CN8 rocket car that would take Donald past the sound barrier on land as well as for a new four-point hydroplane with retractable wheels, the plan being to raise both records with one vehicle. Donald was finding it increasingly difficult to impress both the public and press alike with his plans, and when, on 30th October 1966, with the intention of increasing interest in the CN8 car, Donald announced his intention of breaking 300 mph in his ageing K7 hydroplane, the reaction was of near total disinterest. Something had changed in Donald Campbell. He had aged considerably, his hairline had receded and had started to grey, and unusually he was ill at ease with those around him. Apart from a small input from the *Daily Sketch*, the whole venture was financed by Donald himself, and the mixture of money problems, marriage difficulties and years of inactivity were taking a heavy toll on the man. The project itself suffered public apathy because of the wider interest in circuit racing, manned space flight, and the tremendous speeds being reached with modern experimental aeroplanes.

At Coniston only the *Daily Sketch* banner flew, looking somewhat bedraggled as it dipped into the water. The support vehicles were the ones from the original land speed attempts, plus ones that had been begged or borrowed for the occasion. Donald was nearly forty-six years old but, instead of reaching the pinnacle of his career, he arrived at Coniston to find he was already on the downward slope. He appeared more lined, and the stress was apparent in his face. He greeted questions with guarded answers. He was suspicious of the press, constantly looking for the hidden agenda in their questions.

He appeared to be always uneasy and on the defensive. Winter in the Lake District was never the perfect time to make an attempt on the Water Speed Record, and the weather changed almost as soon as Donald and his team arrived. There were instant press claims that the 300 mph attempt was a cut-price effort when, on one of the first occasions that the engine was run, the air intakes collapsed. Yet more press sniping was to come when, in an effort to cure a balance problem, a run was made with sandbags tied to the stern, as his father had done. To some, it appeared a Heath Robinson affair. Radio and television interviews took on the air of interrogations or accusations of deliberately holding back. It is nothing short of miraculous that Donald did not snap. After years of building himself an identity outside that of simply being Sir Malcolm Campbell's son, he was fighting to keep it.

The Last Days

It is a sad reflection on today's society that most have based their appraisal of Donald Campbell upon his last days. It can never be easy for a son to follow in his father's footsteps, and it is even more difficult when the footsteps are so large. One could accuse Donald of making a rod for his own back, but that is to ignore his achievements, usually attained under far greater pressure and in the face of a greater fear than his father had endured. In an attempt to quantify this we must look at some simple facts.

In all, there have been 61 successful, officially recognised attempts on the Land Speed Record. Similarly, there have been 44 successful and officially recognised attempts on the Water Speed Record, making a total of 105 officially held world records. Of these, 20 are attributed to Sir Malcolm and Donald Campbell. Sir Malcolm set a total of thirteen records, of which four were on water and nine were on land, which is felt to be the easier of the two media. Donald set eight records, of which one was on land. Considering how few multiple record holders there have been, it is instantly apparent that both of the Campbells' success rates were above average. Donald was certainly not that far behind his father, yet he is still very often considered a failure by comparison.

Some have said that Donald was out of his time, a throw-back to the past, but those who were close to Donald felt that his only problem was to have chosen to follow in his father's very considerable footsteps. Perhaps there would have been no such problems had he been Sir Malcolm's brother, and had been competing directly against him, although it certainly never worked that way with the Arfons brothers. Why, then, is Donald's image based on his supposed failures, his personal failings, and his violent and very public death, rather than his undeniable successes?

To many, who have no personal recollection of the man, Donald was not the man his father was: incapable of the same success, incapable of the same engineering excellence and therefore incapable of generating the same public praise and support that were so freely given to his father. Donald had, at all times, to compete with the past. His financial backing was at best sparse, and his team small, but the technology was at the leading edge. All but one of his successful attempts were on water, not the most predictable of mediums, yet even though he succeeded against these odds, he is not remembered for his talent or success.

Fear played a much larger part in Donald Campbell's attempts than we can ever really know, yet not once did he draw back from the edge. He is often quoted as saying that once having started, you were already past the point of no return. One can only imagine how the two abortive attempts on the Land Speed Record can have affected him. He did speak publicly on the fear he felt while piloting his *Bluebirds*, but privately he often gave the impression that perhaps he should never really have followed that particular path. Surely a man who flies in the face of his own fears on so many occasions, and succeeds, is a very rare breed of man indeed.

Without doubt, Donald's popularity was greatly affected by the times he lived in. In Sir Malcolm's day – say, 1935 – the fastest machine in the World was the Supermarine S5 aeroplane, which was not that much faster than Campbell's car. Perhaps it could be seen that Sir Malcolm, a privateer, with no official government support, was pitting himself against all other nations on behalf of Great Britain. He was in the forefront of speed and technology, and was there when such behaviour was lionised. Yet, just as Sir Malcolm turned to the water, his popularity began to wane. He was going through a very public and messy divorce, in which his estranged wife used his daughter as a device to gain public sympathy. And in the world of speed, the new god was the test pilot in his jet fighter. Even when Malcolm tried the new jet engine in his converted K4 hydroplane, he suffered his first complete failure and, with both Britain and the United States striving to break the sound barrier, record-breaking on land and water became a far less newsworthy affair. When Donald walked onto the empty stage left by his father's death, he cannot have been expecting an easy ride, but surely he was not prepared for the near total apathy that greeted him. Perhaps his father's parting shot was to kill the last vestiges of public interest, by failing in his final record attempt. In the *Boys' Own* world of the fifties and sixties, Donald's attempts to shine out from his father's shadow, were dimmed, as the world looked first skyward to the likes of Chuck Yeager and Neville Duke, and then higher into space to Yuri Gargarin and Alan Sheppard, men who travelled at thousands of miles per hour. Who needed a car that could reach 400 mph, or a boat that could touch 250 mph? Donald Campbell was never going to compete.

As already mentioned, Ken and Lewis Norris were already planning a rocket-powered *Bluebird* to exceed the sound barrier, but the idea met with a lukewarm response, even though the Jamaican Government had promised to build a fourteen-mile runway for the attempt. In addition, Campbell planned to run CN7 there as well, to prove she was capable of recording 450 mph. When it became obvious that the CN8 rocket car was going to take a lot longer to reach fruition, Campbell's mind drifted to the standing start record, again using *Bluebird* CN7, but Ken Norris felt that any increase would be marginal, and the idea was finally dropped when Dunlop could not justify producing the necessary tyres.

On 19 June 1966, *Bluebird* CN7 was to be the star attraction at a Motor Sport Gala to be held at RAF Debden, in Essex. Campbell was suffering from a bout of flu and asked his friend, Peter Bolton, to demonstrate the car for him. The day before, Campbell gently rolled *Bluebird* down the runway, with Bolton sitting alongside in the open cockpit, to familiarise him with the controls. The car was turned around, and the 'new boy' climbed in, with strict instructions not to touch the throttle pedal. Ray Govier, a Bristol Siddeley technician who had been with the project since the first day, witnessed what happened next.

"I remember, I started the thing up for him, and away he went. I jumped into a Land Rover, with the late lamented Leo Villa, and off we went in pursuit, with me standing up in the back. I said something like, 'I can't see him Leo, he's gone, he's gone off the end of the bloody runway', and indeed he had. The car had gone straight out through a hedge at the end of the runway, across a main road, through another hedge, through a corn field, bounced over a ditch, and came to a halt. Leo and I went straight across and were the first people there, and the driver was in a very sorry state, although unharmed, but pale and very shaken. He was convinced he had suffered a brake failure, but we found them 100%. In fact, when we took the covers off the brakes, it was obvious the brakes had been on, and on very hard indeed. I can only assume that he had a very large foot and had his foot on the brake, and the throttle at the same time. The car was in a very sorry state. It was a sad day all round."

Alan Howe was driving past Debden, on his way home in Newmarket. "I couldn't believe my eyes. It flew over the road about ten feet off the ground at an incredible speed. It jumped clean over the road, not even touching the tarmac, clearing it by at least fifteen feet".

The air intake had taken a severe knock, the underside was badly dented, and the rear suspension was wrecked. The car was patched up in time for Campbell to give the demonstration as planned the next day, but repairs for another record attempt would cost more than £50,000. To Campbell, whose spirits were already low, it was a further blow. He had already consigned the K7 hydroplane to the museum, and it looked like the car would join her. Donald made no secret that he preferred to be behind the wheel of his beloved hydroplane, always giving the impression that he was uncomfortable in the *Bluebird* car. K7, or the 'old girl' as he often referred to her, had never really let him down. Of course, not every attempt had succeeded in raising the record, but Donald openly admitted that he felt the *Bluebird* boat was fated.

Indeed, he actually gave her credit for saving him from disaster when he felt that he no longer had control. He had told those close to him of one near miss, saying, "After a superb run south I found the turn beyond Peel Island so easy that I gambled that I could beat the rough water and make use of the calm water again. It must have been during this reasonably high-speed turn that the pitot tube became blocked, and so I had no idea of my speed. Everything seemed just so easy, I felt like a passenger. It suddenly occurred to me that I should be readying myself to reduce my speed and drop the rear shoe to further reduce speed and allow me to taxi back to the jetty. I eased off the throttle but *Bluebird* just seemed to keep going, and suddenly I was in danger of running up the beach, or worse still into the rocks at the northern end. I was so convinced that I let go of the wheel and drew my legs back thinking all the time of how hard the impact was going to be. I still don't know how, but just at the right time *Bluebird* just seemed to fall from her points and steer around into a gentle arc, finally drifting to a halt some ten or twenty feet from the rocks. Leo later told me that he thought it was all done deliberately, but it had still worried him. For my part, I just don't know. I always thought the old man was helping me. All I know is it wasn't me that averted a disaster".

Donald had taken to visiting clairvoyants and mediums soon after his father's death and, much to Leo Villa's chagrin, gave credit for several incidents to those 'on the other side'. This was a statement echoed by Donald's second wife many years later. After their divorce, Dorothy McKegg returned to New Zealand, where she still lives today. She relates a story, with the utmost conviction, of a time when, while driving alone along a deserted road in thick fog, she lost control on a notorious bend. "I thought I was going to leave the road for sure, when two hands grabbed the wheel and steered the car to a safe halt. There was a wedding ring on one of those hands. It was Donald's". Even though this event occurred some years after Donald's death it is still difficult to argue with her sincerity.

Donald had told his third wife, Tonia, that he intended to retire from record-breaking, and suggested opening a restaurant in Southampton, where both *Bluebirds* would be on display. It therefore came as a shock to Leo Villa when Campbell announced he would go for 300 mph on water with the old K7, equipped with a new Orpheus engine. The attempt that was to be Campbell's last.

1960 – 1967

Leo Villa, the man behind the Campbells. Probably the most experienced man that record-breaking has ever known *(© Kevin Desmond)*

Donald and Leo at Goodwood in 1960. Later, Donald would drive *Bluebird* around the circuit, at 80 mph, with the brakes on! *(by kind permission of Ray Govier)*

The Dunlop test rig for the tyres of *Bluebird CN7*. Later, the tyres for *Concorde* would also be tested on the very same rig *(© Dunlop Tyres plc)*

Donald talks to the press (out of shot) as Ray Govier, to his left, listens in *(by kind permission of Ray Govier)*

Some experts claim that CN7 was always intended to have a tail fin. However, this shot from Goodwood in 1960 shows that there were no mountings in the tail to accommodate such an appendage *(by kind permission of Ray Govier)*

Early morning, 1964. CN7 ready for a trial run *(© Campbell Collection)*

Goodwood, 1960. The split panel in the air intake of CN7. This panel would later save Leo Villa when he was sucked into the intake *(by kind permission of Ray Govier)*

A superb shot of Donald between runs in 1963. Just visible in the top of the windscreen is the head-up display. It was removed when Donald noticed the glass was green! *(© BP plc)*

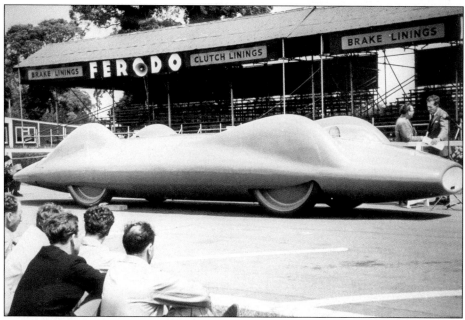

The *Bluebird* team (Ray Govier extreme right in the foreground) looks on as Raymond Baxter conducts an interview behind *Bluebird* (© *Leo Villa Collection*)

Leo Villa with Lord Montagu and *Bluebird* in 1974 (© *Dunlop Tyres plc*)

Orpheus engine number 709 being finally removed after *Bluebird's* air intakes collapsed. She was coaxed to run once more to test the rebuilt intakes, then discarded *(© Leo Villa Collection)*

Bluebird K7 after a run in Perth Harbour. In this rare shot of the underneath of the hull, the razor-sharp fins can be seen in-board of the Sonard planing shoes. A camera has been temporarily fitted to the tail fin. Beneath, Donald can just be seen *(© Leo Villa Collection)*

Dumbleyung, 1964. The double in Australia was a close-run thing
(by kind permission of K.W. Norris)

Bluebird, Coniston, 1967. The repaired intakes a different shade of blue, and with the new flat splash shields. Beautiful, even at rest *(© Paul Allonby)*

6.

Bluebird K7

The focal point for Donald Campbell's challenge for the Water Speed Record was Burgess Hill in Sussex. It was here that Lewis and Kenneth Norris, after their separate introductions into record-breaking, had joined forces with their other brothers and formed their own engineering company, logically called Norris Brothers. When Lewis left his position at Kine Engineering, Campbell sold his half share in the company, and started to investigate the prospect of a new *Bluebird* with the fledgling company. Early in 1952, Bill Coley, Campbell's life long friend, had suggested that, as John Cobb was undoubtedly going to succeed in raising the Water Speed Record, then perhaps Campbell should regain the Harmsworth Trophy from the Americans. By mid-1952 Norris Brothers had produced several schemes of what was to become the new *Bluebird* and, after much discussion it was decided to follow what had been titled the 'C' boat idea. Both Ken and Lewis Norris had decided that a three-point hydroplane was the best route to follow, which would again use the prop-rider technique. This meant that, through necessity, the design would have to be 'conventional' in that two planing surfaces would have to be forward-mounted to reduce the impact loads.

Even in the design's early days, the craft's appearance was quite different from that of a 'normal' hydroplane. It was decided to 'cut away' the surface area from between the forward planing shoes to ensure totally neutral aerodynamics. This meant that these surfaces had to be out-rigged on arms, or spars, and mounted in floats or sponsons. The main body of the craft was to be no higher than the engine, which was selected to be a Rolls-Royce type 65 Griffon, with a standard power output of 2200 bhp which, with the skill of fuel expert Commander Rod Banks, could be increased by some considerable amount for short periods. Directly in front of the engine sat the cockpit, much the same as on a modern Grand Prix car, although it was envisioned as being fully enclosed. Above the canopy protruded a ram intake for the engine's supercharger. Propulsion was to be taken from the crankshaft through a 3:1 'up and over' gearbox directly to the prop'. When he first saw the designs for the new boat, Leo Villa was moved to comment, "it's a bit like a lobster, isn't it?". The Norris brothers designed a scale hull to test the prop-riding principle of this new scheme and employed a 30 c.c. motor that produced 3.3 bhp at 15,000 rpm, which in turn required the to-scale propeller to spin at a staggering 40,000 rpm.

On 29 September, news came to the design team that Cobb and his jet-powered *Crusader* had crashed on Loch Ness, and 'Big John' had been killed (see page 23). All work on the new project ground to a halt while the magnitude of what had happened sank in. Donald Campbell was certain that the Americans had a clear path to the record, and gradually concluded that the new *Bluebird* would have to be designed to go faster than had originally been thought. By early October, it had started to become clear that a piston-engined craft could succeed in raising the record, but only by a very small margin, and only if some very major hurdles could be overcome. Power from the 37 litre Griffon would have to be increased considerably, and the propeller would have to withstand spinning at an unheard of 18,000 revolutions per minute. The Norris brothers had set out from the very beginning to design a structure of enormous strength to house both engine and driver, and set about studying the crash that had befallen Cobb's *Crusader* and building up a huge library of data.

The team began to consider how they could obtain more power. In a portent of the CN7 car, the Bristol Siddeley Proteus was considered, placing the propeller directly onto the end of the output shaft, and thereby predating by some years a technique now used throughout the world of the American unlimited hydroplanes. But still the problem of propeller speed could have been insurmountable. Even today, the submerged propeller-driven record is only just above 200 mph. Saunders Roe had been testing a tank model of the boat for some time, and were about to start trials with a free-running, radio-controlled model, but test tank superintendent, Bill Crago was having great difficulties in finding a small enough engine to achieve the correct scale speeds. He agreed with Donald that a small rocket motor would be much easier to use, but added that the results would be a lot closer to that of a full-scale jet-engined craft.

The First Model

Campbell was keen to develop new ideas and would have been desperate to succeed where his father, and poor Cobb, had failed, in harnessing a jet engine. The jet also scored highly because it did away with the need for propellers and shafts and their associated handicaps. And so, by the end of May 1953, the free-running model was ready, complete with a 6lb thrust, cold hydrogen peroxide rocket motor.

The basic outline of the design remained as originally envisaged, with its twin forward-mounted sponsons outrigged on arms, and a single, central planing shoe at the rear. For the first tests, a rough approximation of the body design was all that was needed. But once the decision had been made to go with a jet engine, and the design was finalised for the spaceframe sub-structure, Saunders Roe produced a model that was not only scale in dimension, but in weight as well. These models were to be Saunders Roe's last input into the project. Since Sam Saunders had founded the company that carried his name, production of motorboats had always been limited to wooden-hulled, propeller-driven vessels. Regardless of the fact they were being asked to use the ground-breaking development work that they had started with their jet-powered SRA/1 flying boat fighter, Saunders Roe felt that they could not be seen to be involved with this unconventional type of powerboat. Testing the models then fell to Donald and his small team. The radio-controlled version had simple controls for left, right, and on or off for the motor. After several accidents, there were not enough pieces left to rebuild the model, and testing became confined to the Imperial College of Science and Technology's wind tunnel, under the supervision of Professor Squire, the Haslar towing tank, and the pond at Donald's home.

Set-up costs alone had eaten up over £5,000 of Donald's own money, and so he started 'doing the rounds of mine, and the old man's previous backers' in an effort to proceed. True to form, Bill Coley deposited the first cheque in the *Project Bluebird* account, which in turn drew Joseph Lucas, Dunlop, Samlesbury Engineering, Bloctubes, and Siebe and Gorman into the fray. C.C. Wakefield, more commonly known as Castrol who, through Lord Wakefield of Hythe, had supported not just record-breaking, but Sir Malcolm Campbell in the past, offered their support with the proviso that George Eyston, who had been Cobb's project manager during his fateful attempt, be allowed to see the design, and be made a member of the team. Eyston, who had already helped Donald by letting him have the last remaining Rolls-Royce R-type spares, recommended that Castrol should become further involved, but the eventual decision was to pull out altogether.

Jet Propulsion

The decision to go with jet propulsion allowed work in Burgess Hill to take off in earnest. Around the basic design outline, general arrangements were penned for the Rolls-Royce Nene and Avon RA3, the Bristol Siddeley Sapphire and the Metropolitan-Vickers Beryl. This last engine had been suggested by none other than Rod Banks as the ideal engine for the job.

The Metropolitan-Vickers Electrical Company had been producing axial flow steam turbines for generating purposes for some years. Frank Whittle had been using similar principles to develop the world's first jet engine, although his first experimental units used a radial flow technique. Once convinced of the possibilities of the jet as a motive force for aircraft, the Royal Aircraft Establishment commissioned Metropolitan-Vickers, amongst others, to use their know-how to design and build a fully operational, airworthy engine.

The first fruits of their programme were coded B10 and D11 of 1939 and 1940 respectively, the data being used to start work on the first of the precious 'stone' series of engines, the Beryl. The design was the work of Dr D. M. Smith, Dr I. S. Shannon and Mr K. Baumann, the first prototype being run in December 1941. The radial flow jets being developed by Rolls-Royce, and Rover Cars, used, as the name suggests, the airflow through chambers around the outside of the main combustion chamber. They were easier to produce than their axial cousins, but created an untidy, short, very large diameter engine that caused installation problems. The axial flow engine used a system of spinning blades mounted in rows on a common shaft to compress the air fuel mixture into a combustion chamber at the very end of the unit. Although this produced a slightly longer engine, it was considerably tidier, smaller in diameter and much easier to install. The Germans had already produced an axial flow engine for the Heinkel He178, the world's first jet-powered aircraft, but the Beryl was far more efficient. For all that, by the time the final production go-ahead came through, it was too late for the engine to make any difference to the outcome of the war.

At the end of the World conflict, hostilities continued in the Far East. Here, the problem of stationing air forces was exacerbated by the lack of suitable airfields. The British Government approached Saunders Roe to produce a jet-powered flying boat fighter that became the SR A/1, and the Beryl was selected as the ideal engine to power it. Development work produced the Beryl F2, series IV, with a ten-stage compressor, and a static thrust of between 3500, and 4000 lbs at 8000 rpm. It measured 141 inches long, with a diameter of 36½ inches and weighed a mere 1,780 lbs. Approximately eleven were built. The first aircraft to fly was coded TG263, and was soon attaining speeds far in excess of contemporary flying boats at 512 mph. A further two airframes were built, but were lost in accidents, after which TG263 was mothballed.

After a further development period, the project was eventually scrapped, and TG263 went to the Airframe College at Cranfield. When, on Rod Banks' advice, Donald Campbell approached the Ministry of Supply to purchase a Beryl, he was offered no less than three! The starboard engine (MV47) was removed from the SRA/1 and the port engine, MV 38, is now in the Science Museum. The MV47 was given to the *Bluebird* project along with a spare (MV 54), and a further engine for spares. This final unit had been used for arms testing, which put simply meant that having once been bolted down and started; it was shot at until it would no longer work! Along with these engines came the support of Metropolitan-Vickers who not only rebuilt the engines for the project, but also sent along two technicians. Both men, James Whiteman, and a Mr Bozzonie had worked with Sir Frank Whittle on his first, experimental jets, and Whiteman had learnt his craft perfecting the supercharger impeller on the Rolls-Royce R-type, which rotated at a jet-like 23,904 rpm.

* * * *

Meanwhile, the design drawings of Norris Brothers were beginning to take shape. Construction of the spaceframe was undertaken by Accles and Pollock after an offer by Leslie Hackett, one of their directors, to complete it free of charge, using high-tensile, box-section molybdenum steel. This was to be precision welded to produce a structure with twice the strength of a supersonic jet fighter. Incorporated into the design of the frame was the means to adjust the position of several of the major components, specifically the engine, so that adjustments to trim could be made in the field. On completion of the frame, construction was moved on to Samlesbury Engineering, then a subsidiary of the Lancashire Aircraft Corporation, who specialized in aircraft wings and alloy coach and bus bodies. Under the direction of Edward Player, Birmid Industries supplied the Birmabright steel, and light alloys which were attached to the frame with a mixture of special alloy rivets (over 70,000) and sealing compounds. The craft's flat underside used the same alloy sheet but, but with the addition of a corrugated metal base to add to the torsional rigidity of the completed structure.

Alongside the engine mounts, water tanks had been included which could be flooded in sections, adding to the possible adjustments of the trim once the craft was launched. Directly behind, and to each side of the cockpit were the intakes for the jet engine leading to the ducting to take the required air (in the region of 3 tons per minute) into a single engine inlet. Built around this intake, in a horseshoe shape, was the fuel tank with a capacity of 48 imperial gallons – quite small when one considers the consumption was in the region of 650 gallons of paraffin per hour. On average, the two runs required for a record attempt would take eight and a half minutes, leaving a safety margin of approximately two gallons if the two runs were made back-to-back. The fuel tank was positioned at the centre of gravity, and constructed in such a manner as to be self-balancing. It was also designed to be as small as possible, accounting for only 300lbs of the all up-weight of 2½ tons when full.

The three planing shoes were machined from single billets of aluminium to increase their strength, the rear shoe being bolted directly to the hull's substructure. The front shoes were to be an integral part of the forward sponsons. These were made in a similar fashion to the hull and attached to a forward-mounted, one-piece cross beam, that went the entire width of the boat. At the rear of the sponsons, two immensely strong arms supported the critical planing area. Again, much like the hull, these sponsons could be moved forward or back to alter the 'wheelbase' of the planing surfaces. On the inside edges of both forward planing shoes were stainless steel stabilising fins, with razor-sharp leading edges. At full speed, these fins could support *Bluebird*'s entire 2½ tons. In the cockpit, the pilot was confronted with a simple dashboard of very few instruments, partially obstructed by a Bluemel steering wheel. To the pilot's right lay an auxiliary hand throttle and a ship-to-shore radio, installed by Harry Sturgeon of Ultra Electric. To the left, there was a set of watches and the pilot's emergency oxygen bottle. Dunlop supplied an air-cushioned, 'Dunlopillo' seat for comfort, and an Irvin safety harness for safety. Each system was tested as it was installed, with only the steering arrangement needing modification.

On Friday, 26 November 1954, Eric Ryland dutifully carried out the handing-over ceremony, and at 11.30 am, Lady Wakefield unveiled *Bluebird* to the world's press. Campbell was quick off the mark, and announced an appeal to raise yet more money to return the World Water Speed Record to Britain. It was enough to persuade Castrol to do an about-turn, and it also encouraged Joseph Lucas to contribute further funds. Lloyds of London insured the craft for a ridiculous £750.00.

Behind the scenes, Leo Villa had organised a collection, and on Bob Coley's seventy-sixth birthday, the loyal *Bluebird* team presented Donald Campbell with his very own St Christopher. After this had been fitted to the dashboard, Adams Brothers of New Malden prepared to transport *Bluebird* to the Lake District.

Bluebird dips her Feet

The plan had been for Donald's wife, Dorothy, to christen *Bluebird* on Monday, 7 February 1955, followed by the boat's first run but, with the appalling timing that was to dog Campbell's ventures, it had snowed. The following day, the waters of the lake were considered too choppy to make any runs, so the team occupied themselves by conducting a full dress-rehearsal until they found that the launch rails were buckled where they ran over a deposit of silt. The next day, the local fire brigade arrived to remove the silt with high-pressure hoses. All morning the flat waters beckoned *Bluebird*, but by the time the bulky canvas hoses were being packed, wind had produced a violent chop on the surface of the lake. It rained all day on the Thursday.

The next morning, Friday, 11 February 1955, was bitterly cold as the *Bluebird* team gathered to see K7 finally launched onto the freezing waters of Ullswater. Once the customary champagne had been broken over the bow, Donald was eager to get on with running his new charge. After three and a half years, there was to be one further delay, but by late afternoon, regardless of a slight swell, the Skipper gave the order to tow *Bluebird* out to her starting position. A sticking starter solenoid, and the induction of water into the engine reduced the first run to 15 mph, and the ignominy of having to be towed back to the jetty. All the while Donald had been on the R.T. (ship-to-shore radio), and in the most colourful of language was giving the rest of his team his thoughts. Sadly, no one told the team that it had been decided to patch these conversations over the public address system!

The First Record, and more

Doubt was cast on the electrically operated spray shields, and excessive rearward buoyancy of *Bluebird*. Several major water leaks had to be cured, and a considerable amount of weight had to be trimmed from the bows. The splash shields were removed and the buoyancy tanks cut away from the stern, lifting the bows by a small degree. When *Bluebird* returned to the water on 22 February, Ullswater was covered in patches of ice. The bows still had a tendency to dip under acceleration, with the accompanying spray dousing the engine. Even the addition of weighed blocks to the transom failed to get K7 onto her points.

Sitting around a pub table that night, several ideas were proffered, but ultimately it was Leo Villa who came up with the answer. In an effort to increase aerodynamic lift, and prevent water entering the engine, Leo suggested filling in the space between the spar arms. The Norris brothers' slide-rule confirmed the idea, as long as the speed was kept to below 150 mph. And so, on 14 March, *Bluebird* left her blocks and raced across Ullswater, planing perfectly as soon as Donald pressed the throttle. After several runs, Donald brought *Bluebird* back to the jetty in a masterly manoeuvre, taxiing to within feet of the jetty on just her forward planing shoes. During the afternoon, Campbell's confidence was high, but several more runs showed a tendency for *Bluebird* to go down at the bows. Neither Leo, nor Ken, nor Lewis Norris could confirm his observations, and so it was decided that the next day Leo would pilot *Bluebird* so that Donald could see for himself. This proved that the team was on the right path, and that *Bluebird*'s cockpit needed further waterproofing!

With K7 safely locked in a boat shed, the team returned south to find a more permanent solution. The Norris brothers attacked the problem with a slide rule and a wind tunnel, while Donald and his team were back on the pond at Abbotts, and the conclusion was that the forward spar would have to be raised. The calculations and drawings were done quickly and a Glaswegian panel beater from Carlisle was employed to carry out the modifications. The one-piece cross-beam that held the forward part of the sponsons was moved up and back, producing a hump in the top of the floats where the beam and sponsons joined. The nose-section also become shorter and more rounded and grew what Ken Norris referred to as 'dragon's teeth' on its lower surface. These guides were designed to direct water under the main hull, rather than around it, and up into the intakes. On 9 June, *Bluebird* K7 returned to the water of Ullswater with high hopes of success. Leo Villa, with his son, Tim, took on the role of Clerk of the Course, and from then on was stationed in the middle of the measured mile, reporting on the changing conditions by radio.

Maurice Parfitt, Andy Brown and Don Woolley were given the task of starting the engine from an adjacent dinghy, as the on-board starting system had been removed to save weight. As the whine of the Beryl began to fill the air the thought of further failure was cast aside as *Bluebird* shot off down the lake faster than she had ever travelled before. Less than five minutes later, Donald stepped from the cockpit, beaming. Instantly he was confronted with a barrage of press questions. By 23 July the team was ready for an attempt on the World Water Speed Record. Phil Mayne had informed Campbell that this would be the last day his timekeepers would be available, which kept modifications down to a reduction in the size of the stabilising fins and rudder. Ullswater had already begun to prove unsuitable for the attempt, being much narrower than Coniston so, to ease Campbell's concern, it was decided to have Andrew Holliday survey a shorter, kilometre course. The morning of the 23rd had broken grey and dull and by the time Donald Campbell had arrived at the jetty, Leo and his son were already stationed in the middle of the lake. Campbell's recurring back problem had flared up again, and he passed his time stretching himself from the hook of a crane. After checking radio communications, the Beryl stirred the air once more and *Bluebird* rocketed toward the marker buoys. It was the first time the throttle of *Bluebird* had been floored in anger, and she was quickly up to over 200 mph. Almost immediately, both the air speed indicator and the radio aerial ceased working.

Campbell's main concern was his speed, but Villa's was that he had no way to inform the Skipper of the course conditions. He had no need to worry, as it took twenty minutes to turn and restart *Bluebird* before the return run could be made. His first run logged 215.13 mph, but on the return the Beryl would only rev to 6900 rpm, giving a run of 189.57 mph, but still enough for a new record of 202.32 mph. At last Donald Campbell had achieved his ambition and broken the record, but it had not been as planned. He had hoped to set a record in excess of that held by Stanley Sayres, and then travel to America to exceed the 200 barrier on live American television, but beggars could not be choosers. So, at Mobil Oil's expense, the *Bluebird* team prepared to travel west. For Campbell's part, he became the darling of the British press, sought after by newspapers and television alike. All through these interviews, Campbell referred to 'we' rather than 'I', giving full credit to his team.

To Lake Mead, the Bottom, and the Record

The invitation to run *Bluebird* in America revolved around a two-fold challenge. The first leg was a straight race between Campbell, the new world record holder, and an American by the name of Jo Schoeneth, in a prop-rider called Gale V, for a prize of $10,000.

After this, assuming the correct conditions, Campbell would attempt the Water Speed Record on live television. He stood to make a great deal of money from the venture, which he was more than happy to be part of, as Mobil Oil were bank-rolling the whole attempt.

The chosen venue, Lake Mead, Nevada, was a huge man-made reservoir created to produce electricity for nearby Las Vegas, but it suffered as a record-breaking venue because of its size. The area was prone to high winds, which could create extremely choppy conditions out on the water. It was in such conditions that *Bluebird* made her first run on 14 October, Campbell being anxious not to let the American television audience down. This first run confirmed that there were still problems with getting *Bluebird* up onto her planing shoes, as well as the entry of water into the engine intakes and, once running, she was still curiously unstable. Leo Villa had been given the task of producing a pair of curved perspex deflectors to be mounted either side of the cockpit, just forward of the intakes. However, as a temporary measure, *Bluebird* was wearing some aluminium panels, in much the same place. Conditions were far from ideal for running *Bluebird*, but Campbell was a man of his word, and after a very wide turn, he returned at about 150 mph, receiving a very bumpy ride, made far worse by the amount of spectator crafts dotted along the course.

At the end of the run, Campbell attempted his usual bow-up taxi to the jetty, only to find the engine flaming out; it was restarted but again was put out by the amount of water being thrown up. Leo Villa decided to take his boat back to the jetty in an attempt to make a clear path for the Skipper, but *Bluebird* had shipped so much water she began to slip beneath the surface, finally disappearing from view 40 yards from safety. Within hours, divers had located the hull, and before nightfall she was back on dry land. She was missing her jet exhaust nozzle, which had to be located later. Her engine cover was buckled, and her angular cockpit canopy was cracked in several places. To make matters worse, the waters of Lake Mead were very high in mineral content, and all of K7's bright steel external fittings had already turned black. The condition of the engine became a major concern, and it became crucial that the hull was stripped, drained and cleaned as soon as possible. Luck was, for once, on Campbell's side. An English Squadron Leader, Peter Carr, was stationed at nearby Nellis Air Force base, where he was instructing pilots in the United States Air Force. He arranged for the Nellis workshops to carry out the required work, an offer Campbell would have been mad to ignore. The process took nearly a month, by which time the match race with Schoeneth had been forgotten. By 16 November, *Bluebird* was again running on the bright blue waters of Lake Mead. Campbell, wearing a bright yellow American air force helmet given to him by Carr, paid his thanks to the Americans with a record of 216.2 mph. It was now the turn of the American press to clamour for Campbell's attention, who made no secret of the fact that he was immensely proud to have beaten the record in Uncle Sam's back yard.

1956 to 1964 – and an Annual Income?

Campbell's success earned him a CBE, and *Bluebird* some much-needed modifications. She appeared at Coniston in August 1956 with the cracked and stained canopy replaced with a jet fighter-style bubble, as well as several changes under the skin. On 16 September, Campbell set off on a timed southerly run, aiming to achieve a speed of about 230 mph. As Leo Villa struggled to comprehend the Skipper's commentary over the R.T., *Bluebird* hurtled by him at over 286 mph, leaping wildly from sponson to sponson. Campbell allowed K7 to flop from her planing condition as he turned her in preparation of the return run. During the twenty-minute pause between runs, Campbell confirmed the rough ride Villa had witnessed, announcing *Bluebird* had 'gone crazy'. Regardless of near-perfect conditions on the return, Campbell 'cruised' by the launch at 164 mph, enough for a new record average of 225.63 mph. Each new record brought with it renewed press interest, as well as the cheques. This was because The Butlin Trophy (set up by Billy Butlin of holiday-camp fame) was awarded to anyone setting a new Water Speed Record in any one year, and was accompanied by a cheque for £5,000, topped up by any sponsors' bonuses. Work had begun on the *Bluebird* CN7 car, and Campbell became expert in using the press coverage of the Water Speed Record to attract more sponsors and, in turn, more income. Much like his father in the twenties and thirties, the attempts on the Water Speed Record became almost an annual event. Campbell wanted to return to the United States in 1957 after an invitation to run at Lake Canandaigua, 350 miles from New York. Fittingly *Bluebird* and her entourage travelled west on the liner *United States*, departing the day after Campbell's divorce from Dorothy McKegg was confirmed.

By chance, the first runs of the new attempt were made on the 4 July, but Lake Canandaigua seemed plagued by strange underwater currents which curtailed the effort after a very short time. The team then moved to

Onandago Lake, where the jetty and workshop were aboard a US marine landing craft moored at one end of the lake. Again, *Bluebird* proved strangely difficult to control. Campbell, depressed that the whole venture had been a fruitless waste of time, sent Leo ahead to prepare for an attempt on Coniston Water, where *Bluebird* returned at the end of October. The team dutifully prepared for the Skipper's arrival. At some time during the abortive American venture, however, something had got into the engine causing damage to several of the turbine blades, forcing Leo and his team to change to their spare engine. Conditions on Coniston Water remained perfect for the duration that *Bluebird* was captive in her shore-side workshop. Leo wrote in a letter, "The water has been better that I have ever seen it, ideal for a record. I can't help thinking it might change for the worse just as Don arrives." But for once, it held, and on 7 November, Campbell earned himself a further £5,000 from the Butlin fund, with a record of 239.07 mph.

During 1958 *Bluebird* changed her look more radically. The blown-bubble cockpit canopy remained, but she was given a more purposeful appearance by the addition of more aerodynamic, raised sponson covers. The stern had grown a low tailfin, designed mainly for housing an experimental braking parachute, but it also gave improved aerodynamic stability. It also provided the ideal mount for the air-speed pitot tube. Trials with the parachute proved a failure when the spray kicked up at the stern prevented it from inflating properly. Less obvious was a new, smaller rudder, matched on the opposite side of the transom by a fixed stabilising fin. This had been produced by Vickers Ltd, and served to counteract the turning effect of rudder drag. Its leading edge was razor-sharp to reduce its own drag, and Campbell found that whatever penalty the drag inflicted, it was far outweighed by the rejuvenated stability of the boat. This highlighted just how out of control *Bluebird* must previously have been at very high speed.

British Petroleum had been researching into special lubricants for the CN7 record car, and decided to reinforce this by sponsoring Campbell's 1958 effort. Trials during October offered no new problems and, on 10 November, Campbell again received the Butlin Trophy, setting a record of 248.62 mph. He was amazed by the transformed handling, caused by forcing the bows to push down into the water, and maintaining contact between the forward shoes and the water. He therefore started to make noises about raising the record to 300 mph, to match his father's achievement of being the first to 300 mph on land.

During 1958 Campbell had married for the third time, to Belgian-born cabaret singer Tonia Bern, whom he took on a skiing honeymoon while his other love, *Bluebird*, toured the major cities of the north and midlands. The desire to run the revitalised *Bluebird* was strong enough to draw

Campbell back to the Lake District as early April of 1959, which provided the extra benefit of more predictable weather. A new record was set on 14 May at 260.33 mph, this being the only record that Campbell achieved with relative ease. The boat had required no modifications, had run fault-lessly, and the weather had been nearly perfect. Perhaps this £5,000 had been 'a piece of cake'. While the construction of the *Bluebird* CN7 car pro-gressed, the K7 hydroplane took a back seat. Campbell's plan was to take both car and boat to America, set a Water Speed Record on Lake Mead, fly to the Bonneville salt flats, and then set a Land Speed Record on the same day. The plan crashed along with Campbell, however, when the CN7 rolled off the course at 360 mph. On his return to England, Donald threw himself into the reconstruction of the land speed car, further curtailing any development to his trusty hydroplane. Work on CN7 reach its climax in 1964 when CN7 established a new record on Lake Eyre, Australia, in such appalling conditions that the best Campbell could hope for was to achieve the double in the same year, let alone the same day, but this left him with a scant five months to capture the second part of the double.

In Search of Water

Campbell's Land Speed Record made a tremendous impact on the Austra-lian people, which in typical fashion he used to great effect. He announced the search for a suitable lake on which to run the *Bluebird* hydroplane, as well as enlisting the help of several major Australian establishments to check all was well with the hull structure. The second leg of the double was set to take place at Barmera, on Lake Bonne, some 150 miles from Adelaide. Just over two months after the Lake Eyre suc-cess, Campbell, his team and *Bluebird* were on the shores of Lake Bonne. On 13 November the still morning air of the remote lake was shattered by the whine of the Beryl as Campbell edged out onto the lake. He returned after one run of 210 mph, but described the run as, 'the worst bloody ride of my life'. Over the next days the weather ranged from terrible to awful and Campbell's mood blackened as he saw his chance of a unique double slipping away.

On 8 December, the team decamped in search of a new venue. It was not until 20 December that *Bluebird* was launched onto Lake Dumble-yung, some 1,600 miles from Lake Bonne. The most obvious problem appeared to be the copious wildlife at the new venue. The simple solution was to empty several shotguns into the air before each run, but there was no easy solution to the 'Albany Doctor'. This was the name given to a curi-ous wind that would appear and disappear without warning from the direction of the town of Albany. It was to stymie several attempts on Dumbleyung. Campbell's mood worsened until 31 December, the last day of the year. None of the trial runs were nearly fast enough to secure the record, and with the lake blown up by a squall, the weight of failure upon him, Campbell was forced to concede defeat. He decided that he and his wife would to fly to Perth, leaving instructions that the team might as well pack up. Even to Leo Villa it was a bitter pill to swallow, until water skiers returned from the centre of the lake reporting that conditions looked perfect. John Davies, a local reporter chased off to the airfield in order to radio Campbell to return, while Leo briefed the team in readiness. Within an hour, Donald Campbell, still wearing his casual polo shirt, was strapped into the cockpit, and in conditions described by Leo as 'only about 80%' *Bluebird* accelerated onto her points. The first run was much faster that she had travelled before in Australia and, to make use of the small patch of calm water, Campbell played the gamble he had rehearsed before in tests, and turned around without refuelling, to return immediately. He set a record of 276.3 mph – the first and last time the gamble paid off.

* * *

Campbell had achieved a unique double, both the Land and Water Speed records broken in the same year, but on his return to England the reception was not as he had expected. Gone were the days of his father's triumphant returns from the beach of Daytona, and the ecstatic crowds. Gone also it seemed was the press coverage, and the knighthood. Just how much Donald Campbell coveted this award is a matter of conjecture. Those close to him say that if it had happened, he would have simply accepted it; others and, interestingly, those on the outer edge of his circle of associates, claim that he actively sought it. Either way, Campbell had to make do with his records and the Segrave Trophy, for the impact of his achievement having been greatly diminished by the American Craig Breedlove, and his jet car *Spirit of America*.

Bluebird CN7 had been designed and built to the letter of the regulations. It had four wheels, two of which controlled direction, and it was propelled by those wheels, which were driven by the engine – it was what Campbell considered to be a car. Breedlove had decided that the record was for the fastest vehicle on Earth. The *Spirit* was a three-wheeler with a pure thrust jet engine, resembling a grounded fighter plane with its wings removed. The FIA had no class for thrust-powered vehicles and, by definition, Breedlove's was a motor cycle and side car! He maintained his argument that the record should be for the fastest vehicle, as did many others, regardless of the means of propulsion or how it interfaced with the ground. Indeed, some, to prove a point, announced jet-powered vehicles to run on skies or blades, on snow or ice. Finally, a new class was created, but the shine of Campbell's achievement was dulled considerably. The double should have been his crowning achievement, and perhaps the perceived lack of recognition added to the growing apathy towards record attempts and this forced Campbell into a period of reflection.

He had thought about displaying his *Bluebird*s at a restaurant in Southampton, or sending them to his friend Lord Bristol for his proposed motor museum, but they remained with Lord Montagu at his museum at Beaulieu while Donald considered his options. The sabbatical didn't last long, however. Spurred on by the efforts of the Americans, as well as by the fertile mind of Ken Norris, Campbell started to consider an attempt at the sound barrier with a rocket-powered car. There were also plans for a vehicle with sloping wheels for stability, and more outlandishly a four-wheel, four-point amphibian vehicle to attack both records. Campbell, Norris, and Villa had formed Bluebird Marine to develop the *Jetstar*, a water-borne runabout powered by a submerged water jet. The annual attempts had ceased, and Campbell's reputation began to slip. His mood was further reduced by the accident involving the *Bluebird* car during a demonstration run at RAF Debden, the estimated repair bill of £50,000 being a further body blow.

Rumours that his marriage was in trouble as well as the lukewarm reaction to the CN8 rocket car coincided with a further ebb in his spirits. But against this background came the renewal of his ambition to be the first man to exceed 300 mph on water. The decision must have been made in late 1965, as initial design work began early in 1966. As early as 6 May 1966, approaches had been made to Bristol Siddeley for an Orpheus jet engine to replace the ageing Metropolitan-Vickers Beryl. Campbell succeeding in purchasing a Folland Gnat aircraft (as used by the Red Arrows of the time) complete with an Orpheus engine for £200 from the Ministry of Defence in July of the same year. In an effort to raise the much-needed cash for the project, Campbell sold the rights to the film 'How Long A Mile' to British Petroleum. The film was a diary of the Land Speed Record; it had been funded by Campbell, and had won several film prizes.

In an echo of Campbell's need to sell his father's car in 1949, he felt it more important to invest in a future project, and the income it might bring. *Bluebird* K7 was taken to Norris Brothers in Haywards Heath, where she was installed in a wooden extension to the main building for the conversion work. To cut costs, Campbell endeavoured to use as many of his own team as he could. But the work was to be very specialised , so Leo Villa and his team were joined by the Norris Brothers employees, Peter Pateman, Bill Izatt, and Mike Okenden, under the supervision of Tony James. *Bluebird*'s hull was soon joined by the Gnat jet trainer, brought down from Dunsfold by truck and dismembered in the Norris Brothers car park. The remains of XM691 remained outside until Ken Norris suggested that perhaps the tailfin from the aircraft could be uti-lised in the conversion, providing a quick and cost-effective means of further improving K7's aerodynamic stability. After the failure of the braking parachute, Norris developed a hydraulically operated water brake to arrest *Bluebird*'s speed after leaving the measured mile. The drag effected by pushing up to six inches of two-inch diameter steel rod into the water at 250 mph was aptly described by Campbell thus: "I suggest that if you pull a sixpence through the water edge-on, and then compare the results if you turn the sixpence sideways, you may well get some idea of how effective it really is".

Bluebird started to take on a yet more purposeful appearance, looking more futuristic and capable than ever before. During October, the residents of Burrell Road were warned that the Orpheus would be started to check its installation before an attempt on the record the following month. With her gleaming new paintwork, she was prepared for the press launch and transportation to Coniston. The press presence was minimal and again Campbell's mood reflected it. He took Tony James to one side and commented, "I hope this lot don't look at the bow, Tony. Some fool looks like they have painted the flags at half-mast. Get it sorted old boy would you?" If Campbell was really as superstitious as he made out, he might not have taken it quite so well.

7.

K7 at Coniston

Bluebird K7 had her last run in the salt waters of Perth harbour, Australia, in 1964, after which Campbell had more or less consigned the boat to a museum. Indeed, from storage at Bill Coley's yard in Hounslow, she had been on display at Lord Montagu's National Motor Museum in Beaulieu, prior to being removed and taken to the Norris Brothers works in Haywards Heath in readiness for her conversion.

Bluebird finally arrived on her slipway at Coniston during the afternoon of 2 November 1966, conveyed as ever by Adams Brothers of New Malden. Campbell's two full-time employees, Leo Villa and Maurice Parfitt had been up at Coniston for over a week preparing the 'boat shed', the term being a touch grand for the structure that was to house *Bluebird*. The slipway was used previously by the 'Lady of the Lake', a lake steamer piloted by Coniston boatman Goffy Thwaites. But the boathouse had since become the property of Arthur Wilson, and the steamer had ceased plying her trade. Wilson had had a large garage built at the very end of the slipway, but it was by no means big enough to house the K7 hydroplane. Instead, over the rails used to launch *Bluebird*, a large scaffolding structure had been erected that was covered in plastic sheeting. Leo had not been relishing the idea of being in the Lake District during the early winter.

His new 'workshop' was draughty and could only be warmed by the use of a huge space heater, burning ten gallons of paraffin a day, and leaving the air heavy with fumes. Campbell arrived the following day, keen to give the engine a test and reacquaint himself with his faithful *Bluebird*. The new power plant, the Bristol Siddeley Orpheus, although smaller and lighter, produced over 1000 lbs of thrust more than the old Beryl, but it became apparent the installation had affected the trim as she seemed down at the bows. *Bluebird* now had an onboard, compressed-air starting system which allowed for about six attempts at getting the Orpheus running. In the workshop in Haywards Heath, the engine had been started and tested by Jack Lavis, a Bristol Siddeley technician, but Donald still had the engine running first go. As soon as he applied the throttle, however, the engine instantly flamed out, a scenario that was repeated six times before Campbell called to be towed in. Lavis and his assistant, Ken Pearson, were promptly informed that the Orpheus was not giving anywhere near full revs. But, more seriously, an inspection showed evidence that something very hard had been ingested into the engine, and a static engine test was scheduled for the following day, Saturday. *Bluebird* was held in place by steel hawsers attached to the Land Rover winch vehicle, and the engine technicians were issued with pilots' headgear to communicate throughout the test. The rest of the team lined up on the jetty hoping that it was going to be a straightforward task to recover the lost revs and that any engine damage was minimal. Lavis soon had the Orpheus at full revs, but no sooner had the noise become ear-splitting, than it was suddenly cut. It soon became obvious that something had gone seriously wrong. The increased demands of air had taken their toll on the intakes, and they had collapsed, releasing a handful of rivets into the spinning engine.

The team did have a spare, engine number 711, which was in the remains of the Gnat trainer in Haywards Heath. Of more concern was just how bad was the damage to the intakes, and how quickly it could be rectified. As Pearson, Lavis and the *Bluebird* team readied themselves to remove the engine Campbell gave a televised interview. His demeanour was obviously that of a man whose thoughts were elsewhere, and his answers were terse, as if humouring the interviewer – but he was unrepentant, indicating that this was by no means the end of the project. Details of the required modifications were telephoned through to Norris Brothers and the intakes dispatched south by lorry for the necessary work to be carried out. A friend of Sir Malcolm Campbell's, Ted Hamel, was at Coniston at the invitation of Donald. He was soon asked to lend his electrical experience to the task of removing the engine intakes, as the wiring loom was in one piece and it had never been thought likely that the engine intakes would have needed to have been changed. He reported to Leo Villa the next morning to inspect the wiring diagram, and instantly became a member of the team.

The roads from Coniston through nearby Ambleside were, and still are, narrow and twisting, switching back on themselves as they climb and fall over the hills that surround each lake. The truck taking the intakes left the boathouse at 4 am but did not arrive in Haywards Heath until the early evening. Knowing there would be a delay, Campbell returned south in his Jaguar the same day, while those temporarily without a job returned either to the Black Bull Inn or to The Sun Hotel to drink coffee and write their reports. To the owner of The Sun, all of this was nothing new. Sir Malcolm Campbell had stayed with the Robinsons in 1939, and Donald had also stayed in the family-run hotel for all of his attempts at Coniston.

For 1966, Donald was invited to take over the family's bungalow, while his team ensconced itself in the Sun. This left those on the outer circle of the attempt, reporters, security personnel and the like to make use of the Yewdale Hotel and the Black Bull Inn. Connie Robinson's son Tony, usually referred to as Robbie, was, as always heavily involved, becoming unofficial team chauffeur, and helmsman for Leo Villa in the Fairlaine.

The intakes arrived at Norris Brothers for modification on the 6 November, but it was not simply a case of strengthening them. On the recommendation of Bristol Siddeley, several other factors had to be taken into account. It was crucial that the intake area was a minimum of 337.10 square inches, which meant enlarging the inlet orifice, at the same time as increasing the thickness of the lip around the intake's outer edge. Bristol Siddeley also pointed out something that was to have repercussions later in the project. In a report numbered PP/INST/131, issued to Norris Brothers in copy form, great emphasis was put on section 2, which stated, 'Care should be taken in throttling back to avoid possible bucketing associated with intake spilling and pre-entry separation of the intake ramp.' Put simply, sudden closing of the throttle would cause instability similar to the effect created by stamping on and off the throttle pedal of a car. A further problem was that the new engine required a header tank for fuel, to act as a sort of one-way valve, allowing fuel to be pumped up to the tank above the engine from the main fuel tank, and then fed by gravity into the combustion chamber of the new Orpheus. There was a degree of guesswork involved at arriving at the size of this tank, but by using the consumption figures as a baseline a reasonable size of header tank was installed, and the fuel system became more or less a fully pressurized system which, it was thought, would go some way to preventing this surging effect.

The lorry returned from Norris Brothers with the spare engine the same day, and this, along with the damaged unit (709) was put in Arthur Wilson's garage ahead of *Bluebird*'s boathouse, awaiting the return of the intakes. Early one morning, Campbell telephoned from his Surrey home to instruct Leo and his team to put the 709 engine back into *Bluebird*'s hull as he did not want to risk his only good engine in a static test, keeping the unused engine until he was absolutely certain the intakes were up to the job. The team rolled up their sleeves and, having removed the top casings and fettled the engine as much as possible, replaced the old engine. According to Leo's diary: "We had to locate and file by hand every damaged blade from both the compressor, and the hot wheel, and in one instance removed every second blade that was beyond repair, while keeping the thing in balance enough to prove the new intakes before putting our only good engine in". So the 709 was able to run, but only well enough for the test of the intakes.

By 18 November, the re-constructed air intakes had arrived back at the slipway. They had been painted by a coachworks in Sussex, and arrived a good couple of shades darker than the rest of the hull. It was not the only disaster on the paintwork. One of the Union flags on the tail fin had been painted upside down, the signal for distress, and while the team awaited the intakes, this had to repainted before a member of the press spotted it, 'the Skipper' being concerned that they would have, 'a bloody field day'.

As was usually the case, Campbell had *Bluebird* back on the water as soon as possible, and having been towed out into his start-up position Campbell applied the throttle while being shadowed by Leo Villa and Robbie Robinson in a Fairlaine 19, lent to the project by Oundle Marine. The engine ran faultlessly, as did the air intakes, but still the trim seemed bow heavy and the splash shields proved inadequate. The daily report was telephoned through to Norris Brothers, and a new shape of splash shield suggested, which Ken Norris later christened 'The Dame Edna Everidges'. During the duration of this attempt, these shields developed a series of baffles to redirect water away from the engine without affecting aerodynamic lift. Yet again the team were put to work changing the engine, replacing the rather soiled engine number 709, which had only done 113 hours, with engine 711 the original power plant of Donald's second-hand Gnat trainer. The engine swap proved to be a difficult task to accomplish, made all the more trying as a bitterly cold wind from the north-east began tearing at the plastic sheeting, ripping it in several places.

Everyday at eleven o'clock, Robbie would drive down to the boathouse with hot coffee and a tin of biscuits, giving the team a small respite. At lunchtime everyone would try a cram into the caravans for lunch, usually soup and steak and kidney pie, and to try to recover some of their lost body heat. The trusty Morris Traveller would return at 4.30 pm with tea and cakes, and if work continued until late, as it had a tendency to do, it would arrive again to bring yet more coffee and biscuits. Copious amounts of cigarettes, the other popular commodity, were supplied from the glovebox of Donald's Jaguar.

If all had gone well during the day, the routine was for everyone to gather in the lounge or, more commonly, the bar of the Sun. This area was a shrine to *Bluebirds*, past and present, the walls being covered in photographs of both Sir Malcolm and Donald in their various cars and boats. There was even a blue-rimmed steering wheel that had seen service on Sir Malcolm's last car, and on both the K3 and K4 boats, and which now hangs in Robbie's hotel, The Coniston Lodge, built on the site of the Robinson family bungalow. Donald was always the last to arrive, having stopped off to chat or make a call to either Tonia or Ken Norris. He had taken to matching his thickly padded anorak with a blue-and-white striped pom-pom hat which had earned him the nickname 'Noddy'. As the Skipper entered the room, so it would mirror his mood. If the day had gone well, everyone was happy but, on the bleak days of failure and set-back, the room where Campbell held court was not a nice place to be. As if sensing the way his mood impressed itself on those about him, he insti-gated a campaign of practical jokes, starting with the introduction of a plastic spider into a fellow guest's soup. Things quickly escalated and, before long, Leo Villa and Maurice Parfitt began to take most of the flak, which more often than not originated from the female staff of the Sun. Apple pie beds were frequent, as was black soap, but the final straw was the introduction of some bed-time companions for two of the team's mechanics, when pillows were dressed in bra, pants, and blonde wigs.

Ever-present was Campbell's long-serving butler, Louis Goossens, whose daily tasks could range from making the morning coffee, usually spiced up with a drop of cognac, to donning overalls and refuelling *Blue-bird*. The boathouse became a scene of frantic activity, which Leo likened to 'mending a watch in the middle of a dance floor'. The congestion was made worse by the presence of the Army in the shape of two officers and two other ranks lent to the team to handle radio communication.

As the team began to solve the problems, so the test runs assumed a routine. At around 6.30 am, Louis Goossens would leave the bungalow in Station Road and drive his Citroën down to the lakeside, returning via the Sun to inform Leo and Maurice of the conditions. If suitable, the team would assemble in Connie Robinson's kitchen for some very hurried coffee and toast. The Skipper would either remain at the bungalow pre-paring himself or, if he needed to discuss anything, he too would be in the Sun's kitchen, joking with Connie and encouraging his team.

These early mornings were recalled some years later as Leo Villa taped his recollections of the 1966/1967 attempt. "It was really all down to how Don felt. It didn't matter if we had worked late the night before, or just had a late night talking in the lounge, it was more to do with his mood. If he was feeling low he would stay at the bungalow and drive himself down to the boat shed, but if he was on an up then he would spring into Connie's kitchen and ,as usual, take the place over, stealing a sausage, wrestling Robbie, and telling us to get a bloody move on!".

The team would bundle into whatever cars were available and bounce down the rough track from the Ambleside road to Arthur Wilson's house and the slipway. Even in the still of the morning, the launches were car-ried out in a strange silence, everyone knowing their job, and when to do it. If Campbell had arrived with the team he would be involved in every aspect of the operation, embarrassing many with the speed with which he would organise the procedure. If he had stayed on at the bungalow, he would jump from his Jaguar fully kitted out, ready for the run. He would quickly be in the cockpit, waiting for everyone to be at their stations as soon as he felt there was sufficient light. During the early runs, *Bluebird* failed to reach the planing condition, usually as a direct result of the engine flaming out and the bows seemingly being forced down into the water. The team would be dispatched back to the Sun, while Campbell would stare dejectedly at either the boat, which had failed him, or the lake if conditions had let him down. According to the journals kept by both Maurice Parfitt and Ted Hamel, on one such morning *Bluebird* had failed to run cleanly and had been returned to the slip. The team left for the Sun Hotel, and breakfast, while Campbell stood drawing on one of the cigars he had taken to smoking, while looking at the transom of K7. The kitchen table had just been covered with several plates of sausages, bacon and an assortment of eggs when the telephone rang – it was the Skipper demanding that the team should return at once.

The Traveller and the Citroën pulled into the yard next to the boathouse to see *Bluebird* already halfway down the slipway, the Skipper operating the Land Rover winch himself. Before anyone had placed a foot into the mud surrounding the cars, Campbell was directing them down the jetty to prepare for a run. The jetty was treacherous with frost, but the Skipper's demeanour indicated some urgency was needed, until someone noticed two sandbags tied to the transom. It was probably a joint decision between Campbell and Villa, who had used a similar ploy with the post-war K4 jet to alter the trim temporarily, but here it was being proposed on a boat capable of well over two hundred miles an hour. Maurice Parfitt announced that, "Heath Robinson is alive and well and living in the Lake District", Campbell shot him a glance that convinced everyone this was very serious indeed.

For the second time in a matter of hours, *Bluebird* started up and began moving towards the centre of the lake. Quite suddenly she was seen to dart out of a great plume of spray and rocket down towards Peel Island and the southern end of Coniston Water, hitting 160 mph, before returning, minus one of the sacks. Regardless of that it was a success, *Bluebird* had reached the planing condition and light could be seen at the end of the tunnel. The mood as the team returned to complete breakfast was far more upbeat. Campbell was astonished that he had reached 160 mph in little over 250 yards – he was a little boy with a new toy.

At the Sun, Leo was instantly on the telephone to Ken Norris who, on the information given to him, calculated where to add the ballast, and how much of it, should be added to the stern to permanently alter *Bluebird*'s trim.

Campbell took Louis Goossens to one side and disappeared from the kitchen with the expression of a man on a mission. Within hours, a truck arrived at the jetty loaded with scrap lead. Yet again Louis was dispatched to return this time with eight biscuit tins, and was instructed, to his utter amazement to discard everything except the lids. Without direct orders being made, as if everyone instantly knew what to do, the process began of melting the lead, casting it into slabs using the lids as moulds, and drilling mounting holes into the slabs. Once the ballast weights were ready, the task of fitting them became the next problem as access to the mainframe was obstructed by the engine. Campbell was, as usual, in at the sharp end, spanner in hand, not only supervising, but installing the weights himself. While Villa and Parfitt were melting down lead and organising the necessary fittings, Campbell's long-suffering butler was pressed into action as engineer.

Access to the inside of the hull was extremely limited and both men had to contort themselves to succeed in fitting the lead slabs. If the engine had been removed the job would have been straightforward, but would have taken days rather than painful hours. Therefore, both men could be seen, faces pressed into the bodywork while their hands were thrust deep into the hull, the language becoming coarser as the task became harder. Goossens was on one side, his head hard against the body, glasses askew, arm down the side of the engine, while Campbell was in a similar position on the other side, straining with something while Villa and Parfitt tried to keep straight faces.

One exchange went as follows:

"Louis, what *are* you doing?"

"I am trying to get my fingertips around the bolthead Mr Campbell."

"You're not", said Campbell,"'you're faffin' around like some bloody old woman at a christening party." Both men were deadpan and looking serious. To the casual observer Campbell's comments were quite vehement, especially in contrast to his butler's monotone replies.

"Go on – grab the bloody thing", came the Skipper's instruction.

"I am doing my best, Mr Campbell", came the retort in true straight-man fashion.

"No you're not, we'll be here until January if you don't. Oh bollocks, someone get the magnet, I've dropped the spanner inside the boat."

"No, I have it Mr Campbell."

"Well about bloody time too, Louis."

Campbell's face was pressed so hard into the bodywork that it had started to turn red, while, opposite, Goossens' face was still expressionless, as if all in a day's work for a butler. He was totally oblivious to his employer's verbal barrage, knowing it was not aimed at him, but at the job in hand. Campbell had no patience for simple tasks made more difficult by circumstance. In this situation, he would revert to an alternative vocabulary. It was full, powerful, and wholly satisfying in both composition and execution. It was never argued with by those about him, and it certainly left no room for a retort of any type. On hearing it, those present gave the deliverer their full attention and 100% effort. It was a useful tool as well as a weapon. It was rude, but never personal, and the situation where it was being used was, without doubt, no place for a lady. The Campbell/Goossens double act gave many hours of entertainment to the team, with its unintentional, subtle humour.

"Louis" enquired the Skipper, drawing on a cigar.

"Yes, Mr Campbell."

"You're smoking too much."

"Yes, Mr Campbell." As usual, deadpan, but staring at the cigar.

"How many do you smoke a day?"

"Twenty Mr Campbell."

"Well that's far too many."

"Yes it is, Mr Campbell."

"You ought to be ashamed of yourself Louis."

"Oh, I am Mr Campbell, I am."

Even to the immediate team, Campbell never gave direct orders, but got things done either by leading by example, or suggesting that it 'might be a good idea' to do a specific job. The continuous modifications to the splash shields, as well as the need to install the extra ballast, led to several late-night stints in the wind-torn boat shed. Even in the glare of the arc lights, everyone's breath was visible, and the sounds of spanners making metallic contact with bolt heads was mixed with the constant rubbing of hands, when it could be heard above the incredible din made by the plastic sheet beating on the scaffold poles of the temporary structure.

On one such night, the hard core of the team – Campbell, Villa, Parfitt, and Hamel – were struggling to refit the splash shields for the umpteenth time. The thought of the warm lounge of the Sun led to an increased urgency to finish. Again without formal instruction, Campbell had teamed up with Ted Hamel on one side, while Villa and Parfitt tackled the other. Campbell had devised a plan to ensure that his side would be finished first, and implemented his game plan with good humour, the banter being continuous from both sides of the boat. Hamel's every move was coached by the Skipper until both men could stand back and admire their work, instantly noting an error. "Ted"', accused Campbell, "you've made a cock of it". It was meant, and taken in good humour, all four men completing the Skipper's side before adjourning to the warmth of the Sun.

The same night as the splash shield race, the weather conspired to go from bad to worse, and it was already appalling. The water on the lake rose to such an extent that the boathouse was nearly cut off from the 'mainland'. The wind ripped through the plastic sidesheets and the rain filled the roof area with such a quantity of water that the weight buckled the scaffold poles holding up the roof. This trapped *Bluebird* inside, which meant that the following day's main task would be repairing the damage. In all the time that everyone was occupied in repairing the roof, the waters of the lake were perfect, but the weather then began extending the project well beyond the planned timescale. The press, and some ill-informed members of the public, started to voice opinions chiding Campbell, insisting that anyone with an ounce of courage would have taken the boat out. But they had never driven *Bluebird* in perfect conditions, let alone in foot-high waves.

Ted Hamel had once found Campbell puffing on a cigar looking at a perfectly calm lake by brilliant moonlight. When asked what was on his mind Campbell replied, "You know Ted, I wonder if we could run at night, it always seems spot-on at this time of night". Quite how serious he was, or what Leo Villa would have said, we can never know.

With the weather closing in day by day, Campbell again returned south, ostensibly because of the prevailing conditions, but also because he needed treatment for his recurring back problem. He stayed there until he got the call from Leo suggesting that perhaps the weather had broken at last. Campbell returned and the early morning runs, 'down to the seaside', began again. On 29 November, everything gelled for the first time and *Bluebird* made two high-speed runs, planing easily and proving the new reduced-manpower launching method, allowing Leo, Robbie, and Louis more time to get to their stations, and the accompanying wakes to die down. After a busy day down at the boathouse the following day, strict instructions were left for everyone to assemble in the bar of the Sun Hotel by 4 o'clock, while Leo was summoned to Campbell's bungalow. It was 'Unc's' birthday. As the Skipper and his faithful chief engineer entered the lobby of the hotel, there was a barrage of champagne corks, and a chorus of 'For he's a jolly good fellow'.

On the days *Bluebird* could not run, groups would gather around various log fires in sundry hotels and pubs around Coniston village. It became quite common to see Campbell's secretary, Pam Cripps, in a huddle with Alan Weeks of the BBC, Raoul Crelerot of Longines and any number of newspaper reporters, drinking coffee and glancing toward a rain-battered window. The scene would change the instant Campbell walked into the hotel, people acting as if they had been caught asleep in class, everyone trying to find something useful to do. At last, the speeds began inexorably to rise. At 2.45 pm on 12 December, *Bluebird* left the jetty for an officially timed trial covering the north-south run in 8.92 seconds, an average of 250.778 mph. After a fairly leisurely seven-minute turnaround she returned at 237.720 mph. Campbell, suitably buoyed by the performance, decided to run the following day, the thirteenth. This was a day much like a Friday, days when the superstitious Campbell would never normally run. Regardless, he recorded 197 mph, and on the following days the speeds peaked at 267.25. Surely an attempt on the record was not far off. Several teething problems with the radio system were cured, but more importantly Campbell experimented with quick turnarounds at the southern end of the lake. These were on the same lines as his return run in Australia and he managed to get the time down to three minutes on one occasion, without refuelling. On 14 December, Campbell staged a dress rehearsal of the record attempt, recording a timed southerly run of 8.37 seconds. Then, as he had done on several other trials, he steered around the refuelling boat, leaving Louis Goossens redundant, and taxied back toward the course, entering the measured kilometre just under 4 minutes later, and completing the course in 9.13 seconds at an average 256.12 mph. Obviously, Campbell was planning something.

* * *

Yet again the weather began to deteriorate, prompting the Longines team to depart for their Swiss base on 21 December. Campbell felt considerably let down, and conceded that his team might as well disband for the Christmas period. His wife, Tonia, was in cabaret in Somerset, and the Skipper was invited to stay with the Robinson family for the festivities, an offer he was quick to accept. Leo Villa left for his Derby home convinced his 'guv'nor' was up to something. "I just had a feeling that if the water looked anything like reasonable, he'd have the boat out".

Campbell didn't disappoint, launching the boat on Christmas Day with the help of Robbie and Dr Stephen Derbyshire, and reached some very respectable speeds. Further south, the boffins at Bristol Siddeley had further developed the booster pump for the fuel system of the Orpheus, which would allow Campbell 110% power during his short duration sprints. It would simply be a case of waiting for the conditions on Coniston to allow *Bluebird* to show her mettle.

The timing crew from Longines became two young trainees who would be on hand to assist Norman Buckley, and Stephen Derbyshire, who were to act as official timers for the attempt. To Buckley, a long-time friend of Campbell, it was nothing new, having set many class records on nearby Windermere, with the help of Campbell himself.

The blackboard in the lobby of the Sun Hotel became a focal point, and soon attracted the attention of the jokers within the team. Leo Villa was most amused by a photograph of the launching of a ship that appeared on it one evening. Ken Norris had skilfully added sponsors and the name *Bluebird* to the ship, and had converted the attending crowd into K7's team, capped with Donald himself, complete with pom-pom hat, sitting on top. Most of the prose and poetry that appeared on the board cannot be repeated! The morning of 31 December was up to the usual standard, and it was obvious that there would be no chance of a run and so, by lunchtime, attention was drawn to the blackboard. The message read, "Notice. The team, staff and hangers-on are invited to a fancy dress party to be held in the lounge at 10 o'clock, New Year's Eve. Your hostess, Lady Aitken. Your Host, Old misery himself. Note: Staff will be on duty at 7.00 am New Year's Day. The Skipper.'

That evening, Campbell became an outrageous French waiter, while the Express reporter, David Benson, was a very convincing Batman. Dr Derbyshire remained a doctor, but a witch doctor with an enormous headdress, while Louis Goossens struggled with a mini-skirt. Perhaps the tension of the much-delayed project prevented the party attaining the usual Campbell standard, reducing it to just a normal New Year's Eve 'bash'. The tension was readily apparent on Campbell's face as he roved around, making sure everyone had charged glasses but, as Leo Villa recalled years later, "He wasn't his usual centre-of-attraction self that night. He even had a go at one of the press boys, claiming that they weren't there to see *Bluebird* succeed, but to see him turn the boat on her back".

Conditions on 2 January 1967 kept *Bluebird* undercover, but a static engine test realised full revs for the first time, and the mood around the project began to assume a determination and purpose. Yet again, the next day prevented anything other than fettling to *Bluebird* ready for an all-out attempt on the record. A frost settled on the grass during the early evening, a sure sign that early morning conditions the next day would be good enough for a dawn call.

January 4, The Final Curtain

The morning of 4 January 1967 broke still and clear, and by 6.30 am all of the team were in the kitchen of the Sun attacking tea, coffee, and toast. By 7.30, the timekeepers were on their way courtesy of Ted Hamel and the Morris Traveller. Campbell remained in the bungalow going through his ritual of donning his overalls, rubbing the belly of his mascot Mr Tiki, and clutching his father's St Christopher. He was pre-occupied; it was time to put up or shut up. The silent activity of the boathouse had *Bluebird* ready well before the blue Jaguar swept into the compound. Campbell strolled through the boathouse and out of the other side until he was standing by the water's edge. Leo Villa sought him out. "'I found the Skipper pulling on his chin, looking grey and lined. I suggested we could wait, as there was a slight popple, but I think he had been hanging around for long enough, and for the first time everything was just about in place. He didn't look away from the lake as he told me to get everyone ready. It struck me as a curt dismissal, but he obviously had a lot on his mind."

Leo, Robbie Robinson, and Geoff Hallawell, a well-known photographer of record attempts at Coniston, set off in the Fairlaine, while Louis Goossens had set off in the refuelling boat some time before. Campbell was already in *Bluebird*, his safety harness secured for him by David Benson and, as the dory towed her out to the lake, he donned his headset and his silver-blue Hunter pilot's helmet. The towrope was cast off, using the quick-release mechanism designed and made by the Skipper himself. At 8.41 am, two rockets leapt skyward, followed by Coniston's wildfowl, and at 8.42 am the Orpheus spun into life. *Bluebird* began to surge forward almost at once, and within yards had darted out of white spray, planing toward the record course.

According to the timing tape, she entered the kilometre at 8.46 am, travelling faster than she had before an averaging 297 mph for the north-south run. What went through his mind in the next minutes we will never know but, as the refuelling boat came into sight, Campbell dropped the stern into what he referred to as the taxiing position. He had obviously decided to use the quick turnaround ploy that he had practised on previous runs, but because of a radio fault he was unable to check on the exact condition of the course. By the time *Bluebird* had circled around Louis' refuelling boat, she was again on her points. A little under four minutes had passed, as he approached the marker buoy, peaking at 327 mph as he entered the measured kilometre at exactly 8.50 am. But *Bluebird* appeared decidedly unsettled, tramping from one planing shoe to the other.

At about one third of the distance into the course, she visibly slowed while her port sponson rose higher than before. The stabilising fin clearly left the water until driven back again by the moment created by the rear fin. The sponson dipped down into the water, its natural buoyancy forcing it to lift again. Then, as if in slow motion, the bows eased away from the lake's surface until they snapped skyward. *Bluebird* flipped through nearly a full 360 degrees, striking the water at an angle and forcing the hull into a series of rolls, before she settled, and dipped, almost gracefully from sight. The surface was covered in ping-pong balls and the plastic flotation foam from inside the sponson covers. Robbie Robinson guided the Fairlaine into the middle of the area, while Leo Villa and Geoff Hallawell scanned the surface hoping above hope that they would find the Skipper. Hallawell nearly fell into the icy water trying to recover Campbell's crash helmet, floating empty among the remains of the cockpit trim. The Dunlopillo seat and headrest bobbed nearby, alongside Campbell's socks, shoes, a glove and his life jacket, its laces ripped open. Finally, Leo recovered Donald Campbell's mascot, Mr Whoppit.

Ken Norris had left Coniston to return south the evening before Campbell's last run, and heard the news shortly after arriving in Sussex. He, and his bother Lewis, instantly set off to return to the Lake District to see what could be done, and to investigate the cause. While the team recovered as much as they could from the lake's surface, the local police arranged for divers to travel down from *HMS Safeguard* in Rosyth, Scotland. The Sun Hotel was quickly taken over by the press, all eager to file their stories as soon as possible, all with their own theories. Bodies filled every available space, every telephone engaged as first the lobby, and then the lounge filled to bursting. Each time the front door swung open all eyes turned to see if it was someone worth interviewing, of just another curious bystander.

When Donald's mother and sister arrived, they were greeted with silence, the look on their faces precluding any thought of questioning them. Leo Villa returned but was in no condition to speak to anyone, all he could do was nod in agreement when his wife Joan told him that he was wanted on a television programme that night. During the early evening, the *Bluebird* team sat in the lounge and watched what had happened out of their view, the commentator having the silent attention of all in the room. Some team members went back down to the lake when the divers arrived at 9 o'clock that night. The team of nine, under the command of Lieutenant Commander A.J. Futcher prepared to dive the next day at 12 o'clock. Bearings had been taken from the timing telescopes, giving an approximation of *Bluebird's* location, but it was not until the fourth dive that the hull was located, resting the right way up in 142 feet of water. From the rear of the cockpit toward the stern the hull was perfectly intact, but the bow, sponsons and forward crossbeam were missing. The cockpit area itself had been completely decimated.

Amongst the twisted remains of torn metalwork barely visible in the gloom, divers found the remains of Campbell's safety harness. The shoulder mountings were torn from the bulkhead, as was one of the waist mountings, the rest only attached by one waist securing bolt, and the buckle was still locked in its closed position. On Saturday, 7 January, the divers located the remains of the bow, the steering wheel and column some 280 feet further south than the main hull. The steering wheel was shattered, twisted beyond belief. The search continued until 16 January. Futcher, working with Leo Villa and Ken Norris, had his team locate and check every splash that had been recorded on film. Most days, parts of the surface of Coniston were frozen over to a depth of a quarter of an inch, and all light from the surface vanished at a depth of 70 feet. A further 70 feet down, the search was made even more difficult by clouds of silt billowing up, making the divers' torches useless. They returned to Rosyth disappointed that, despite their enormous efforts, they had failed to find *Bluebird's* intrepid pilot. Leo's thoughts were that perhaps the Skipper should be left with his boat, although for three months the local police continued to check the shoreline daily.

At the Sun, the lounge was a far quieter place. Small groups remained, but thought replaced conversation as they drank the tea that Connie Robinson brought without being asked. Lady Dorothy Campbell, Donald's sister Jean and her husband, Major Charles Wales, sat with Ken and Lewis Norris, and Leo Villa, with his wife Joan. Finally, Lady Campbell turned to Leo and started to ask "Leo, do you remember when Donald and Jean …" The question raised a wry smile, and further recollection, but the mood remained heavy. Slowly the team disbanded in grief.

In the years that followed the tragedy, each member of the team, and Campbell's family went through the process of restoring some form of normality to their lives. For Leo Villa the process was never going to be easy. He had lost the best friend he had known since 1921. His life had revolved around the preparation of a *Bluebird* of some description for the last 46 years, but now he was alone with his memories, friends, and beloved wife Joan. Campbell had been posthumously awarded the Queen's Commendation for Brave Conduct, and a third Segrave trophy. Villa, for his part, received a Segrave medal, as did other members of the team, and the OBE. He threw himself into recording his many recollections on tape and filing the enormous amount of paperwork that he had amassed, these becoming the basis for two books on his life with the Campbells. He became a consultant to several proposed record projects ranging from motor cycles to the outright Water and Land Speed Record. He gave talks to clubs and societies and tended his garden, growing cucumbers under the redundant splash shields from the K7 hydroplane. Sadly, Joan Villa died of cancer, Leo confessing that he had lost both of his best friends. He died in 1979.

* * *

In the immediate aftermath of Coniston, Ken Norris set about analysing the huge amount of data that had been amassed in an effort to try and pinpoint what had happened on 4 January. In the following years, the loose ends of the Norris brothers involvement with Campbell were tied up and the company diversified into several fields. Norris Brothers, the engineering design consultants, worked on cigarette lighters for Calibre, wheels for BRM, machines to pump concrete, and inflatable buildings. More specialised work led to whole new companies being set up, such as Worcester valves, Norcon Norris, and Agricultural and General Aviation, all of which still flourish today. Much like Leo Villa, Ken Norris was sought out by those that wished to follow Campbell's lead. Norris eventually becoming team manager on Richard Noble's successful Thrust project, as well as the designer of *Quicksilver* – a new challenger to the Water Speed Record.

8.

Cause and Effect

By definition, an accident is an event, or string of events which lead to an unexpected result. That which befell *Bluebird* was no exception. There are instances where one factor can cause a major tragedy. In recent years, one faulty component in an air-tight door of a Douglas DC10 air-craft led to the deaths of many hundreds of people when the door fell from the aircraft over France (although there was some indication that defec-tive service routines may have contributed). Yet in most cases it is a cul-mination of several elements of failure, occurring in an unfortunate sequence that results in catastrophe.

When *Bluebird* left the jetty on the morning of 4 January 1967, she encountered one such string of circumstances that led to just such a tragic conclusion. Like other 'final scenes' that have been played out in public, *Bluebird's* final disastrous run against the clock has led to much specula-tion. Some, with little, if any actual technical knowledge, or only a pass-ing grasp of just some of any data that exists, feel qualified enough to express the 'real' reason, cause or culprit to any number of events, both past and present. Each time a new book is published about the Victorian Whitechapel murders we are told, quite categorically, 'for the first time, the real identity of Jack the Ripper is revealed'. Yet, each time the theories are then picked apart by another expert, who just happens to have his own theory. Those working with more modern history can have as much trouble researching, and qualifying their own theories. John F. Kennedy was assassinated in 1963, yet to this day there are as many theories as to how he met his end, as there has been years since, each with its own mass of evidence. Still, we are no closer to who, if anybody, assisted Lee Harvey Oswald in the murder. Nor for that matter the identity of Jack the Ripper, or what happened to the *Marie Celeste*, each issue being clouded by time, and confused by the shear weight of interest.

With the final chapter of the *Bluebird* story, we are fortunate in that after the accident Ken Norris set about making a full investigation into the events at Coniston. With the same thorough logic that went into design-ing Campbell's hydroplane, he gathered all of the available material relating to the crash which, like any other accident, was the culmination of a tragic sequence of related incidents.

Much has been made of the fact that Donald Campbell had made his last return run without refuelling, or even stopping. Yet it is known that this was a gambit he had used before and had even practised at Coniston over the winter of 1966/67. In Australia, Campbell successfully raised the record using the same quick return method, and so just how much can be read into this one particular occasion is a matter of some considerable conjecture, as is the reduced weight of *Bluebird* due to the lack of fuel. Again, many runs had been made, more so during the final 1966/67 attempt, as part of the quick turnaround experiments, without refuelling. As has already been stated, a major part of the Norris brothers' design philosophy for both of Campbell's *Bluebirds* had been of total aerodynamic neutrality in regard to lift and down-force, so that perfect balance of handling was crucial. For the CN7 car, this was relatively easy to attain, as the interface between vehicle and medium remained reasonably constant, and the only variable was the reduction in weight as fuel was used. In both the car and, more importantly, the hydroplane, much thought went into the positioning of the fuel tanks. Simply because of the nature of the medium in the Water Speed Record, maintaining the precise balance of the vehicle becomes far more difficult. Even if water is absolutely flat-calm, it is never the same twice. What could be perfectly flat on one run, would be totally different on the next run, either from natural, or outside, influence. Therefore, designers of high-speed boats have to make more concessions within the design to compensate for variations in the boat/water interface.

In recent times, the handling of Grand Prix cars had been transformed by the introduction of the now-banned 'active suspension', which acted on the irregularities of the track surface, rather than just reacted to them. This highly complex system used a computer to monitor the position of, and the loads upon the road wheels in relation to the track surface. Then, rather like the muscles of a leg, the position of the wheel could be altered, maintaining the chassis of the car in a perfect position to utilise its aerodynamics and traction, as opposed to the somewhat haphazard pitch and roll of a chassis that occurs with the more common springs and shock absorber system.

It could be argued that if a hydroplane could be fitted with the aquatic equivalent of this system it might be possible to predict water conditions and allow runs in less than perfect water. When one considers that most family cars have more computer power today that the command module of the Apollo moonshots, it is obvious that in the late 1950s to early 1960s, to have such a system would have been extremely farsighted, and prohibitively costly.

For Kenneth and Lewis Norris, the means to effect reasonably predictable handling while running at speeds well in excess of any other craft were few and far between. Aerodynamically, this was limited to the increased size of the tail fin, which would really only affect lateral yaw, keeping *Bluebird* on a straight course. Hydrodynamically, the problems were a good deal more complex. The need to alter *Bluebird's* condition from low-speed, high-drag, to high-speed, low-drag, meant raising the hull from the water as speed increased. Therefore, the leading surfaces of both the hull and sponsons were angled to cause the hull to lift clear of the water into the planing condition. Once the craft was planing, acceleration became more rapid until a tiny wetted area (less than 14 square inches) could support the entire boat. As these areas reduced in size (due to the hydrodynamic lift) there would be a related reduction in stability, which creates what is described as 'porpoising': the boat will rise and fall as the hull alternately drops down, as the support becomes insufficient, and then lifts again as the forward movement, and the angle of the planing surface, repeat the process of reducing drag.

In the case of *Bluebird*, this often became a rolling movement as the process alternated between the sponsons, what Campbell described as 'sponson walking' or 'tramping', much like someone standing still and rocking from foot to foot. This could be induced either by the normal build-up and reduction of lift, or by irregularities in the surface of the water. The three-point planing system used in *Bluebird* placed two support surfaces at the front and one central planing surface at the very stern, all angled in such a way that at optimum speed the main structure of the boat would be held above the water at the correct attitude. But, because of the porpoising, and the natural buoyancy of the hull and sponsons, it became critical that the leading shoes maintained their correct angle of attack, otherwise the bows could lift above the critical safety limit.

The Norris brothers' solution to this problem was two-fold. Firstly, the line of thrust produced by the jet engine was angled very slightly down and, secondly, a stabilising fin was installed on *Bluebird's* transom. As well as countering the drag of the steering rudder, the fixed fin and the engine thrust had the cumulative effect of forcing the bows of *Bluebird* down into the water – the trick being to produce a fine balance between lift on the forward surfaces and the inertia created by the thrust line and fin. The precise centre of gravity was calculated, and designed to be as low as possible and, in an effort to maintain the delicate balance of the craft, this is where the fuel tank was positioned. To ensure that the decreasing fuel load would have a minimal effect on *Bluebird's* handling, the fuel tank was kept as small as possible, and designed to be self-balancing. This kept the fuel load central and low and, negating any forward or rearward shift in balance, ensured that the weight of the tank, no more than 300 lbs fully laden, would have no ill effects on handling or balance. The later addition of the lead ballast to *Bluebird's* every other part of her design, very carefully calculated f and position, as was a reduction in the size of the rudder.

Another theory often put forward as to why the bows suddenly rose above her safe running limit, was that she had struck something in the water, the evidence given being that two large dents were found in the leading edge of the forward planing shoe's stabilising fin. These fins were mounted inboard of the shoes and, on occasion, were the only things supporting *Bluebird* above the water at full speed. They were made of extremely strong stainless steel, their leading edges honed to razor sharpness. The waters of Coniston were swept sometimes as often as twice a day, and it seems unlikely that anything would have been missed, but assuming it had, it would, by definition have to be buoyant enough to float, but hard enough to inflict considerable damage to the steel fins. Had this mystery object been a piece of wood, one can only assume that a razor-sharp fin, travelling at over 200 mph, would simply have sliced through it, possibly unsettling *Bluebird*, but unable to dent a steel fin. On the other hand, if the object were hard enough to cause such damage, it would hardly be likely to float, unless attached to something of considerable buoyancy, which in turn would have been so large it would have been very difficult to miss in the sweeps of the lake before, or after the accident. It seems safe to conclude, therefore, that the fin must have struck another part of the hull during the wild tumbles of the accident, when the sponsons parted company from the hull.

Eye-witness reports of the condition of the lake during both runs were that the actual measured kilometre was flat calm on the first north-south run, and only mildly disturbed during the second and fatal south-north run – no worse than any conditions in which *Bluebird* had run before. The area of water where Campbell had accelerated was a considerable distance from the north marker buoy, and the area where the water brake had arrested his speed was also well out of the course, although close enough for any instability created to be carried into the course.

Careful analysis of the commentary of the last run, timed to all available film to the nearest quarter second, when superimposed over a map of the last run, show that this 'bad' water was between a quarter and a third of a mile from the beginning of the course. This should have allowed enough time for the stability to be restored by the relevant design methods, had not one of these methods failed. After *Bluebird's* sinking at Lake Mead, a slick of the remaining fuel on board rose very quickly to the surface, to the point where it was relatively easy to calculate how much had been left in the tank.

It was noted as early as 09.25 am on 4 January, that no fuel had risen to the surface. The assumption of the RAF crash investigation crew was that

Bluebird might have run out of fuel, robbing her of the vital down-force of the engine. We then also have to go back to the report submitted to the project by Bristol Siddeley in 1966, warning against sudden closing of the throttle due to the adverse effect this would have on the boat's stability in addition to the sudden loss of down force. The report, number PP/INST/131, issued directly to the project stated the following:

> 'Based upon the area of your intakes, 337.10 square inches, the Orpheus 701, at 5000lbs of static thrust will require 87lbs per square inch intake.

Of special note is the following paragraph:

> 1] At the proposed maximum speed of 325 knots the intake will be approximately matched (that is AO/AI=1), therefore care should be taken in throttling back to avoid 'bucketing' associated with *intake spilling and pre-entry separation at the intake ramp'*.

The fuel system had been modified for the Orpheus, and was very nearly a fully sealed and pressurised system, except for the header tank. This tank was very small in relation to the main tank, holding less than a gallon of fuel, and it is almost certain that the 'bucketing' described in the report will have meant a breakdown in the flow of fuel to this tank. In other words, the header tank ran dry. Donald himself had complained of fuel flow problems, reporting throttle hesitation and on two occasions, complete engine cut-out. Bristol Siddeley had fitted a new pump, but it did not completely cure the fuel problems that had been encountered. Again it is also necessary to study the speed graph of *Bluebird*'s last run, showing that she had slowed considerably from her peak speed, which she reached well outside the measured kilometre. This graph also confirms the 'bucketing' (alternate slowing and surging) that Bristol Siddeley had warned against. Two seconds out of the start of the official course *Bluebird* had peaked at 328 mph, but in the following 1.5 seconds she slowed by 10 mph, her speed further dropping to just over 300 mph as her nose began to lift clear of the water.

By the time the bows were above the safe limit, her speed was down to 290 mph, confirming a loss of nearly 40 mph in less than 4 seconds, and 200 yards. The original films of the accident have been edited on so many occasions that it is unsafe to trust the attached sound tracks as to how or, indeed, *if* the engine was running. But, as *Bluebird* reached an angle of some 45 degrees to the water, it is noticeable that there is no jet wash creating the expected plume of spray, which with anywhere between 3800lbs to 5000lbs of thrust, would have been considerable. Again this would appear to confirm that the engine had ceased producing any reasonable thrust. As the hull of *Bluebird* reached a near-normal attitude above the water, there is clearly a puff of vapour from the jet pipe as the hot engine appears to attempt to re-ignite. Having watched a Gnat take off from a wet runway, and noting just how large a jet wash this created, the absence of spray as *Bluebird* lifts one can lead one to conclude that: *either* the fuel pump had not managed to fill the header tank quickly enough, bearing in mind the engine had been set to run at 110%, or a mixture of surging and poor fuel flow had created an air lock in the fuel system. It is quite clear that Donald had closed, or partially closed the throttle. If the intake air had indeed started to spill back out of the intakes, then it is without doubt this, added to a starvation of fuel, that caused the engine to cease producing any form of useful thrust.

Bluebird K7 timed transcript. January 4th 1967

The timing of the run pinpoints and substantiates the above points. Ken Norris relied on film and tapes produced by the BBC, ITN, Border Television and the transcript of Campbell's cockpit commentary supplied by Paul Evans of the Army radio team, *before* they were edited. These tapes were recently subjected to digital enhancement, voice matching and analysis software and digitally filtered. The timings count down in seconds to the impact of *Bluebird* after she completed her somersault.

Time in seconds	Cockpit commentary event and/or speed
-66	'STARTING MY RETURN RUN NOW'
-41	'FULL NOSE UP'
-38	'PITCHING A BIT DOWN HERE, PROBABLY FROM MY OWN WASH'
-35	'ER- GETTING- STRAIGHTENING UP NOW ON TRACK'
-31	'PASSING CLOSE TO PEEL ISLAND AND WE'RE TRAMPING LIKE MAD'
-27	'AND- ER- FULL POWER'
-26	Start of ITN footage
-23	'WE'RE TRAMPING LIKE HELL HERE'
-20	'I CAN'T SEE MUCH, AND THE WATER IS VERY BAD INDEED'
-16	'I'M GALLOPING OVER THE TOP'
-13	'AND SHE'S L......... GETTING A LOT OF BLOODY ROW IN HERE'
-9.75	*Start of Norris Bros analysis* Speed 295 mph
-9	*Bluebird's* bows rise momentarily + slight side roll
-8	'I CAN'T SEE ANYTHING'
-7.25	Speed 328 mph
-6	'I'VE GOT THE BOWS UP'

-5.66	*Bluebird* enters measured kilometre
	Speed 318 mph
-4.66	*Bluebird's* bows begin to rise
	Speed 305 mph
-3.3	*Bluebird's* engine cuts out
-3	'I'VE GONE'
	Speed 294 mph
-2.25	*Bluebird* breaks contact with water
-2	'U-UHH!'
	Bluebird somersaults
0	Impact at 183 mph

By using this transcript, the information gathered, both at the time, and more recently, it is possible to see a near-complete picture of the events of 4 January 1967.

Having completed her first run, *Bluebird* rapidly slowed to about 60 mph and, on spotting the refuelling boat, Campbell dropped the rear planing shoe into his familiar taxiing condition. Then, as had been practised on several occasions, he circled the boat and started to accelerate toward the course. Having regained her planing condition *Bluebird* accelerated rapidly, encountering the patch of water disturbed by the water brake at the end of the first run approximately 25 seconds south of the kilometre. Still accelerating, the rough water created severe tramping, confirmed in Campbell's commentary. *Bluebird's* speed peaked at 328 mph 3 seconds out from the entry into the kilometre and then started to decelerate. 1.5 seconds later the bows lifted momentarily, quite clearly visible in film footage, but the uneasy stability was restored.

Campbell, aware that *Bluebird* was pushing the limits of adhesion, eased the throttle, entering the kilo at 318 mph but as he did so the bows began to rise again, forced up by the bow's inherent buoyancy. In the film footage, the bows appeared to hover as, at first, the thrust of the engine tried to drive the sponsons back down into the water. It was at this point that *Bluebird's* engine appeared to have cut, visible as a change in spray pattern. She was then robbed of her vital down-force, allowing the bows to rise above her six-degree safety limit, and aerodynamics took over. Campbell, aware that all was not well, had already reduced the throttle but, as had happened in the past, *Bluebird's* speed curve had remained level, allowing *Bluebird* to hold her speed. It is at this point that the lack of jet wash would indicate that there was either no throttle being applied or that the engine has ceased working. But a different spray pattern, visible at the stern, indicates that Campbell had the foresight to attempt deploying the water brake. Sadly, it was too late.

Bluebird lifted into the air, rotating nearly a full 360 degrees before striking the water at a speed of approximately 183 mph at an angle of about 45 degrees, nose first. She had also been deflected from her course by some 10 degrees, probably caused by a mixture of the roll effect of the tramping, and the drag of the stabilising fin as the forward fins parted company with the water's surface. As the tips of the forward-mounted sponsons struck the water they were bent downwards and torn away from the forward cross-beam. A split second after this initial contact, the bows then struck the water, again folding downward and breaking the hull at the point where the jet intakes were located. As the sponsons rotated further back, they were torn away from their rear mounts, flying forward out of the enveloping spray. At some point during the collapse of the bow section, the lower rails of the boat's spaceframe snapped, separating the bow from the main hull, which then sank at the point of impact, along with much of the cockpit fittings. The main hull, after partially submarining into the lake, then began to roll forward; the stern rapidly overtook the decimated bow section as it 'dug in', the hull's natural buoyancy keeping it more or less above water. The centrifugal forces as the forward part of the hull rotated end-over-end then tore the twisted remains of the forward cross-beam, devoid of the sponsons, forward and away from the hull, at an angle of about forty degrees to the north-west. The inertia of *Bluebird*'s initial deviation from her course then caused a transition from an end-over-end roll, to a lateral 'barrel' roll. This ended with the remains of the hull coming to rest almost facing the direction she had come from, before sinking some 275 feet from the initial impact point. Not much was left floating on the surface. The two sponsons were found within 100 feet of the impact point, while Campbell's oxygen bottle, seat and headrest were found more or less where *Bluebird* had struck the water, suggesting that they had became separated from the cockpit area as it was destroyed.

Apart from the buoyancy material, the only other items found were parts of Campbell's clothing. These were midway between the impact point and where the hull had sunk, and consisted of a glove, shoes, crash helmet and radio headset, as well as his life jacket, the laces having been torn open. Some twenty feet from the remains, bobbed Mr Whoppit. The divers, sent to try to locate Campbell's body, traced the direction of the accident back from the main hull and in an area some 200 feet either side of the crash line. Apart from the major parts, such as the bow and hull, most of the smaller parts of the wreckage on the lakebed were from the cockpit area. The steering wheel and upper section of its column were found with the bow, but the steering rods, some controls, and parts of the canopy mechanism were even further north than the hull, indicating that they were thrown out of the hull during its gyrations, as can be seen in the film footage of the crash. The cockpit area of the hull was totally destroyed. The remains of the frame rails were found to be bent downward, suggesting that they had at least bent, if not snapped, at the moment the bows struck the water.

More ominous were the remains of Campbell's safety harness. This had been of the four-point type, i.e. two shoulder straps and two waist straps, buckled at the centre of the lap belt. The harness had been designed to withstand over 3G forward momentum, but the accident that had befallen *Bluebird* had not been a simple head-first collision. Both shoulder mounts, and the left-hand lap mounting had been torn from the bulkhead, the bolts still in their holes, the buckle still fastened. The right-hand mounting was still firmly attached to the hull. One can really only speculate what had happened to poor Campbell during the accident, but from the state of the cockpit area, and the way the safety harness had failed, he would have had little chance of survival. Even if the harness had remained attached to the hull, it would have required crotch straps to prevent Campbell submarining out from under the lap belts.

Considering that the forward part of the hull struck the surface of the water at some 185 mph, it is unlikely that anyone could have survived without the protection of the bow section bodywork or being securely held by a harness.

For several days after the accident, plans were made to recover as much as possible from the bottom of Coniston, but after discussions with the Air Accident Investigation crew, it was decided that there would be no further information to be gained from the recovery. Leo publicly announced that it was always the Skipper's wish that in such circumstances *Bluebird* should be left to rest, a sentiment that Tonia agreed with wholeheartedly. The remains that had been recovered were loaded onto a lorry and taken to Norris Brothers' storage facility at Ditchling Common, in Sussex, from where they went missing during the 1970s, probably being used as hardcore to fill a hole for a concrete floor at what is now an industrial estate. This is also where the mock-up of the CN8 rocket car was stored, until it too disappeared. Members of the *Bluebird* team set up a fund to construct a memorial in Coniston village, which took the form of a seat, next to which a plaque was sited.

Beginning and End

During the remaining months of 1967, Lee Taylor drove his jet boat *Hustler* to a new Water Speed Record of 285.21 mph although, as the directional steering for the craft came not from a rudder but from vertical vanes mounted in the jet stream, the boat was operating outside of the regulations. The Land Speed Record was already nearly 200 mph faster than that Campbell had set in 1964 while, in the following year, Apollo 8 took man away from Earth and around the moon. Schoolboy heroes changed their professions, and the record-breaker moved further back than even a back seat. Regardless of this, the name *Bluebird* remained synonymous with speed. Even today, children who are far too young to have witnessed the events of 1967 know the name, some even believing that *Bluebird* is the name of the fastest car ever. There have been others whose untimely deaths have helped them to achieve immortality: had James Dean not lived up to his profession's dictum, 'always leave them wanting more', it is unlikely that his acting abilities would have made him the icon he has become. He was indeed a 'rebel without a cause' who lived, and died young. But as Jimi Hendrix had once said, "The best career move you can make is to die".

Donald Campbell lived his life in a manner few others ever have. As soon as he could walk, talk and understand the world about him, he was eclipsed by the larger-than-life form of his father. Success in the first quarter of the century was hard to come by and fame, on a national level, let alone internationally, was the domain of very few. Media coverage was far sparser than today, and available to an extremely small percentage of the population. Real fame was the preserve of royalty and film stars, and even then only by reputation.

Sir Malcolm Campbell attained a status in the eyes of his own country-men not far short of the Royal family. After the death of his father, Donald decided, for whatever reasons, to follow Sir Malcolm onto the same stage. For a novice, the stage lights would have been dim, but the lights that con-fronted Donald were still burning brightly from his father's performance. That Donald was not blinded, nor stage-struck, was the first indication that here was a man of unusual bravery. Sir Malcolm had started at rela-tively low speeds, although still faster than any man had driven before. By the time Donald sat in the cockpit of his father's old *Blue Bird* hydroplane, he did not have the option of building up speed slowly. His first runs were at near-record speeds. He succeeded on a regular basis, usually against far higher odds than his father. He competed against his own fear of what he was doing, something his father claimed that he never had to overcome. After the Utah accident of 1960, he also had to compete against the pain of his various serious injuries, which caused him blinding headaches and back pain, originating from his two motorcycle crashes. Not once did he give up, and not once, when he felt there was the slightest chance of suc-cess, did he fail to make a run. Unlike his father, he never erred on the side of caution. It is very unlikely that Sir Malcolm Campbell would have ever driven his *Blue Bird* on the wet salt of Lake Eyre, or in conditions remotely near those that his son did. Campbell senior always put his responsibili-ties to himself first, whereas Donald would always consider others and what he felt they were owed before all else, even if it were members of the public who had simply turned up to watch.

Yet Donald has never been seen in the same light as his father. To sug-gest he only achieved a fraction of what his father had is nonsense, yet it is an accusation that is often made. Donald's successes were not always visible to the public. In his father's day, money was relatively easy to come by; Sir Malcolm never used his own money to finance record attempts, and made a handsome living from them. Donald somehow managed to extract money from individuals and firms alike, in difficult economic times, and would use all of his own money if he felt it was needed. He could change the mood of a room simply by entering it, but that meant those present would mirror his mood, good or bad. But still it is perceived that he was not from the same mould as his father, regardless that he managed to succeed in harder times, and in the face of vicious criticism. Because of this, or perhaps in spite of it, his followers today lionise him as strongly as any living hero. It has been over thirty years since *Bluebird* powered across Coniston at speeds only one man has exceeded, and lived to tell the tale – yet today, children know the name and adults still remember her pilot. It is ironic that, like so many others, Donald Campbell is better understood in death rather than life.

* * *

I finished writing this story, in 1992, never expecting that anything would change. Then, early in April 2001, I received a telephone call from Donald Campbell's nephew, Don Wales, informing me that K7 had been 'found', and that it had been decided to recover the wreck. I probably always knew that it would happen one day, but it still came as a shock. Gina made it clear that, once *Bluebird* was recovered, the Skipper should be found as well. I understood this. I watched the final moments of *Bluebird*, sitting on my dad's lap as a seven-year-old, dragged away from my game to see, 'the end of a very brave man, and the end of an era'. I was not impressed, but my father died on 10 January 1967, six short days later, and so the two events were always linked. I could see Gina's need for what I had always had, somewhere to go and to know that my father was there.

When I saw the wreck for the first time I was shocked to realise how accurately Commander Futcher had described it, especially as so little could be seen at that depth in 1967. But I drew little consolation from the fact that, as more information came from the remains of this once great craft, how my theory took on a more solid appearance, especially the fact that the water brake was found to have been deployed. But it actually serves no purpose to know why *Bluebird* crashed, just that it took away one of Britain's last, truly great heroes, even if too 'unsung' for many. What has come from the recovery of both *Bluebird*, and her Skipper, is the knowledge that there are so many more souls that have followed, and exalted the achievements of Donald M. Campbell than I ever thought, and that a whole new generation can see first-hand just how courageous he was.

Lake Eyre, 1963. *Bluebird's* loading ramp is in the foreground. The dry salt flats are already under threat from cloud *(by kind permission of Ray Govier)*

Ray Govier (on top of car) and Leo Villa (back to camera) contemplate *Bluebird's* Proteus engine as a dry lake beckons *(by kind permission of Ray Govier)*

Donald Campbell talks to Ken Reeks, just after landing on Lake Eyre
(by kind permission of Ray Govier)

The original U.I.M. certificate, ratifying Donald Campbell's 1958 record
(by kind permission of Don Wales)

A happy Tonia, waiting for Bluebird to make a run. She is holding the happy couple
– Mr Whoppit and Mrs Whacko *(by kind permission of Ray Govier)*

Donald Campbell sits dejectedly atop K7. The repaired intakes are a success, but K7 has failed to plane correctly. The *Daily Sketch* banner reflects the mood *(by kind permission of Tony James)*

Tony James supervises the Orpheus engine change on the slipway at Coniston, while Leo Villa chats with Clive Glynn. Note the painted water brake
(by kind permission of Bill Vanryne)

K7 is rolled out, ready for the trip to Coniston. Note the unpainted water brake assembly and the *Bluebird* roundel below the tail fin *(by kind permission of Tony James)*

Geniuses together. On the right, Ken Norris; on the left, master modeller, Fred Harris. *Bluebird K3* is in the background *(author's collection)*

A rare shot inside *Bluebird* with the engine removed. The self-balancing fuel tank surrounding the air intakes is clearly visible *(by kind permission of Tony James)*

Early morning, December 1966. Wrapped up against the cold, Leo Villa opens his mail as another long day begins *(by kind permission of Tony James)*

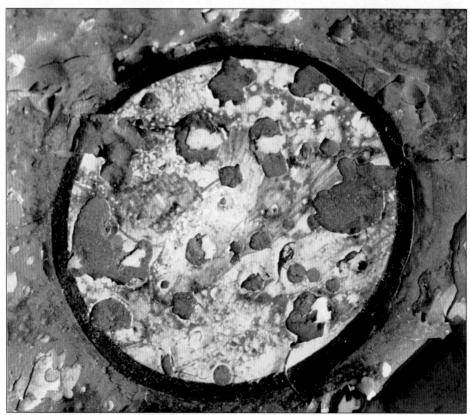

Defiantly visible after over thirty years in Coniston Water, the Union Jack – note the orientation –
and the *Bluebird* roundel on the starboard side of the hull *(both pictures reproduced by kind
permission of Andy Griffin © 2001)*

Appendix 1

Absolute Human Speed

Compiled and researched by S.A. Holter

Date	Person or Vehicle	Location	Speed (mph)
6500 BC	Running		25
6600 BC	Sledging	Southern Finland	25
3000 BC	Skiing	Fenno-Scandia	35
1400 BC	Horse-Riding	Turkey	35
1600 AD	Ice Yachts	Netherlands	50
13/11/1839	Steam train, *Lucifer*	Staffs, GB	59
16/12/1845	Steam train, *Ixion*	Berks, GB	71
1/6/1846	Steam train, *Great Western*	Wilts, GB	74.5
11/5/1848	Steam train, *Great Britain*	Wilts, GB	78
?/6/1854	Steam train 'No 41'	Somerset GB	81.8
?/3/1873	Tommy Todd (skier)	Cal, USA	87.8
20/6/1890	Steam train 'No 604'	FR	89.48
?/?/1901	Siemens und Halske electric train	Berlin, GER	101
6/10/1903	Siemens und Halske electric train	Berlin, GER	124.89
23/10/1903	Siemens und Halske electric train	Berlin, GER	128.43
27/10/1903	Siemens und Halske electric train	Berlin, GER	130.61
26/1/1906	Marriot, Stanley; Steam Car 'Rocket'	Daytona, USA	150
1918-1919	WWI Fighter planes (dives included)	FR	210
25/9/1921	Sadi Lecointe (Nieuport bi-plane)	FR	210.64
21/9/1922	Sadi Lecointe (Nieuport bi-plane)	FR	211.91
18/10/1922	Brig. General. W. Mitchell (Curtis HS D12)	Detroit, USA	243.94
4/11/1923	Lt. A Williams (Curtis R2 C1)	Long Is, USA	270.5

4/11/1923	Lt. A. Brown (Curtis HS D12)	Long Is, USA	274.2
11/12/1924	Adj. Chef. F. Bonnet (Ferbois V-2)	Istres FR	278.47
26/9/1927	Flt Off Webster (Supermarine S5)	Venice, IT	284.21
6/11/1927	Maj. Mario de Bernardi (Macchi M32)	Venice, IT	313.59
7/11/1927	Lt A Williams (Kirkham racing plane)	Long Is, USA	322.6
30/3/1929	Maj. Mario de Bernardi (Macchi M32)	Venice IT	348.6
7/9/1929	Flt Off Waghorn (Supermarine S6B)	Solent, GB	370
13/9/1931	Flt Lt Bootham (Supermarine S6B)	Solent, GB	380
13/9/1931	Flt Lt G.H. Stainforth (Supermarine S6B)	Ryde, GB	388
29/9/1931	Flt Lt G.H. Stainforth (Supermarine S6B)	Ryde, GB	415.2
10/4/1934	Wing Off. F. Agello (Macchi-Castoldi 72)	Lake Garda, IT	430.32
18/4/1934	Col Bernasconi (Macchi-Castoldi 72)	Desenzano, IT	434.96
23/10/1934	Sec Lt Agello (Macchi-Castoldi 72)	Lake Garda, IT	441.22
30/3/1939	H. Dieterle (Heinkel He 100 V8)	Oranieuburg, GER	463.94
26/4/1939	F. Wendel (Messerschmitt Bf 209R)	Augsburg, GER	469.22
3/7/1939	H. Dittmar (Heinkel 176)	Peenemunde, GER	525
?/8/1941	H. Dittmar (Me 163 V-1 Komet)	Peenemunde, GER	571.78
2/10/1941	H. Dittmar (Me 163 V-1 Komet)	Peenemunde, GER	623.85
?/7/1944	Georg Adam (Me 262 V-12)	Linter, GER	624.62
27/9/1946	G. de Havilland (DH 108)	Kent, GB	660
20/8/1947	Cdr T.F. Caldwell (Skystreak D558-1)	Muroc, USA	652.6
14/10/1947	Maj M.E. Carl (Skystreak D558-1)	Muroc, USA	653.4
14/10/1947	Capt C. Yeager (Bell XS-1)	Muroc, USA	670

– MACH 1 –

26/3/1948	Capt C. Yeager (Bell XS-1)	Muroc, USA	967
?/6/1951	W.B. Bridgeman (Skyrocket D558-II)	Muroc, USA	1,135
11/6/1951	W.B. Bridgeman (Skyrocket D558-II)	Muroc, USA	1,181
?/6/1951	W.B. Bridgeman (Skyrocket D558-II)	Muroc, USA	1,221
7/8/1951	W.B. Bridgeman (Skyrocket D558-II)	Muroc, USA	1,238
?/12/1951	W.B. Bridgeman (Skyrocket D558-II)	Muroc, USA	1,241
14/10/1953	A.S. Crossfield (Skyrocket D558-II)	Muroc, USA	1,272
14/10/1953	A.S. Crossfield (Skyrocket D558-II)	Muroc, USA	1,328
12/12/1953	Maj C. Yeager (Bell X-1A)	Muroc, USA	1,612
23/7/1956	Lt Col Everest (Bell X-2)	Muroc, USA	1,934
27/9/1956	Capt Milburn Apt (Bell X-2)	Muroc, USA	2,094
12/5/1960	J. Walker (X-15)	Muroc, USA	2,111
4/8/1960	J. Walker (X-15)	Muroc, USA	2,196
7/2/1961	Maj R.M. White (X-15)	Muroc, USA	2,275
7/3/1961	Maj R.M. White(X-15)	Muroc, USA	2,905

– SPACE FLIGHT –

17/4/1961	Flt Maj Y. Gagarin (Vostok 1)	17,560
3/10/1962	Cdr Schirra (Sigma 7)	17,558
12/10/1964	Yegorov, Feoktistov (Voskhod I)	17,600
18/3/1965	Belyayev, Leonov (Voskhod II)	17,750
14/9/1966	Conrad, Gordon (Gemini VII)	17,943
21/12/1968	Borman, Lovell, Anders (Apollo VIII)	24,226
27/12/1968	Borman, Lovell, Anders (Apollo VIII)	24,752
27/5/1969	Cernan, Young, Stafford (Apollo X)	24,791

Abbreviations: *GB, Great Britain; FR, France; GER, Germany; IT, Italy; USA, United States*

Appendix 2

The World Land Speed Record

Speeds in italics are unofficial or timed by non-sanctioned equipment

Date/ Location	Car/ Make or name/ Constructor	Driver/ owner/ designer/s	Engine(s) & type	Speed/ Weight/ Total bhp
18/12/1898 Acheres FR	Jeantaud Jeantaud Jeantaud	Chasseloup-Laubat Chasseloup-Laubat Jeantaud	Fulmen Electric	39.24 mph 3300 lbs 30 bhp
17/1/1899 Acheres FR	C.I.T.A - Jenatzy	Jenatzy Jenatzy Jenatzy	Electric	41.42 mph 3960 lbs 30 bhp
17/1/1899 Acheres FR	Jentaud Jentaud "Duc Profilée" Jentaud	Chasseloup-Laubat - Jeantaud	Fulmen Electric	43.69 mph 3300 lbs 30 bhp
27/1/1899 Acheres FR	C.I.T.A - Jenatzy	Jenatzy Jenatzy Jenatzy	Fulmen Electric	49.92 mph 3960 lbs 30 bhp
4/3/1899 Acheres FR	Jeantaud 'Profilee' Jeantaud	Chasseloup-Laubat Chasseloup-Laubat Jeantaud	Fulmen Electric	57.60 mph 3190 lbs 30 bhp
29/4/1899 Acheres FR	C.I.T.A No 25 'La Jamais Contente' Jenatzy	Jenatzy Jenatzy Auscher	Fulmen x2 Electric	65.79 mph 3300 lbs 68 bhp
13/4/1902 Nice FR	Serpollet 'Ouef de Paques' Gardner/Serpollet	Serpollet Serpollet Serpollet	Serpollet Steam	75.06 mph ??? lbs 20 bhp
5/8/1902 Ablis FR	Mors - Mors	Vanderbilt Vanderbilt	Mors Piston	76.08 mph 2420 lbs 60 bhp
5/11/1902 Dourdan FR	Mors - Mors	Fournier - -	Mors Piston	76.60 mph 2420 lbs 60 bhp
7/11/1902 Dourdan FR	Mors - Mors	Augieres - -	Mors Piston	77.13 mph 2420 lbs 60 bhp

Date / Place	Car / Name	Driver	Engine	Performance
7/3/1903 Clipstone GB	Mors - Mors	Rolls - -	Mors Piston	82.84 mph 2420 lbs 60 bhp
17/7/1903 Ostend BEL	Gobron-Brillie 'Gobbling Billie' Gobron-Brillie	Duray - -	Piston	83.47 mph 2189 lbs 110 bhp
?/7/1903 Dublin IRL	Mors 'Dauphin' Mors	de Forest - -	Piston	84.09 mph 2200 lbs 70 bhp
?/10/1903 Clipstone GB	Mors 'Dauphin' Mors	Rolls - -	Piston	84.73 mph 2200 lbs 70 bhp
5/11/1903 Dourdan FR	Gobron-Brillie 'Gobbling Billie' Gobron-Brillie	Duray - -	Piston	84.73 mph 2189 lbs 110 bhp
12/1/1904 L St Clair USA	Ford 'Arrow'(999) Ford/Wills	Ford Ford Ford/Wills	Ford Piston	*91.37 mph* 4136 lbs 100 bhp
27/1/1904 Daytona USA	Mercedes Mercedes Mercedes	Vanderbilt -	Mercedes/ Maybach Piston	*92.30 mph* 2189 105 bhp
31/3/1904 Nice FR	Gobron-Brillie 'Gobbling Billie' Gobron-Brillie	Duray - -	Piston	88.76 mph 2189 lbs 110 bhp
31/3/1904 Nice FR	Gobron-Brillie 'Gordon Bennett' Gobron-Brillie	Rigolly - -	Piston	93.20 mph 2189 130 bhp
31/3/1904 Nice FR	Gobron-Brillie 'Gordon Bennett' Gobron-Brillie	Rigolly - -	Piston	94.78 mph 2189 lbs 130 bhp
25/5/1904 Ostend BEL	Mercedes - Mercedes	De Caters - -	Piston	97.25 mph 2189 lbs 105 bhp
21/7/1904 Ostend BEL	Darracq 'Gordon Bennett' Darracq	Baras - -	Darracq Piston	101.67 mph 2189 lbs 100 bhp
21/7/1904 Ostend BEL	Gobron-Brillie 'Gordon Bennett' Gobron-Brillie	Rigolly - -	Piston	103.55 mph 2189 lbs 130 bhp
13/11/1904 Ostend BEL	Darracq 'Gordon Bennett' Darracq	Baras - -	Darracq Piston	104.52 mph 2208 lbs 100 bhp
24/1/1905 Daytona USA	Napier L48 Napier	Macdonald - -	Napier Piston	104.65 mph 2156 lbs 142 bhp
25/1/1905 Daytona USA	Mercedes 'Flying Dutchman II' -	Bowden - -	Mercedes x2 Piston	*109.75 mph* 2640 lbs 130 bhp

Date / Place	Car / Name / Entrant	Driver / Team	Engine	Speed / Weight / Power
31/1/1905 Daytona USA	Mercedes 'Flying Dutchman II' -	Bowden - -	Mercedes x2 Piston	108.58 mph 2640 lbs 130 bhp
30/12/1905 Arles FR	Darracq Darracq V8 Darracq	Hemery - -	Piston	109.65 mph 2208 lbs 200 bhp
23/1/1906 Daytona USA	Darracq Darracq V8 Darracq	Hemery - -	Piston	115.30 mph 2208 lbs 200 bhp
25/1/1906 Daytona USA	Darracq - Darracq	Chevrolet - -	Darracq V8 Piston	117.64 mph 2208 lbs 200 bhp
26/1/1906 Daytona USA	Stanley 'Rocket' Stanley Steam Co	Marriot Stanley Bros -	Stanley Steam	121.57 mph 1595 lbs 120 bhp
8/11/1909 Brooklands UK	Benz Benz No1 -	Hemery - -	Benz Piston	125.95 mph 3190 lbs 220 bhp
16/3/1910 Daytona USA	Benz Benz No1 -	Oldfield - -	Benz Piston	131.27 mph 3190 lbs 220 bhp
23/4/1911 Daytona USA	Benz Benz No1 -	Burman - -	Benz Piston	141.37 mph 3190 lbs 220 bhp
24/6/1914 Brooklands UK	Benz Benz No3 -	Hornsted - -	Benz Piston	124.10 mph 3190 lbs 250 bhp

Official records now set by average speed, calculated over two runs *(unofficial speeds shown in italics)*

Date / Place	Car / Name / Entrant	Driver / Team	Engine	Speed / Weight / Power
12/2/1919 Daytona USA	Packard '905 'Liberty Racer ' -	De Palma	Packard Piston	149.87 mph 3388 lbs 244 bhp
27/4/1920 Daytona USA	Duesenberg 'Twin-Duesey' -	Milton - -	Duesenberg x2 Piston	156.03 mph ???? lbs 188 bhp
6/4/1922 Daytona USA	- - -	Haugdahl - -	'Wisconsin Special' Piston	162.09 mph ???? lbs 254 bhp
17/5/1922 Brooklands UK	Sunbeam 350 hp Sunbeam -	Guinness Sunbeam Co Coatalen	Sunbeam Piston	133.75 mph 3542 lbs 360 bhp
23/6/1923 Fano DK	Sunbeam **Blue Bird** Sunbeam	M. Campbell M. Campbell Coatalen	Sunbeam Piston	136.31 mph 3542 lbs 360 hp
19/6/1924 Saltburn UK	Sunbeam **Blue Bird** Sunbeam	M. Campbell M. Campbell Coatalen	Sunbeam Piston	145.25 mph 3491 lbs 360 bhp

Date / Place	Car / Name / Entrant	Driver / Constructor / Modifier	Engine / Type	Performance
26/6/1924 Arpajon FR	Leyland Leyland-Thomas No1 JGP Leyland/J.G.P. Thomas	J.G.P. Thomas Thomas Leyland Mod's by Thomas	Piston	133.78 mph 3630 lbs 200 bhp
6/7/1924 Arpajon FR	Delage 'La Torpile' Delage	R Thomas - -	Delage Piston	143.31 ???? lbs 280 bhp
12/7/1924 Arpajon FR	Fiat 'Mephistopheles II' Fiat	Eldridge - -	Fiat Piston	146.01 mph 3196 lbs 320 bhp
25/9/1924 Pendine UK	Sunbeam **Blue Bird** Sunbeam modified by Campbell	M. Campbell M. Campbell Coatalen	Sunbeam Piston	146.16 mph 3542 lbs 360 bhp
21/7/1925 Pendine UK	Sunbeam **Blue Bird** Sunbeam modified by Campbell	M. Campbell M. Campbell Coatalen	Sunbeam Piston	150.76 mph 3542 lbs 360 bhp
16/3/1926 Southport UK	Sunbeam 'Tiger' Sunbeam	Segrave Sunbeam Co -	Sunbeam Piston	152.33 mph 2046 lbs 310 bhp
27/4/1926 Pendine UK	Thomas Special BABS Zborowski/Rubery Owen	J.G.P. Thomas J.G.P. Thomas -	Liberty Piston	169.30 mph 3575 lbs 450 bhp
28/4/1926 Pendine UK	Thomas Special BABS Zborowski/ Rubery Owen	J.G.P. Thomas J.G.P. Thomas -	Liberty Piston	171.02 mph 3575 lbs 450 bhp
4/2/1927 Pendine UK	Napier Campbell **Blue Bird** Vickers/Campbell	M. Campbell M. Campbell Villiers/Mainia	Napier Lion Piston	174.88 mph 6490 lbs 644 bhp
29/3/1927 Daytona USA	Sunbeam '1000 hp Mystery Racer' or SLUG Sunbeam	Segrave Coatalen	Sunbeam Matebele x2 Piston	203.79 mph 8492 lbs 880 bhp
19/2/1928 Daytona USA	Napier Campbell **Blue Bird** Vickers/Campbell	M. Campbell M. Campbell Villiers/Mainia	Napier Lion Piston	206.95 mph 5588 lbs 943 bhp
22/4/1928 Daytona USA	White Triplex 'Spirit of Elkdom' J.H. White	Keech White J.H. White	Liberty x3 Piston	207.55 mph 8052 lbs 1308 bhp
11/3/1929 Daytona USA	Irving Napier Golden Arrow K.L.G	Segrave Lord Wakefield J.S.Irving	Napier Lion Piston	231.44 mph 7796 lbs 925 bhp
5/2/1931 Daytona USA	Napier Campbell **Blue Bird** Thomson & Taylor	M. Campbell M. Campbell R Railton modified	Napier Lion Piston	246.09 mph 7920 lbs 1320 bhp
24/2/1932 Daytona USA	Napier Campbell **Blue Bird** Thomson & Taylor	M. Campbell M. Campbell R Railton modified	Napier Lion Piston	253.97 mph 8162 lbs 1370 bhp

Date / Place	Car / Builder	Driver / Designer	Engine	Performance
22/2/1933 Daytona USA	- **Blue Bird** Thomson & Taylor	M. Campbell M. Campbell R Railton modified	Rolls-Royce R Type No R33 Piston	272.46 mph 10879 lbs 2260 bhp
7/3/1935 Daytona USA	- **Blue Bird** Thomson & Taylor	M. Campbell M. Campbell R Railton modified	Rolls-Royce R Type No R37 Piston	276.82 mph 9504 lbs 2535 bhp
3/9/1935 Bonneville USA	- **Blue Bird** Thomson & Taylor	M. Campbell M. Campbell R Railton modified	Rolls-Royce R Type No R37 Piston	301.13 mph 9504 lbs 2535 bhp
19/?/1937 Bonneville USA	Thunderbolt Beans	Eyston Eyston/Andreau	Rolls-Royce x 2 R Types R25,R27 Piston	312.00 mph 15312 lbs 4000 bhp
28/8/1938 Bonneville USA	- Thunderbolt Beans	Eyston - Eyston/Andreau	Rolls-Royce R25 & R27 Piston	345.50 mph 13200 lbs 4800 bhp
15/9/1938 Bonneville USA	Railton Thomson & Taylor John Thompson Ltd	Cobb Cobb Railton	Napier Lion x2 Piston	350.20 mph 6985 lbs 2534 bhp
16/9/1938 Bonneville USA	Thunderbolt Beans	Eyston - Eyston/Andreau	Rolls-Royce R25 & R27 Piston	357.50 13200 lbs 4800 bhp
23/8/1939 Bonneville USA	- Railton Thomson & Taylor John Thompson Ltd	Cobb Cobb Raiton	Napier Lion x2 Piston	369.70 mph 6985 lbs 2534 bhp
16/9/1947 Bonneville USA	Railton Mobil Special Thomson & Taylor John Thompson Ltd	Cobb Cobb Railton	Napier Lion x2 Piston	394.20 mph 8082 lbs 2636 bhp
5/8/1963 Bonneville USA	- Spirit of America Breedlove	Breedlove Breedlove Breedlove	GE J47/15 Jet	*407.45 mph* 6705 lbs 5200lb/t
17/7/1964 Lake Eyre AUS	**Bluebird CN7/62** Coventry Motor Panels	D. Campbell D. Campbell Norris Bros	Bristol Siddeley Proteus 425 Gas Turbine	403.10 mph 9581 lbs 4310 bhp
2/10/1964 Bonneville USA	- Wingfooot Express W Arfons	Green W Arfons W Arfons	WH J46 Jet	413.10 mph 4774 lbs 6200lb/t
5/10/1964 Bonneville USA	- Green Monster A. Arfons	A. Arfons A. Arfons A. Arfons	GE J79 3A Jet	434.20 mph 6490 lbs 15000lb/t
13/10/1964 Bonneville USA	- Spirit of America Breedlove	Breedlove Breedlove Breedlove	GE J47/17 Jet	468.72 mph 6705 lbs 5700lb/t

15/10/1964		Breedlove	GE J47/17	526.28 mph
Bonneville USA	Spirit of America	Breedlove	Jet	6705 lbs
	Breedlove	Breedlove		5200lb/t
27/10/1964		A. Arfons	GE J79	536.71 mph
Bonneville USA	Green Monster	A. Arfons	Jet	6490 lbs
	A. Arfons	A. Arfons		15000lb/t
2/11/1965	Spirit of America	Breedlove	GE J79	555.48 mph
Bonneville USA	Sonic I	Breedlove	Jet	8980 lbs
	Breedlove	Breedlove		15000lb/t
7/11/1965	-	A. Arfons	GE J79 3A	576.55 mph
Bonneville USA	Green Monster	A. Arfons	Jet	7040 lbs
	A. Arfons	A. Arfons		15000lb/t
15/11/1965	Spirit of America	Breedlove	GE J79	600.60 mph
Bonneville USA	Sonic I	Breedlove	Jet	8980 lbs
	Breedlove	Breedlove		15000lb/t
23/10/1970		Gabelich	RDI hp/LNG	622.40 mph
Bonneville USA	Blue Flame	RDI	Rocket	6985 lbs
	RDI	RDI		13000lb/t
4/10/1983		Noble	Rolls-Royce	633.48 mph
Black Rock USA	Thrust II	Thrust Cars	Avon	8580 lbs
	Thrust Cars	Thrust Cars	Jet	17000lb/t
		(John Ackroyd)		
17/12/1979	Budweiser Rocket	Barrett	Romatec V4	*739.666 mph*
Rodgers DL USA		Needham	Rocket	5069 lbs
		Needham/		25000lb/t
		Von Fredrich		
15/10/1997	Thrust SSC	Green	Rolls-Royce	763.035 mph
Black Rock USA	G Force/Thrust Cars	Thrust Cars	Avon x2	4988.616 lbs
		Ayers	Jet	50000lb/t

Abbreviations: *AUS, Australia; BEL, Belgium; DK, Denmark; FR, France; GER, Germany; IRL, Ireland; IT, Italy; UK, United Kingdom; USA, United States*

Appendix 3

Significant Land Speed Failures

Year	Car	Driver	Cause
1902	Baker Electric "Torpedo"	Walter Baker	Accident
1913	300 HP Fiat	A. Duray	Mechanical breakdown
1927	BABS	P. Thomas	Fatal accident
1927	Djelmo	G. Foresti	Accident
1928	Stutz Blackhawk	F. Lockhart	Fatal accident
1929	Blue Bird	M. Campbell	Insufficient speed
1929	White Triplex	L. Bible	Fatal accident
1930	Silver Bullet	K. Don	Insufficient speed
1932	Enterprise	F. Smith	Insufficient speed
1960	Bluebird CN7	D. Campbell	Accident
1960	Challenger 1	M. Thompson	Mechanical breakdown
1960	City of Salt Lake	A. Graham	Fatal accident
1960	Flying Caduceus	N. Ostich	Insufficient speed
1961	City of Salt Lake	O. Anzjon	Accident
1962	Cyclops	A. Arfons	Insufficient speed
1962	Valkyrie	Hatcher	Insurance problem
1962	Infinity	G. Leasher	Fatal accident
1962	Flying Caduceus	N. Ostich	Insufficient speed
1963	Bluebird CN7/62	D. Campbell	Track/weather conditions
1965	Wingfoot Express II	B. Tatroe	Insufficient speed
1965	Green Monster	A. Arfons	Accident
1965	Green Monster	A. Arfons	Accident
1976	SMI Motivator	H. Needham	Insufficient speed
1977	SMI Motivator	H. Needham	Insufficient speed
1978	Anderson Pea Soup Monster	Gardner	Insufficient speed
1981	Thrust II	R. Noble	Insufficient speed
1982	Thrust II	R. Noble	Insufficient speed

Appendix 4

The World Water Speed Record

Year	Craft/ Builder	Pilot/ Owner	Location/ Engine	Speed (mph)/ Designer
1897	*Turbina* Brown & Wood	C.A. Parsons C.A. Parsons	Spithead UK Parsons Steam Turbine	39.1 Parsons
1903	*Napier Minor* Tanners	C Muir S.F Edge	Cork UK Napier	24.9 Linton Hope
1904	*Trefle a Quatre Feuilles* Seyler	M Thery H. Brasier	Monaco MC Richard Brasier	26.65 Seyler
1905	*Challenger* Smith & Mabley/Crane	*P Smith* Smith & Mabley	*L Worth USA* Simplex	29.3 Crane
1905	*Napier II* Yarrow	Tucker S.F Edge	Greenwich UK Napier	29.93 Yarrow
1905	*Dubonnet* Tellier	Dubonnet Dubonnet	Monaco MC Delahayes x 2	32.46 Tellier
1906	*Legru Hotchkiss* Legru		R Seine FR Hotchkiss x2	34.17 Linton Hope
1907	*Dixie* Smith & Mabley/Crane	Pearce Schroeder	L Worth USA Simplex Franquist modified	31.78 Crane
1908	*Dixie II* B. Frank Wood	Crane Schroeder	Bayonne USA (H) Crane V8	36.6 Crane
1910	*Ursula* Saunders	Robbins Duke of Westminster	Monaco MC Wolseley x2	43.6 S.E Saunders
1911	*Dixie IV* Staten Island Shipbuilders	Burnham Syndicate Owned	Huntingdon USA (H)Crane/Whitman V8 x2	45.21 Crane
1912	*Maple Leaf IV* Saunders	Sopwith M. Edgar	Cowes UK Austin x2	46.51 Fauber S.E Saunders

1913	*Maple Leaf IV*	Sopwith	Cowes UK	57.45
	Saunders	M. Edgar	Austin x2	Fauber
				S.E Saunders
1914	*Santos Despujols*	Despujols	Monaco MC	59.96
	Despujols	Despujols		Despujols
1915	*Miss Minneapolis*	Smith	Putin Bay USA	66.66
	C.C Smith	Syndicate	Stirling	C.C. Smith
		Owned		
1919	*Hydrodome IV*	Baldwin	Beinn Bhreagh USA	70.86
	Bell/Baldwin	A.G Bell	Liberty x2	A.G Bell
1920	*Miss America*	Gar Wood	Detroit River USA	77.85
	Smith/Wood	Gar Wood	Liberty x2	Smith/Wood
1921	*Miss America II*	Geo Wood	Detroit River USA	80.57
	Smith/Wood	Gar Wood	Liberty x4	Smith/Wood
1924	*Farman Hydroglider*	Fischer	R Seine FR	85.56
	Farman	Farman	Hispano-Suiza	Farman

All Records that follow have been homologated by I.M.Y.U (UIM) Brussels

1928	*Miss America VII*	Geo Wood	L George USA	92.84
	Lisee/Garwood Inc	Gar Wood	Packard x2	Wood
1929	*Miss England*	Segrave	Venice IT	FAILED
	British Powerboats Ltd	Scott-Paine	Napier Lion	Cooper/
				Scott-Paine
1929	*Miss America VII*	Gar Wood	Indian Creek USA	93.12
	Lisee/Garwood Inc	Gar Wood	Packard x2	Wood
1930	*Miss England II*	Segrave	Windermere UK	98.76
	Saunders Roe	Lord	Rolls-Royce x2	Cooper
		Wakefield	R-type, Nos R17 & 19	
1930	*Estelle V*	Carstairs	L Muskuka CDN	FAILED
	Carstairs	Carstairs	Napier Lion	Hawker
	Sylvia Yard			
1931	*Miss* America IX	Gar Wood	Ind Creek USA	102.25
	Lisee/Garwood Inc	Gar Wood	Packard x2	Wood
1931	*Miss England II*	Don	R Parana BR	103.49
	Saunders Roe	Lord	Rolls-Royce x2	Cooper
		Wakefield	R Type Nos R17 & 19	
1931	*Miss England II*	Don	L Garda IT	110.28
	Saunders Roe	Lord	Rolls-Royce x2	Cooper
		Wakefield	R Type Nos R17 & R19	
1932	*Miss America IX*	Gar Wood	Ind Creek USA	111.71
	Lisee/Garwood Inc	Gar Wood	Packard x2	Wood
1932	*Miss England III K1*	Don	L Lomond UK	117.43
	Thornycroft	Lord	Rolls-Royce x2	Cooper
		Wakefield	R Type Nos R17 & R19	

1932	*Miss England III K1* Thornycroft	Don Lord Wakefield	L Lomond UK Rolls-Royce x2 R Type Nos R17 & R19	119.81 Cooper
1932	*Miss America X* Lisee/Garwood Inc	Gar Wood Gar Wood	L St Clair USA Packard x4	124.48 Wood
1937	*Blue Bird K3* Saunders Roe	M. Campbell M. Campbell	L Maggiore IT Rolls-Royce R Type No R39	126.33 Cooper/Railton
1937	*Blue Bird K3* Saunders Roe	M. Campbell M. Campbell	L Maggiore IT Rolls-Royce R Type No R39	129.56 Cooper/Railton
1938	*Blue Bird K3* Saunders Roe	M. Campbell M. Campbell	Hallwyl SW Rolls-Royce R Type No R39	130.93 Cooper/Railton
1939	*Blue Bird K4* Vosper	M. Campbell M. Campbell	Coniston UK Rolls-Royce R Type No R39	141.74 Cooper (Du Cane)
1939	*Empire Day II* R. Malcolm Ltd	E Spurr E Spurr	Windermere UK Napier Lion	FAILED E Spurr
1947-8	*Blue Bird K4* Vosper	M. Campbell M. Campbell	Coniston UK De Havilland Goblin Jet	FAILED Cooper Du Cane
1949	*Aluminium First* Ventnor Boat Wks	Lombardo H Kaiser	L Placid USA Allison	FAILED Lauterbach
1949	*Blue Bird K4* Vospers	D. Campbell D. Campbell	Coniston UK Rolls-Royce R Type No R37	FAILED Cooper Du Cane
1950	*Blue Bird K4* Vospers (two seat conversion by Campbell)	D. Campbell D. Campbell	Coniston UK Rolls-Royce R Type No R 37	FAILED Cooper Du Cane
1951	*Blue Bird K4* Vospers (prop-rider conversion)	D. Campbell D. Campbell	Coniston UK Rolls-Royce R Type No R 39	FAILED Cooper Du Cane L. Norris/Railton
1952	*Whitehawk K5* Hanning-Lee	Hanning-Lee Hanning-Lee	Windermere UK Whittle/ Rolls-Royce Derwent jet	FAILED K.Norris Hanning-Lee
1952	*Crusader K6* Vospers	J Cobb J Cobb	L Ness UK De Havilland Ghost jet	FAILED Du Cane Railton
1950	*Slo-Mo-Shun IV* Jensen Motor Boat Co	Sayres Sayres	L Washington USA Allison	160.32 Jones
1952	*Slo-Mo-Shun IV* Jensen Motor Boat Co	Sayres Sayres	L Wasington USA Allison	178.49 Jones

1954	*Moshettiere*	E Selva	L Como IT	FAILED
	Selva & Sons	Selva & Sons	Alfa Romeo	L.Selva
1954	*Mercedes*	Castoldi	L Iseo IT	FAILED
	Timossi	Castoldi	Mercedes	Timossi
1954	*Laura III*	M Verga	L Iseo IT	FAILED
	Timossi	M Verga	Alfa Romeo x2	Timossi
	Stella Coachworks & Radice			
1955	*Bluebird K7*	D. Campbell	Ullswater UK	202.32
	Samlesbury Eng	D. Campbell	Metro-Vickers	Norris Bros
	Accles & Pollock		Beryl jet	
1955	*Bluebird K7*	D. Campbell	Lake Mead USA	216.23
	Samlesbury Eng	D. Campbell	Metro-Vickers	Norris Bros
	Accles & Pollock		Beryl jet	
1956	*Bluebird K7*	D. Campbell	Coniston UK	225.63
	Samlesbury Eng	D. Campbell	Metro-Vickers	Norris Bros
	Accles & Pollock		Beryl jet	
1957	*Bluebird K7*	D. Campbell	Coniston UK	239.07
	Samlesbury Eng	D. Campbell	Metro-Vickers	Norris Bros
	Accles & Pollock		Beryl jet	
1958	*Bluebird K7*	D. Campbell	Coniston UK	248.62
	Samlesbury Eng	D. Campbell	Metro-Vickers	Norris Bros
	Accles & Pollock		Beryl jet	
1958	*Tempo Alcoa*	Lombardo	Pyramid Lake USA	FAILED
	Kwakawin Wood Products	Staudacher	Allison J35 jet	Staudacher
	Staudacher			
1959	*Bluebird K7*	D. Campbell	Coniston UK	248.62
	Samlesbury Eng	D. Campbell	Metro-Vickers	Norris Bros
	Accles & Pollock		Beryl jet	
1959	*Bluebird K7*	D. Campbell	Coniston UK	260.35
	Samlesbury Eng	D. Campbell	Metro-Vickers	Norris Bros
	Accles & Pollock		Beryl jet	
1960/61	*Miss Stars & Stripes*	Staudacher	L Hubbard USA	FAILED
	Kwakawin Wood Products	Staudacher		R Evans/
	(Staudacher)			Staudacher
1964	*Bluebird K7*	D. Campbell	Dumbleyung AUS	276.33
	Samlesbury Eng	D. Campbell	Metro-Vickers	Norris Bros
	Accles & Pollock		Beryl jet	
1967	*Bluebird K7*	D. Campbell	Coniston UK	FAILED
	Samlesbury Eng	D. Campbell	Bristol-Siddeley	Norris Bros
	Modified by Norris Bros		Orpheus jet (709 & 711)	
1967	*Hustler*	Taylor	Guntersville USA	285.21
	Hallet	Taylor	Westinghouse	Hallet
			J46 jet	

1967	*Green Submarine*	A. Arfons	L Hubbard USA	FAILED
	A. Arfons	A. Arfons	General Electric	A Arfons
			J 79 jet	
1969	*Hustler*	J. Beaudoin	L Isabelle USA	FAILED
	Hallet	J. Beaudion	Westinghouse	Hallet
			J 46 jet	
1977	*Capt Crazy*	K O'Niel	Walker Lake USA	FAILED
	(Formerly Hustler)	J. Diest	Westinghouse	Hallet
	Hallet		J 46 jet	
1977	*Spirit of Australia*	Warby	Blowering AUS	288.17
	Warby	Warby	Westinghouse	Warby
			J34 jet	
1978	*Spirit of Australia*	Warby	Blowering AUS	317.18
	Warby	Warby	Westinghouse	Warby/ Fink
			J34 jet	
1980	*US Discovery II*	Taylor	Lake Tahoe USA	FAILED
	Taylor	Taylor	Hydrogen	Williams/ Taylor
	(McDonnell Douglas)		Peroxide Rocket	
1982	*British Pursuit K8*	T. Fahey	Coniston UK	FAILED
	Blue Fin/Roevin	T. Fahey	Rolls-Royce	J Tyrer
			Viper jet	/ R Nangia
1989	*Rain-X Challenger*	C Arfons	L Jackson USA	FAILED
	C Arfons (DIVA based)	C Arfons	Westinghouse	C Arfons
			J 85 jet	

Abbreviations: *AUS, Australia; CDN, Canada; IT, Italy; MC, Monaco; SW, Switzerland; UK, United Kingdom; USA, United States*

Appendix 5

Blue Bird Propeller details

Blue Bird K3 & K4

Diameter	Pitch	Details
12 inch	20 inch	Steel (Loch Lomond)
13 inch	20 inch	Steel (Maggiore records)
14 inch	20 inch	Bronze (failed)
14 inch	20 inch	Steel (1939 record & 49)
15.25 inch	19 inch	Bronze (74.5 sq in area "prop rider")
13 inch	20 inch	Bronze (70 sq in area "prop rider")
12 inch	21 inch	Bronze (Last run, "prop rider")

Appendix 6

Rolls-Royce R-type Engine

As used in the Supermarine S6 and S6B: two wins in the Schneider Trophy and two air speed records. Also used in *Miss England* II and III, *Blue Bird* K3 and K4 motor boats, breaking nine World Water Speed records and winning the Oltranza Cup. Fitted in two *Blue Bird* cars to achieve three World Land Speed records.

Design

Designed by Royce and Rowledge.

12-cylinder 60-degree Vee, water cooled, supercharged with four valves per cylinder, sodium-cooled exhaust valves.

Bore 6 inches, stroke 6.6 inches, cubic capacity 36.765 litre (36,765 cc). Compression ratio 6:1. 2,240 cubic inches. Cylinder pressure. 1929 = 225 lbs per sq inch. 1931: 254 lbs per sq inch.

Horsepower (Shaft)

Max power = 2,750 hp (assuming air speed exceeds 280 mph).　　1929 = 1,900hp

1931 = 2,350hp

(Sprint engine) 1931 = 2,700hp

Marine engine at 120 mph: 2,000hp

Power at 150 mph: 1,800 hp at 3000 rpm.

Engine data

Engine speed (at crankshaft): 1929 = 2,900 rpm. 1931 = 3,200 rpm.

Supercharger manifold pressure = 72.3 per square inch.

Tickover 475 rpm with induction pressure of 32.7 psi.

Boost pressure (Induction pipe). 1929 = +13 lbs per sq inch. 1931 = +18 lbs per sq inch.

Sprint fuel mix = 30% Benzol, 60% Methanol, 10% Acetone, plus 4.2 cc of tetra-ethyl lead per gallon as an anti-knock agent.

Fuel consumption:	1929 = 3.6 gallons per minute.
	1931 = 14 gallons per minute (240 gallons per hour).
	6 pints/horsepower/hour.
Oil consumption:	1929 = 12 gallons per hour on sprint setting of pure castor oil.
	1931 = 14 gallons per hour on sprint setting of pure castor oil.
Weight	1.530 lbs (1929 spec) 1,635 lbs (1931 spec).

Apendix 7

Run Logs for Bluebird K7 1966/67

Recorded by Norman Buckley

12ᵗʰ December 1966

Run 1, north to south	14.45 GMT	8.92 seconds	250.778 mph

7 minute turn-round

Run 2, south to north	14.52 GMT	9.41 seconds	237.720 mph

13ᵗʰ December 1966

Run 1, north to south	14.10 GMT	11.31 seconds	197 mph

4 minute turn-round

Run 2, south to north	14.14 GMT	8.56 seconds	261.325 mph

14ᵗʰ December 1966

Run 1, north to south	11.33 GMT	8.37 seconds	267.250 mph

4 minute turn-round

Run 2, south to north	11.37 GMT	9.13 seconds	245.009 mph

(Turn-round time not recorded after this run)

Run 3, north to south	7.52 seconds	297.000 mph

(This was written down by Norman Buckley, and is also in Leo Villa's notes; it is, however, a remarkable coincidence that the speed was precisely the same as on 4ᵗʰ January. Could it have been a back-calculation or an estimate?)

3 minute turn-round

Run 4, south to north   *(no data recorded; Campbell executed the particularly fast turn-round as a practice manoeuvre and then drove back to the start.)*

4ᵗʰ January 1967

Run 1, north to south	08.46 GMT	7.525 seconds	297 mph

4 minute turn-round

Run 2, south to north	08.50 GMT	Incomplete (accident)

(GMT times refer to when Bluebird entered the measured distance)

Index

Limited Edition Prints of Paintings by Arthur Benjamins

"One Hell of a Job": Malcolm Campbell in the 1933 *Blue Bird* on Daytona Beach. Print size 19" x 25"

"And to Hell with You Too": Donald Campbell at the helm of *Blue Bird K4* during the 1950 Oltranza Cup Race. Print size 19" x 23"

"Full Power": Donald Campbell with *Bluebird K7* on Coniston Water during 1966.

"The Christmas Run": *Bluebird K7* passing the Old Man of Coniston. Print size 18" x 25"

One Hell of A Job, unsigned	£25
Signed & numbered by the artist	£45
And to Hell with you Too, unsigned	£25
Signed and numbered by the artist	£45
Full Power, unsigned	£25
Signed & numbered by the artist	£45
Signed & numbered by the artist, and countersigned by Mr Ken Norris	£85
Signed & numbered by the artist, and countersigned by both Mr Ken Norris & Mrs Jean Wales	£125
The Christmas Run, unsigned	£25
Signed & numbered by the artist	£45
Signed & numbered by the artist, and countersigned by Mr Ken Norris	£85

Further information on these and other prints can be obtained from:
Blue Bird Publications, 162 Swievelands Road, Biggin Hill, Kent TN16 3QX, UK.
Tel: 01959 574414; Fax: 01959 571077; e-mail: bbirdpubl@aol.com

Orders, with cheques payable to "Blue Bird Publications" should be sent to the above address. Post & packing for each order: UK £3.50. Europe £6. Worldwide £12.

Also from Sigma Leisure:

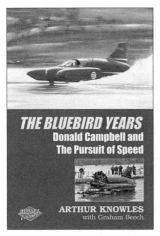

THE BLUEBIRD YEARS:
Donald Campbell and the Pursuit of Speed
Arthur Knowles, with Graham Beech

This best-seller is the complete story of Donald Campbell's heroic attempts to take the world water-speed record past 300 mph and of how the wreck of his jet-boat *Bluebird* – and his remains – were recovered from Coniston Water more than 34 years later. It includes the entire text of 'With Campbell at Coniston' – the classic account by Arthur Knowles of the preparations and the final tragic attempt when success seemed within Campbell's grasp. New material and photographs have been added, including an eye-witness description by co-author Graham Beech of the recovery operation that took place in March 2001 and the funeral in September of the same year.

The challenges that faced the designers of the record-breaking jet-boat are included, together with suggested reasons for the crash revealed by Ken Norris, co-designer of Bluebird K7. There are comprehensive listings of water-speed records plus information on how record attempts have been measured from the 1960s to the present day. The human story is also featured: the Campbell family and the Bluebird heritage – from museums and web sites to the exclusive K7 Club, Britain's foremost promoter of speed records.   *£9.95*

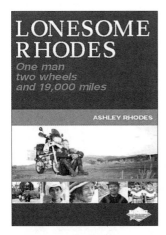

LONESOME RHODES
– one man, two wheels & 19,000 miles
Ashley Rhodes

Whether you're a traveller, an armchair traveller, a biker or a would-be biker, this book is for you. Picture yourself as the pillion passenger on a bold, brave, daring and defiant journey across the longest continuous landmass in the world … the Americas.

Read about the author's struggles against the forces of nature; loneliness in empty Patagonia; prison visits in Bolivia; sinister goings-on in Peru; dodging guerrillas in Colombia … and Mormons in Utah. Along the way he met dozens of entertaining characters from walnut-faced *campesinos* to the world's most beautiful women.

"Ashley Rhodes has written an enjoyable account of his own marathon, packed with incident and observation. If I had anything to do with inspiring it, I accept the responsibility with pleasure and pride." – *Ted Simon (author of* Jupiter's Travels).   *£8.95*

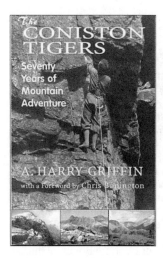

THE CONISTON TIGERS
A Harry Griffin MBE

This is the life story of A Harry Griffin MBE, much loved as Country Diary writer for *The Guardian*. As much of interest to lovers of the great outdoors, and to those who simply enjoy writing of the highest calibre, "The Coniston Tigers" features period photographs of climbers from the 1930s with their minimal climbing gear - some nonchalantly smoking their pipes as they balance on the most delicate ledge.

"A very special book . . . a living history of modern Lakeland climbing" – Chris Bonington. "The book which thousands have been willing Harry Griffin to write." – Alan Rusbridger, Editor of *The Guardian*. "Prose tumbles off the page as clear as a mountain stream – a classic of mountain literature" – Bill Birkett, mountain writer & photographer. "Harry Griffin is one of the great outdoor writers of the century." – Cameron McNeish, Editor of *The Great Outdoors*. £9.95

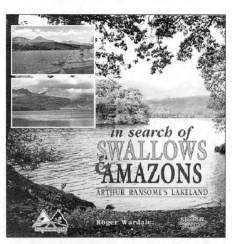

IN SEARCH OF SWALLOWS & AMAZONS: Arthur Ransome's Lakeland

This is a new edition of a popular book originally published in 1986. Additional material has been added to satisfy even the most avid reader of "Swallows & Amazons" – three decades of Ransome hunting with text and photographs to identify the locations of the ever-popular series of books. There's a two fold pleasure in this book– enjoying the original stories and discovering the farms, rivers, islands, towns and hills that formed their backdrop. £7.95

All of our books are available through booksellers or direct from Amazon.co.uk. In case of difficulty, or for a free catalogue, please contact: SIGMA PRESS, 5 ALTON ROAD, WILMSLOW, CHESHIRE SK9 5DY Phone/Fax: 01625-531035

E-mail: info@sigmapress.co.uk
Web site: http//www.sigmapress.co.uk